Computer Science Logo Style
Beyond Programming

Brian Harvey

Computer Science Logo Style

SECOND EDITION

Volume 3
Beyond Programming

The MIT Press
Cambridge, Massachusetts
London, England

For information on program diskettes for PC and Macintosh, please contact the Marketing Department, The MIT Press, 55 Hayward Street, Cambridge, Massachusetts, 02142.

Copyright credits for quoted material on page 349.

This book was typeset in the Baskerville typeface.

The cover art is an untitled mixed media acrylic monotype by San Francisco artist Jon Rife, copyright © 1994 by Jon Rife and reproduced by permission of the artist.

Library of Congress Cataloging-in-Publication Data

Harvey, Brian, 1949–
  Computer Science Logo Style / Brian Harvey. — 2nd ed.
    p.   cm.
  Includes indexes.
  Contents: v. 1. Symbolic computing. — v. 2. Advanced techniques —
  v. 3. Beyond programming.
  ISBN 0–262–58151–5 (set : pbk. : alk. paper). — ISBN
  0–262–58148–5 (v. 1 : pbk. : alk. paper). — ISBN 0–262–58149–3 (v.
  2 : pbk. : alk. paper). — ISBN 0–262–58150–7 (v. 3 : pbk. : alk.
  paper)
  1. Electronic digital computers–Programming. 2. LOGO (Computer
programming language) I. Title.
QA76.6.H385   1997
005.13′3—dc20   96–35371
                                                       CIP

Contents

Appendices

Preface

The phrase "computer science" is still, in some circles, battling for acceptance. Some people, not necessarily antagonistic to computers, consider it an illegitimate merger of two disconnected ideas (much as I feel myself about the phrase "computer literacy"). They don't see where the *science* comes in; what is taught in computer science departments is mostly how-to tricks of the trade, comparable to medical or legal training. Such training is valuable to the individual and to society, but the trainees are not learning to be scientists.

My own feeling is that there is some truth on both sides. There *is* some science in computer science. Abelson and Sussman, in *Structure and Interpretation of Computer Programs,* use the words "complexity" and "process" to explain what it is that computer scientists study. A process need not take place inside a computer, but it happens that computer processes are particularly amenable to formal study and they shed light on the idea of process in general. On the other hand, Abelson and Sussman are exceptional. A great deal of what is called computer science *is* much more a matter of programming techniques; many computer science students are first offered courses in several different programming languages and then taught specific techniques for particular problem domains, like graphics or data base systems or compiler construction. And many students who find themselves in computer science departments because they love programming computers are impatient with theory and weak in mathematical sophistication. Such students are perfectly satisfied with the how-to approach. (I don't mean this as an insult. I have in mind some excellent students I've taught who are brilliant programmers, very intelligent people, but happen not to have a theoretical bent.)

My goal in this book is to provide a bridge over which a lover of practical programming can cross into the world of theory. I envision someone who got bored or confused early in the high school math curriculum and was left with a distaste for formal thinking, but who is nevertheless a closet formalist when programming, getting the same joy from representing an intellectual problem in executable form that a traditional mathematician gets from representing a similar problem in an axiom system. I've tried to discuss the concerns of more abstract computer science using the language of concrete Logo programs that embody those concerns. This is an ambitious goal and I'm not sure how well I've succeeded.

For example, in automata theory there is an elementary result called Kleene's Theorem that establishes the equivalence of two different representations for a certain class of problems. One representation, the finite-state machine, is a *procedural* one, a sequence of steps, like a Pascal program. The other, the regular expression, is *declarative*, describing the desired result rather than the sequence of steps needed to get there, like a Prolog program. The representations are equivalent in the sense that any problem that can be described as a regular expression can be solved by a finite-state machine, and vice versa. (Not all problems are in this category.) Automata theory texts offer a formal proof of Kleene's Theorem using mathematical induction. What I offer is a Logo program that takes a regular expression as input and actually works out an equivalent finite-state machine for that particular expression. The program and the formal proof are similar in structure, embodying many of the same ideas. But the program is concrete and manipulable.*

Don't get the impression that the book contains nothing but formal mathematics, even in executable guise. The first two chapters (on automata theory and discrete mathematics) concern relatively abstract topics, although each has practical applications; the later chapters are more directly about the process of computer programming.

About This Series

The book you are reading is the final volume in a three-volume series, *Computer Science Logo Style*. In the introductions to the earlier volumes I have distinguished two approaches to computer science: the software engineering approach and the artificial intelligence approach. The former makes the idea of *algorithm* the central one. It thrives in a context of well-defined problems; a computer program proposed as a solution to such a problem

---

* Of course, computer programs are not concrete for everyone. Despite what I said above about students who like programming but don't like abstraction, anyone who has learned to see programs as concrete objects is well on the way to mastering mathematical abstraction too; that's what gives me hope about this enterprise. The fact that the Piagetian boundary between concrete objects and abstract ideas is not the same for everyone, and that what was formerly abstract can become concrete in a suitable learning environment (such as the one made possible by computers), was the insight that led Seymour Papert to espouse computer programming as an activity for children.

can be clearly judged correct or incorrect, and it can be more or less efficient than some other proposed solution. The artificial intelligence approach is harder to describe in one sentence. It embraces vaguely defined problems; it emphasizes an interactive process in which the programmer and the computer are participants.

Of course the terms in which I describe the two approaches are not value-free. A software engineer would use different language. Nor would all experts necessarily accept my dichotomy in the first place. Alan Perlis says, in his foreword to *Structure and Interpretation,* "After all, the critical programming concerns of software engineering and artificial intelligence tend to coalesce as the systems under investigation become larger. This explains why there is such growing interest in Lisp outside of artificial intelligence."

I have also described the sequence of stages through which I think an apprentice programmer travels. Volume 1 of this series, *Symbolic Computing,* teaches the rules of the game. It is addressed to a reader who has probably done some computer programming before, but is just starting to get serious about it. It differs from most introductory Logo programming books in that the latter focus attention on a particular programming goal, usually turtle graphics, and try to make the language itself as transparent as possible. I prefer to make the rules of the language an explicit object of study, since the design of any language embodies the designer's ideas about the structure of computer science.

Volume 2, *Advanced Techniques,* combines additional tutorial chapters about advanced Logo features with a collection of more or less practical programming projects. As in any field, apprentices learn by doing more than they learn by reading books; yet they require the attention of a master to see that they are learning a good style of work and not practicing bad habits. To speak of apprenticeship in this century sounds quaint, and in fact most of our master programmers do not take on apprentices. That's a pity, I think; too many would-be apprentices don't find suitable guidance. (They sometimes try to fill the gap by learning how to break into some company's computer, and then they get in trouble.) No book can be as good as living contact with a master programmer, but Volume 2 is my attempt.

This volume, *Beyond Programming,* is for the reader with a few substantial programming projects, or more than a few, behind him or her, who is starting to feel bored with programming for its own sake but isn't sure what to do instead. Some people never do experience that sense of constriction, and that's okay, as I said earlier. But I love mathematics myself, and I confess that I'm always a little disappointed if one of my best students doesn't come to share that love. In this volume my goal is to tempt them.

How to Read This Book

Slowly.

Each chapter introduces some rather sophisticated ideas. You may find that reading the chapter once leaves you with only a vague understanding. There are two things you can do about that: Read it again and experiment with the programs in the chapter. Test the limits of the programs; see what problems you can solve that are similar to the ones I solve, and what problems don't yield to the techniques I use. Think about how you could extend the techniques. You should understand how each program works, but don't fall into the trap of thinking that the program is the most important thing in the chapter. You should also understand how the program fits into a broader theoretical framework—how it embodies the *ideas* of the chapter.

The programs in each chapter are available on diskette and through the Internet along with Berkeley Logo, a free Logo interpreter that runs on PC, Macintosh, and Unix systems. Please note, though, that in a few places I show alternate versions of a program in the text. In those situations the diskette contains the final version, but it's worth your while to work through the development of the program by typing in the earlier versions yourself. (I don't do this with enormous programs.)

Most of the chapters concentrate on a single idea selected from a broad topic. Earlier I mentioned Kleene's Theorem as an example; that theorem is a very small piece of automata theory, but it takes up the bulk of the chapter. Only in the final pages do I hint at some of the other topics within automata theory. I think it's better to teach you one idea in depth than to give a handwavy picture of an entire area of study. You should expect to have to explore each area further by reading books about that topic; this book ends with a bibliography to help you.

The specific ideas I present are generally not at the cutting edge of current research in computer science; instead, they are older, more fundamental ideas. In part this is inherent in the introductory nature of the book. In part it reflects the limitations of my own knowledge. And in part it reflects the limitations of the home computers I expect my readers to have available to them. Then, sometimes the older ideas are easier to present in a complete, coherent, concrete form. For example, in the chapter on artificial intelligence I present an implementation of a program from 1964. In that program, the method used in the understanding of English sentences is closely connected to the particular problem (solving algebra word problems) that that program handles. A more modern English sentence parsing program is not only slower and more complicated but also is hard to demonstrate unless it's attached to an equally slow and complicated expert system or other purposeful program. I hint about the newer techniques, but I don't demonstrate them.

Chapters make occasional references to earlier chapters, so it's best if you read the book in order, although the references are rarely so substantial that you can't survive skipping a chapter. (But definitely read Chapter 4 before Chapter 5.)

What Isn't Included

When I first conceived of this series I described the third volume as "the first chapter of every graduate computer science course." As it turned out, the actual book does not pretend to cover anything like the entire field of computer science. It contains a selection of topics that I know about and find most worthwhile.

Some topics are omitted because I just don't care about them personally. For example, I don't have anything to say about numerical analysis. I'm glad there are people in the world who are concerned to ensure that when I use the square root primitive in Logo I get the right answer, but I am not such a person myself. That doesn't mean you have to share my taste, but if you want to know about numerical analysis you'll have to read someone else's book.

Other topics are omitted because I couldn't find any way to illustrate the topic through Logo programming on a microcomputer, which was one of the constraints I set for myself in planning this series. For example, one of the areas of computer science I find *most* interesting is operating systems. My high school students in Sudbury had access to a Unix timesharing system on a minicomputer and they did significant software development in that environment. But I don't know how to make that particular experience available on a single-user microcomputer in which the operating system is someone's trade secret.

Finally, some topics just didn't fit. I originally planned to have a chapter on graphics programming, but I decided that there are many books on the subject at both a popular and a professional level of expertise, and I had less to say about it than about some other areas.

The bibliography in Appendix A includes some pointers to information about some of the missing topics. In any case, the purpose of this book isn't to teach you everything there is to know about computers. It's to nurture in you a sense of what computer science is like, or at least one approach to computer science, in the hope that you'll be inspired to pursue the study in the "regular" college-level texts.

Computers and People

Steve is a college sophomore, an engineering student who had never thought much about psychology. In the first month of an introductory computer-science course he saw how seemingly intelligent and autonomous systems could be programmed. This led him to the idea that there might be something illusory in his own subjective sense of autonomy and self-determination.

Steve's classmate Paul had a very different reaction. He too came to ask whether free will was illusory. The programming course was his first brush with an idea that many other people encounter through philosophy, theology, or psychoanalysis: the idea that the conscious ego might not be a free agent. Having seen this possibility, he rejected it, with arguments about free will and the irreducibility of people's conscious sense of themselves. In his reaction to the computer, Paul made explicit a commitment to a concept of his own nature to which he had never before felt the need to pay any deliberate attention. For Paul, the programmed computer became the very antithesis of what it is to be human. The programmed computer became part of Paul's identity as not-computer.

Paul and Steve disagree. But their disagreement is really not about computers. It is about determinism and free will. At different points in history this same debate has played on different stages. Traditionally a theological issue, in the first quarter of this century it was played out in debate about psychoanalysis. In the last quarter of this century it looks as though it is going to be played out in debate about machines.

—*The Second Self: Computers and the Human Spirit,* Sherry Turkle, p. 23.

The psychology of computer programming, the sociology of the computer-intensive society, the economics of automation, the philosophy of mind, the ethics of computer use: these are the topics I find most interesting and most important in thinking about computers. That's why I'm a teacher instead of a computer programmer in industry.

In the original plan for this book there was to have been a chapter called "Computers and People" at the end of the book. I feel strongly that it's irresponsible to train people in the skills of computer technocracy without also encouraging their sensitivity to the human implications of their work. I ended up not writing that chapter, for several reasons. First, it would have to be very different in tone from the hands-on, experimental style of the rest of the book. I was afraid that, tacked on at the end, it would sound preachy, or worse, tokenistic and hypocritical. So instead there is this shorter discussion in the preface, where an author is allowed to sound preachy.

Second, I'm not sure that the relevant issues can be presented usefully to apprentices in the form of abstract reading. There is a lot of literature on this side of computing, some of which is listed in the bibliography. But the books, like all theoretical psychology or philosophy, are hard reading for people whose relevant practical experience is just beginning. Instead I think the best way to teach about the human side of computing is through sensitive adult attention to the actual experiences that take place in the computer center. (In general I've tried to write these books in a way that leaves open exactly who is reading them. I think this sort of approach to computer science can be useful to a wide range of people, kids and adults, in and out of formal educational settings. But I guess right now I am talking primarily to the teachers of high school students and undergraduates.)

At my high school computer center the kids liked to write video game programs. For a while some of the authors of these games included in the programs a list of which other kids were or weren't allowed to play the games. This practice let the game authors feel powerful and important, but of course it wasn't very helpful to the community spirit in the computer center. I didn't want to forbid the practice, making the issue one of rules and authority. Instead, in conversation with the students I tried to turn their attention away from ideas of intellectual property and entitlement—"It's my program and I have the right to decide who can use it"—and toward a sense of their own need for a strong community. Every time you write a program you're building on the work of last year's students who developed some of the techniques you use, on the work of people outside the school who designed the programming language, operating system, and so forth, and on the generosity of the adults in your community who paid for the equipment you use. In the end, I think the issue was settled not so much by my eloquence as by the example set by some other students who became important members of the community through their willingness to help others by teaching, encouraging, and sharing their own work. The kids all learned that it's possible to be respected, admired, and loved instead of respected but resented.

At many schools, when teachers express concern about the social issues in the computer center, the main focus of that concern is around the question of software piracy. Kids show up at school with a pirated version of the latest microcomputer game program, very proud of themselves for having it, and the teachers try to get the kids not to be proud of their theft of intangible property. But it seems to me that the other side of the issue, the spirit that's held up to kids as good computer citizenship, is marked by secrecy, distribution of programs in compiled form only, copy protection that works against networking, paranoia, and plain greed. I don't like *either* side of that dichotomy.

By contrast, in the university computer centers built around timesharing systems or networked workstations I see much more of a spirit of sharing, openness, community, programs provided with source code so that people can build on other people's work, trust, and an ideal of service to the community. That's another reason I chose to set up a Unix system in Sudbury. The ethical issues that arise in such a setting revolve around privacy of information. Kids find it a challenge to break into other people's accounts just as they do in the real-world computer systems that get into the newspapers, but at school the person who gets angry is another student rather than some faceless administrator. And students also experience the positive moral force of software sharing and collaboration.

I'm exaggerating the differences; I know that there is cooperation among microcomputer users and greed in the large computer world. Also, recent hardware developments are making the boundary less clear; home computers and workstations are built using the same processor chips. But the software is different and I think the style of human interaction is different as well. Still, the technical details of the facility are less important than the teacher's willingness to be a humane model and not just a fount of expertise. One of the virtues of that quaint idea of apprenticeship was that the apprentice was involved in the *entire* way of life of the master; there was no artificial separation between professional concerns and human concerns. What goes on among the people in a computer center is at least as important as what goes on between person and machine.

Acknowledgments

As for the previous two volumes, my greatest debts are to Hal Abelson and Paul Goldenberg. Both of them read the manuscript carefully through several drafts. Hal is great at noticing the large problems; he makes comments like "throw out this whole chapter" and "you are putting the cart before the horse here." Paul's comments were generally on a more detailed level, pointing out sections in which potentially valuable content was sabotaged by a presentation that nobody would understand. Together they have improved the book enormously.

Some of the examples in this book are ones that were posed to me by other people in other contexts. Horacio Reggini raised the issue of listing (not merely counting) the combinations of r elements of a list; Dick White asked me to investigate just how secure the Simplex lock is; Chris Anderson taught the probability class where the question about multinomial expansions arose. I'm grateful to Anita Harnadek, whom I've never met, for a logic problem I use to demonstrate inference systems. (She is, by the way, the author of a fantastic textbook called *Critical Thinking* that I recommend to teachers of almost any subject: math, English, or social studies.) Jim Davis's Logo interpreter in Logo (in the *LogoWorks* anthology I co-edited) was an inspiration for the Pascal compiler.

I'm grateful to Dan Bobrow, Sherry Turkle, and Terry Winograd for permission to quote from their work here. In particular, Bobrow's doctoral thesis forms the basis for my chapter on artificial intelligence, and I'm grateful for the program design as well as my extensive quotations from the thesis itself. He was also very patient in answering technical questions about details of a program he wrote over 20 years ago.

Mike Clancy taught me about generating functions and used them to find the closed form definition for the multinomial problem; Michael Somos, via the `sci.math` newsgroup, provided the closed form solution to the Simplex lock problem. Paul Hilfinger straightened me out about parser complexity.

Computer Science Logo Style
Beyond Programming

1   Automata Theory

Program file for this chapter: `fsm`

As I explained in the preface to the first volume, one of my purposes in writing this series of books has been to urge computer hobbyists away from the view of computer expertise as the knowledge of obscure characteristics of some particular computer—how to program it in machine language, what magic numbers can be found where in its memory, how to overcome the copy protection schemes on its disks, and so on. The trouble with this sort of machine-specific expertise is that it becomes obsolete when your favorite computer does. From my point of view, one of the virtues of Logo as a programming language is that its high level data structures direct your attention away from questions about what goes where in memory, allowing you to focus instead on a more abstract description of your problem.

Automata theory is a further step in abstracting your attention away from any particular kind of computer or particular programming language. In automata theory we consider a *mathematical model* of computing. Such a model strips the computational machinery—the "programming language"—down to the bare minimum, so that it's easy to manipulate these theoretical machines (there are several such models, for different purposes, as you'll soon see) mathematically to prove things about their capabilities. For the most part, these mathematical models are not used for practical programming problems. Real programming languages are much more convenient to use. But the very flexibility that makes real languages easier to use also makes them harder to talk about in a formal way. The stripped-down theoretical machines are designed to be examined mathematically.

What's a mathematical model? You'll see one shortly, called a "finite-state machine."

The point of this study is that the mathematical models are, in some important ways, *equivalent* to real computers and real programming languages. What this means is that any problem that can be solved on a real computer can be solved using these models, and vice versa. Anything we can prove about the models sheds light on the real problems of computer programming as well.

The questions asked in automata theory include these: Are there any problems that no computer can solve, no matter how much time and memory it has? Is it possible to *prove* that a particular computer program will actually solve a particular problem? If a computer can use two different external storage devices (disks or tapes) at the same time, does that extend the range of problems it can solve compared to a machine with only one such device?

There is also a larger question lurking in the background of automata theory: Does the human mind solve problems in the same way that a computer does? Are people subject to the same limitations as computers? Automata theory does not actually answer this question, but the insights of automata theory can be helpful in trying to work out an answer. We'll have more to say about this in the chapter on artificial intelligence.

What is a Computation?

What kinds of problems can we give to our abstract computers? In automata theory we want to focus our attention on computation itself, not on details of input and output devices. So we won't try creating a mathematical model of a video game.

We will play a game, though. In this game the computer has a rule in mind. You type in strings of letters, using only the letters A, B, and C. The computer tells you whether each string follows the rule or not. Your job is to guess the rule. For example, suppose you have done these experiments:

accepted	rejected
ABC	CBA
AAA	BBB
ABCABCABC	BCABCABC
A	BBBBBBB
ACCCCCCCC	CAAAAAAAA

You might guess, from these examples, that the rule is "The string must begin with A." Once you've made a guess you can test it out by trying more examples.

The program to play the game is called game. It takes one input, a number from 1 to 10. I've provided ten different rules. Rules 1 to 3 should be pretty easy to guess; rules 8 to 10 should be nearly impossible. (Don't feel too frustrated if you don't get them.)

A string can be any length, including length zero (the empty string). Each time you type a letter the program lets you know whether the string you've typed so far obeys the rule. The program indicates whether the string is accepted or rejected by displaying the word `accept` or `reject` on the screen. In particular, as soon as you start `game` the program will tell you whether or not the empty string is accepted by this rule. If you type the string `ABC` you'll really be testing three strings: `A`, `AB`, and `ABC`. You should type one letter at a time to make sure the program has a chance to respond to it before going on to the next letter. To start over again with a different string, press the Return key.

You should stop reading now and try the game. In the following paragraphs I'm going to talk about some of the answers, so this is your last chance. After you've figured out at least some of the rules, come back to the book.

Finite-State Machines

The point of studying this game is that we're going to look at a way to design a special-purpose abstract computer that understands one particular rule. We can then ask questions about how much information the computer needs to handle the job.

You've seen the word *state* before in connection with the Logo turtle. Its state includes its position and its heading. So one turtle state might be "position [17 82], heading 90." In principle, the turtle has an *infinite* number of possible states, because its position and heading don't have to be integers. Its position might be [14.142 14.142], for instance.

Anything that holds information can be in different states. As another example, an on-off light switch has two states. Some lamps have four states: off, low, medium, and high. A computer, too, has a certain number of states. The state of a computer includes all the information in its memory at some particular time.

A machine that has only a limited number of states, like the example of the light switch, is called a *finite-state machine*. For almost all of this chapter we'll be dealing with finite-state machines. You might think that that imposes a very severe limit on the kinds of computations we can do. But note that in the game I asked you to play, a rule can accept an infinite number of possible strings and reject an infinite number of others. The accepted or rejected strings can be of any length. (Some rules restrict the length of a string, but others allow any length at all.) In some sense, a finite-state machine can still perform infinitely varied computations.

Consider the third game as an example. The rule is "Accept any string that starts with `AB`." Here is a picture of a finite-state machine that implements that rule:

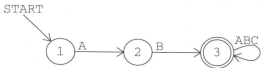

Each numbered circle represents a state. This machine has three states. The **start** arrow indicates that the machine starts out in state 1. State 3 is shown with a *double* circle to indicate that it is an *accepting* state. In other words, when the machine is in state 3 the screen says **accept**. The other two states are not accepting states. Every time you type a character the machine switches from one state to another. The arrow from state 1 to state 2 has an **A** next to its tail. This indicates that when the machine is in state 1, an input of **A** switches it to state 2. (The arrow from state 3 to itself has the three letters **ABC** at its tail. This is a shorthand notation for three separate arrows with heads and tails in the same place, one for each letter.)

This picture is actually incomplete. For a full description of the machine we have to indicate what happens on any input in any state. In other words, each circle should have *three* arrows coming out from it, one each for **A**, **B**, and **C**. I've chosen to adopt the convention that every machine has an unmarked state called **reject**. Any missing arrow goes to that state; once the machine is in the reject state it stays there forever. Here, then, is the complete diagram of the machine for game 3:

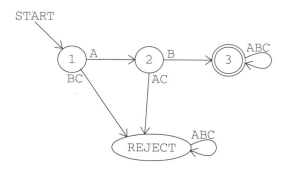

From now on I won't draw the **reject** state, but you should remember that it's really part of the machine description. So this machine requires four states, not three.

If the first input letter isn't **A**, the machine goes to the **reject** state. If the first letter is **A**, the machine goes to state 2. Then, if the second letter is **B**, the machine ends up in state 3 and accepts the string **AB**. This is the shortest acceptable string.

Each of the three arrows from state 3 loops right back into state 3 itself. (Remember, although only one arrow appears in the picture, it is labeled with three letters, so officially it represents three arrows.) This means that once the machine is in state 3 it stays there no matter what inputs it gets. Any string that starts **AB** is acceptable.

Here is a machine for game number 2:

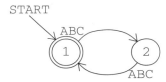

In this machine the *start state* is also an *accepting state*. (Every machine has exactly one start state, but it may have any number of accepting states.) This machine never gets into the `reject` state. That doesn't mean it doesn't reject any strings; all odd-length strings are rejected in state 2. But a rejected string can redeem itself by adding another input character, so state 2 allows a return to the accepting state 1.

Here is a machine for game number 5. (Notice that I'm saying "a machine" and not "the machine"; it is always possible to design other machines that would follow the same rule.)

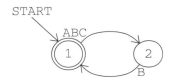

You probably had more trouble discovering rule 5 than rule 2, and it takes longer to say the rule in English words. But the *machines* for the two rules are almost identical. (Remember, though, that the rule-5 machine really has a third state, the `reject` state, which is not shown in the diagram.)

Here are machines for rules 7 and 9. With these machines as hints, can you figure out the rules? Go back to the `game` program to test your hypotheses.

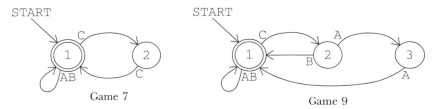

Game 7   Game 9

You should also get some practice translating in the other direction, from English rules to machine diagrams. Here are a couple to work on: Rule 4 is "To be accepted a string must be composed of doubled letters (**AA**, **BB**, and **CC**) strung together." Rule 8 is "To be accepted a string must contain an even number of **A**s."

Nondeterministic Machines

Here is rule 6: "To be accepted a string must begin with A and end with C." Strings accepted by this rule include AC (the shortest possible), ABC, AACC, ACAC, ABCABC, and so on. Between the initial A and the final C an accepted string can have any combination of As, Bs, and Cs. It's natural to think of the string as having three parts: a fixed beginning, a variable middle, and a fixed end. The three parts of the input strings can be represented conveniently with three states in the machine, like this:

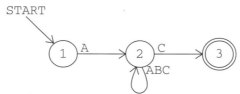

The machine starts in state 1. To be accepted a string must start with A. Therefore, an A arrow leads from state 1 to state 2. Any other input at state 1 leads to the `reject` state.

Once the machine is in state 2 it is ready for the middle part of the string. In this middle part any combination of letters is allowed. Therefore, there are three arrows from state 2 to itself, one for every possible letter.

Finally, a C arrow leads from state 2 to state 3, signaling the end of an acceptable string. A string must end with C to be accepted.

There is a problem with this machine: There are *two* C arrows leading out from state 2. One is a loop back into state 2; the other goes on to state 3. This situation reflects the fact that C serves two different functions in this rule: C is an optional part of the middle section of the string, and it's also the required final input in the string.

A machine with two arrows from the same state for the same input is called a *nondeterministic* machine. Here is how such a machine could work: Whenever there are two choices for the machine's current state and input, the machine clones itself. One of the copies follows each arrow. From then on, if *either* machine is in an accepting state the string is accepted.

Nondeterministic finite-state machines are more complicated than deterministic ones. Does the added complexity "buy" any added power? In other words, can a nondeterministic machine solve problems that a deterministic machine can't? It turns out that the answer to this question is no. Deterministic machines are just as powerful as nondeterministic ones. This is an important theorem in automata theory. I'm not going to prove it formally in this book, but to illustrate the theorem, here is a deterministic machine that carries out game 6:

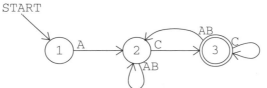

This machine is similar to the nondeterministic version. It has the same number of states and some of the connections are identical. State 3 is more complicated, though. Also, in this machine, it is no longer the case that each state of the machine corresponds exactly to one of three parts of the input string. Specifically, when the machine is in state 3 the string may or may not be finished.

Representing Machines as Logo Lists

The game program uses finite-state machines to represent the rules by which it accepts or rejects strings. (The machines must be deterministic for the program to work.) Logo programs can't read circles and arrows, so a machine is represented as a list. What information is actually contained in an FSM diagram? The diagram shows that there are a certain number of states (the circles), that there are certain transitions from one state to another (the arrows), that one particular state is the start state (the start arrow), and that certain states are accepting ones (the double circles). As in any programming project, I could have chosen many different ways to represent that information in the program.

In the particular representation I chose, the list form of a machine has three members. The first member is the number of the start state. The second member is a list of arrows; each arrow is itself a list, as I'll explain in a moment. The third member of a machine list is a list of the accepting states of the machine. For example, here is the machine for game 3 again, in both forms:

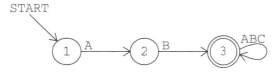

```
[1 [[1 A 2] [2 B 3] [3 ABC 3]] [3]]
```

The number 1 is the start state; the list [3] is the list of accepting states. (This machine happens to have only one accepting state.) Everything else is the list of arrows. Each arrow is also a list with three members: the initial state (the tail of the arrow), the input letter or letters, and the final state (the head of the arrow). The first arrow in this machine is

```
[1 A 2]
```

This is the arrow from state 1 to state 2 associated with the input **A**.

The list [3 ABC 3] in this machine represents three arrows, using the same short-hand as in the circle-and-arrow diagrams. I could equally well have represented these arrows separately:

```
[1 [[1 A 2] [2 B 3] [3 A 3] [3 B 3] [3 C 3]] [3]]
```

As in the circle-and-arrow diagrams, I haven't explicitly represented the transitions to the **reject** state in these lists. The program is written so that if it doesn't find a transition for the current state and input in the list of transitions, it goes into state number −1, its representation for the **reject** state.

Here are some more machine lists:

```
Game 2:    [1 [[1 ABC 2] [2 ABC 1]] [1]]
Game 7:    [1 [[1 AB 1] [1 C 2] [2 C 1]] [1]]
Game 9:    [1 [[1 AB 1] [1 C 2] [2 A 3] [2 B 1] [3 A 1]] [1]]
```

At this point you should stop and play with the program. Make up your own rules. The procedure **fsm** takes a machine list as input and accepts strings based on that machine. (**Game** uses **fsm** with particular machines as inputs.) Try out your new rules to make sure you've designed the machines correctly. Then get a friend to play with your rules. If both of you are reading this book together you can have a competition. (It's easy to design rules that are impossible to guess because there are too many details. If you have a competition you should limit yourselves to three states per machine.)

You might be interested in reading through the **fsm** program, which simulates a finite-state machine when given the machine's description as its input. It's a pretty simple program. If you think of a machine's state diagram as a kind of "wiring diagram" that might be used in building a real version of that particular machine, this Logo program is a kind of *universal* finite-state machine implementation.

Text Editors: a Use for Acceptors

It may seem to you that accepting or rejecting strings isn't much like what you usually do with computers. You may wonder how this mathematical model is related to real computer programming. There are two answers to this question. One is that it's possible to design finite-state machines that have more versatile outputs than simply yes or no. I'll give an example shortly. But the other answer is that there are real situations in which accepting or rejecting a string of symbols does come up in practical computation.

One example is in the implementation of programming languages. When you say that

```
print 2+2
```

is a legal Logo instruction but

```
print 2+
```

is illegal, you're doing a more complicated version of what a finite-state acceptor does.

The *search* command in a good text editor uses finite-state machines. Most text editors have a command that allows you to look through a file for a particular string of characters. Fancier editors allow searching not just for one particular string, but for any string that follows a rule the user can provide. The editor finds a string that matches the rule using a finite-state machine. Of course, people who use editors don't have to specify their search rules in the *form* of a finite-state machine! The editing program accepts search rules in a simpler form and translates them into FSM form. Here is an example, the notation used by *ed,* a standard editor in the Unix operating system.

A string like

```
spaghetti
```

just matches an identical string in the file you're editing. A slightly more interesting case is

```
[Ss]paghetti
```

which matches either "Spaghetti" or "spaghetti" (with a capital or lower case "s"). The square brackets indicate that *any* of the letters inside the brackets will be accepted. In the expression

```
[Ss]paghet*i
```

the asterisk matches *any number* (including zero) of the letter before it (in this case, the letter t). This example would match any of these:

```
Spaghei
Spaghetttti
spaghetti
spagheti
```

You might use this in a search command if you're a bad speller! The bracket and asterisk can be combined;

```
C[AD]*R
```

will match any of

```
CAR
CDR
CADDR
CR
```

Or you could use

```
M[is]*p*i
```

to match the name of a famous river.

Some of the rules from the game I presented earlier can be represented as *ed* search strings according to these rules. In the first game the machine accepted any string made up of As and Bs. The corresponding *ed* expression is

```
[AB]*
```

The third game called for strings beginning with the sequence AB, followed by whatever you like. This can be represented as

```
AB[ABC]*
```

Game 10, which I'm sure you didn't solve, accepts any string that includes the sequence ABCBA within it. In *ed* terms, that's

```
[ABC]*ABCBA[ABC]*
```

I haven't given you a complete description of the *ed* search rules. I included this much only because I want you to see how a "real" program uses the idea of finite-state machines. But in the remaining part of this chapter I want to use a different notation based on Logo words and lists.

Regular Expressions

The notation I'm about to describe allows an acceptance rule, like the rules in the **game** program or the rules for *ed* searches, to be represented in Logo. The representation of such a rule is called a *regular expression*. I'm going to tell you some rules for what a regular expression can look like. Don't be confused: Any particular regular expression is a rule that accepts strings of letters. I'm giving you rules that accept regular expressions—rules about rules. As a rough analogy, "one player is X and the other is O" is a rule about the specific game Tic Tac Toe; "each player should have a fair chance to win" is a rule about what kinds of game rules are acceptable.

Alphabet rule. Any symbol in a machine's alphabet is a regular expression. We represent the symbol as a one-letter Logo word. In our guessing game the alphabet contains three symbols: A, B, and C. So

B

is a regular expression.

Concatenation rule. A list whose members are regular expressions represents those expressions one after another. For example, since A is a regular expression and B is a regular expression,

[A B]

is a regular expression representing the string AB. (Notice that the Logo word AB does *not* represent that string; the alphabet rule requires that each letter be represented as a separate word.)

Alternatives rule. A list whose first member is the word or and whose remaining members are regular expressions represents any string that matches *any* of those expressions. For example,

[OR [A A] B]

matches either the sequence AA or the single symbol B. As a convenience, a Logo word containing more than one letter (other than the word or) is taken as an abbreviation for the oring of the individual letters. For example, ABC is equivalent to [OR A B C].

Repetition rule. A list containing exactly two members, in which the first is the asterisk (*) symbol and the second is a regular expression, represents a string containing any number (including zero) of substrings that match the regular expression. So

```
[* [OR [A A] B]]
```

matches any of these:

```
B
BB
BAAB
AAAAAA
AABAA
      (the empty string)
AABBBBBAA
```

The number of consecutive As must be even for a string of As and Bs to match this expression.

These four rules constitute the definition of a regular expression. It's a *recursive definition.* Just as the effect of a recursive Logo procedure is defined in terms of a simpler case of the same procedure, a complex regular expression is defined in terms of simpler ones.

Here are the ten game rules from the beginning of this chapter in the form of regular expressions:

1. [* AB]
2. [* [ABC ABC]]
3. [A B [* ABC]]
4. [* [OR [A A] [B B] [C C]]]
5. [* [ABC B]]
6. [A [* ABC] C]
7. [* [OR A B [C C]]]
8. [[* BC] [* [A [* BC] A [* BC]]]]
9. [[* AB] [* [C [OR B [A A]]] [* AB]]]
10. [[* ABC] A B C B A [* ABC]]

You should go through these examples carefully, making sure you understand how the regular expression represents the same idea as the English description or the machine diagram you saw earlier.

Rules That Aren't Regular

You may be thinking that *any* rule for accepting or rejecting strings of symbols can be represented as a regular expression. But that's not so. For example, consider the rules for recognizing ordinary arithmetic expressions:

accepted	rejected
2+3	23+
2*(3+4)	2*)3+4(
-5	/6

Think for a moment just about the matter of balancing parentheses. Sometimes you have parentheses within parentheses, as in

```
((3+4)/(5+6))
```

How would you represent this part of the arithmetic expression rule in the form of a regular expression? You can't just say something like

```
[[* () something-or-other [* )]]
```

to mean "any number of open parentheses, something, then any number of close parentheses." That would allow strings like

```
(((7)))))
```

But this string should be rejected because it has too many close parentheses. You're not allowed to use a close parenthesis unless you've already used a matching open parenthesis. You can have any number of nested parentheses you want as long as they're balanced.

It is possible to invent other kinds of formal notation, more powerful than regular expressions, that will allow us to give the rules for well-formed arithmetic expressions. In this section I'll introduce briefly a formal notation called *production rules* that's powerful enough to describe arithmetic expressions. For now, in this chapter, I don't want to discuss production rules in great detail; my only reason for introducing them at this point is to give you a sense of how regular expressions fit into a larger universe of possible formal systems. In the following sections I'll have more to say about regular expressions and finite-state machines. But we'll return to production rules in Chapters 5 and 6, in which we'll need formal notations with which to discuss more interesting languages than the A-B-C language of this chapter. (In Chapter 5 we'll be talking about Pascal; in Chapter 6 we'll take on English.)

The key ingredient that's missing from regular expression notation is a way to *name* a kind of sub-expression so that the name can be used in defining more complex expressions. In particular, a sub-expression name can be used in its own definition to allow a *recursive* definition of the rule.

A production rule has the form

```
name      :  expansion
```

Each rule is a definition of the name on the left in terms of smaller units, analogous to the definition of a Logo procedure in terms of subprocedures. The expansion part of the rule is a string of symbols including both members of the "alphabet" of the system (like the alphabet that underlies a regular expression language) and names defined by production rules.

As an example, here is a set of production rules that defines the language of arithmetic expressions. These rules take into account the "order of operations" for arithmetic that you learned in elementary school: multiplication before addition. An expression like

```
2/3+1/6
```

is ordinarily interpreted as the sum of two *terms,* namely two thirds and one sixth. An expression can be a single term, a sum of terms, or a difference of terms. Here's how that idea is expressed in a set of production rules; I'll discuss the notation in more detail in a moment.

```
expr      :  term | expr + term | expr - term
term      :  factor | term * factor | term / factor
factor    :  number | ( expr )
number    :  digit | number digit
digit     :  0 | 1 | 2 | 3 | 4 | 5 | 6 | 7 | 8 | 9
```

The vertical bars separate alternatives. The first rule, the one that defines `expr`, contains three alternatives. First, an expression can be just a single term. Second, an expression can be a smaller expression plus a term. Third, an expression can be a smaller expression minus a term. The symbols inside boxes are the members of the alphabet of the arithmetic expression language. (I've put them in boxes to make it easier not to confuse them with the punctuation characters—the colons and vertical bars—that are part of the production rule notation itself.)

Do you see how parentheses fit in? If a string like 4+5 is an expression, then (4+5) is a factor, so 3*(4+5) is a term, and so on. Since a factor is a kind of term, and a term is a kind of expression, the factor (4+5) can be considered an expression, and so it too can be put inside parentheses. So ((4+5)) is also acceptable as a factor.

Regular Expressions and Finite-State Machines

I've hinted at something that I haven't actually made explicit: Regular expressions are equivalent to finite-state machines. In other words, if you can express a rule as a regular expression, you can design a finite-state machine that carries out the rule. If you can't write a regular expression for the rule, you can't design a finite-state machine either.

You may be thinking, "so what?" I've introduced two different formal notations, finite-state machines and regular expressions, and now I'm telling you that the two are equivalent. So why didn't I just pick one in the first place and forget about the other? I have a general answer and a specific answer to these questions.

The general answer is that comparing different formal systems is what automata theory is all about. By the end of this book you'll have been introduced to half a dozen or so different formal systems. Some are more powerful than others. The bare assertion that one formal system is equivalent to another, or more powerful than another, isn't very interesting; but if we can understand the *reasons* behind those assertions then we may be able to put the knowledge to work in practical situations. At the very end of this book, in Chapter 6, we'll talk about a particular formal system that's often used in artificial intelligence programs to recognize English sentences. By then you should know enough about formal systems to be able to understand why that particular one is a good choice.

The specific answer is that finite-state machines and regular expressions are *different* from each other in an interesting way. A finite-state machine is an *algorithm,* a sequence of steps, or a procedure that can be followed to test whether some string matches a given rule. It says, "start here, then if this happens do this, then..." just like a procedure in Logo or most other programming languages. (But we've seen that a finite-state machine is like a procedure written in a restricted programming language that isn't as flexible as Logo.) A regular expression, though, is *not* a sequence of steps. It's more like a description of the *result* that we want, leaving open the precise recipe for how to get there. People often pose problems in a similar way. They call the plumber and say, "the drain in my bathtub is backing up." Part of the plumber's expertise is to be able to translate that *declarative* problem statement into a *procedural* form, a sequence of steps needed to clear up the problem. An early stumbling block in artificial intelligence research was the seeming gulf between the procedural knowledge embodied in a computer program and the declarative knowledge needed for human-like behavior. Recently people have invented *declarative programming languages* (the best known is Prolog, but any commercial spreadsheet program is also in this category) that allow the user to state a problem in declarative form. The programming language interpreter then automatically translates this problem statement into a sequence of steps for the computer to perform.

Writing a Prolog interpreter raises many issues beyond the scope of this book. But we can take a smaller step in the realm of translation from a declarative notation to a procedural one. I've written a Logo program, listed at the end of the chapter, that translates from a regular expression to an equivalent finite-state machine. Its top-level procedure, `machine`, takes a regular expression as input and outputs a machine list in the format I showed earlier.

How to Translate

The general claim that regular expressions are equivalent in power to finite-state machines is called Kleene's Theorem, named after the mathematician Stephen C. Kleene, its discoverer. You can find a proof of this theorem in any textbook on automata theory. I'm not going to give a proof here, but I'll indicate how the translation is done in my program. The same kinds of ideas are used in the proof.

Remember that there are four parts to the definition of a regular expression. The alphabet rule provides the fundamental building blocks; the concatenation, alternatives, and repetition rules build large regular expressions recursively out of smaller ones. The translation process follows the same pattern: We start with a procedure to build a trivial two-state machine that only accepts a single letter, then we add three rules for combining smaller machines into a large machine. In the following paragraphs I'll show how each rule is reflected in the `machine` program.

This construction process often produces machines with more states than necessary. The `machine` program eliminates redundant states as its final step.

The alphabet rule says that any member of the machine's alphabet is a regular expression. In the program, a symbol can be any one-letter word other than *. The symbol X is translated into the machine

```
[1 [[1 X 2]] [2]]
```

(You'll see that the program works by combining little machines into bigger ones. Every time the program has to invent a new machine state it uses the next free number. So the state numbers might not be 1 and 2 in a real example.) The procedure `ndletter` handles this rule.

Next comes the *concatenation rule*. The regular expression

`[A B]`

matches a string with two parts; the first substring matches the A and the second matches the B. In this simple example each "substring" matches only a single letter. In a more complicated concatenation like

`[[OR A C] [* B]]`

there are different choices for each substring. For example, that regular expression is matched by the string

`CBBB`

in which the letter C matches the first part of the expression and the substring BBB matches the second part.

To translate a regular expression of this kind (a concatenation) into a finite-state machine, we begin by recursively translating the subexpressions into smaller machines. Then we have to "splice" the two machines together. Procedure `ndconcat` does this splicing.

We'll begin with the simplest possible example. Suppose we want to translate the regular expression

`[A B]`

We have already translated the two symbols A and B into machines:

[1 [[1 A 2]] [2]]   [3 [[3 B 4]] [4]]

The combined machine must start at the start state of the first component machine, state 1. The combined machine should be in an accepting state when *both* component machines have been satisfied; in other words, the accepting states of the combined machine should be those of the *second* component machine. In this case that means only state 4.

To splice the component machines together we must add transitions (arrows) between them. Specifically, whenever the first component machine gets into an accepting state, the combined machine should follow the same transitions that apply to the start state of the second component machine. In this case, when the combined machine gets into state 2 (the accepting state of the first component machine) it should follow the same transitions that apply to state 3 (the start state of the second machine). There is only one such transition, a B arrow into state 4. That means we must add the arrow

[2 B 4]

to the combined machine.

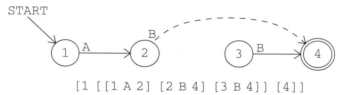

[1 [[1 A 2] [2 B 4] [3 B 4]] [4]]

State 3, although it is still in the machine, is now useless. There is no way for the machine to get into state 3. Later in the translation process another procedure removes such "orphaned" states from the machine.

As a slightly more complicated example, consider the translation of the regular expression

[[OR A C] [* B]]

We start by supposing that we've already translated the two subexpressions separately:

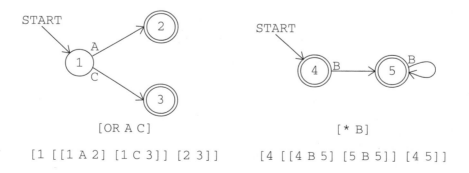

[OR A C]   [* B]

[1 [[1 A 2] [1 C 3]] [2 3]]   [4 [[4 B 5] [5 B 5]] [4 5]]

Chapter 1   Automata Theory

(We haven't yet discussed the alternatives rule or the repetition rule, so I haven't yet explained how these subexpressions are translated. For now, please just take on faith that this picture is correct. We'll get to those other rules shortly.)

The start state of the combined machine is the start state of the first component, state 1. At every accepting state of the first machine we must duplicate the transitions from the start state of the second machine. In this example the start state of the second machine has only the transition

```
[4 B 5]
```

but there are two accepting states in the first machine, so we must add two new arrows:

```
[2 B 5]    [3 B 5]
```

A final detail is that in this example the start state of the second component machine, state 4, is an accepting state. That means that the second substring can be empty. Therefore the accepting states of the first component machine should also be accepting states of the combined machine. Here is the result:

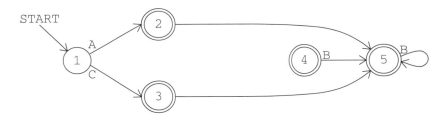

```
[1 [[1 A 2] [1 C 3] [2 B 5] [3 B 5] [4 B 5] [5 B 5]] [2 3 4 5]]
```

Again, state 4 is now an "orphan" and will be eliminated later in the program.

The *alternatives rule* combines two machines in parallel, so to speak, rather than in series. It works by inventing a new state that becomes the start state of the combined machine. Arrows leaving from the new state duplicate the arrows from the start states of the component machines. Procedure ndor handles this rule.

As an example, here is the translation process for

```
[OR A B]
```

(or its abbreviation **AB**). We start with two separate machines:

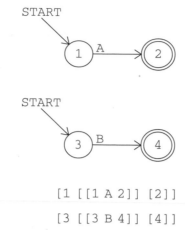

[1 [[1 A 2]] [2]]

[3 [[3 B 4]] [4]]

We combine them by inventing a new state 5:

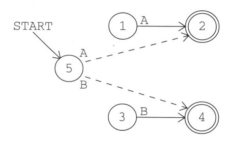

[5 [5 A 2] [5 B 4] [1 A 2] [3 B 4]] [2 4]]

I haven't explained all the details of the construction process. For example, should the new state, state 5, be an accepting state? In this example it shouldn't be. See if you can think of a case where it might be; then read the program listing to see the exact algorithm that makes this decision. Again, this construction process may leave unused states for later cleanup.

A much more serious problem is that an **or** construction is likely to produce a nondeterministic machine. For example, here is the machine for

[OR [A B] [A C]]

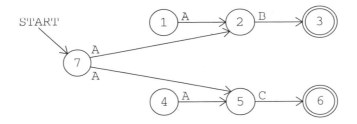

[7 [[7 A 2] [7 A 5] [1 A 2] [2 B 3] [4 A 5] [5 C 6]] [3 6]]

Like the unused states, the problem of nondeterminism is left for the end of the program, when procedure `determine` translates the nondeterministic machine into a deterministic one. (The concatenation rule can also make nondeterministic machines, although it's not as likely.)

The final case to be considered is the *repetition rule*. This rule acts on only one smaller machine, not two machines as in the previous two cases. The rule doesn't require any new states. It has two effects. One is to add the start state to the list of accepting states. The second is to add arrows from the (old) accepting states that mimic the arrows from the start state. (This is exactly like the splicing of two machines in the concatenation rule, but in this case we concatenate a single machine with itself!) Procedure `ndmany` makes this transformation. It, too, can result in a nondeterministic machine.

Here is an example of the rule:

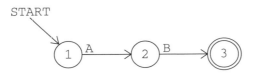

[A B] → [1 [[1 A 2] [2 B 3]] [3]]

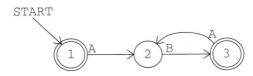

[* [A B]] → [1 [[1 A 2] [2 B 3] [3 A 2]] [1 3]]

These four rules are combined by `nondet`, a procedure whose input is a regular expression and whose output is a (possibly nondeterministic) machine.

```
to nondet :regexp
if and (wordp :regexp) (equalp count :regexp 1) [output ndletter :regexp]
if wordp :regexp [output ndor reduce "sentence :regexp]
if equalp first :regexp "or [output ndor butfirst :regexp]
if equalp first :regexp "* [output ndmany last :regexp]
output ndconcat :regexp
end
```

The top-level procedure `machine` does a little initialization and then does its work with the instruction

```
output optimize determine nondet :regexp
```

That is, first it creates what may be a nondeterministic machine, then if necessary it translates that into a deterministic one (eliminating orphan states in the process), then it gets rid of any redundant states that may have been created.

Making the Machine Deterministic

In the first volume of this series we explored the techniques of depth-first and breadth-first tree traversal. Given a tree structure, these algorithms allow us to "visit" every node of the tree once.

A finite state machine can be viewed as a structure almost like a tree. The machine's start state corresponds to the root node; the states that can be reached by an arrow from a given state are the children of that state. But there is one important difference between trees and machines: In a tree, every node (except for the root node) has exactly one parent. The tree search algorithms depend on that fact to ensure that each node is visited only once. In a machine, arrows from several different states can lead to the same state, so a state may have several "parents." The technical name for an arbitrary collection of nodes with connections among them is a *graph*. If the connections are one-way, as in the finite state machine diagrams, it's called a *directed graph*.

Searching a graph is just like searching a tree, except that we have to keep track of which nodes we've already visited, to avoid examining the same node twice. Procedure `determine` creates a list named `states`, initially empty, into which each state number is added as the program examines that state. The depth first traversal of the machine is carried out by procedure `nd.traverse`; although this procedure looks different from the `depth.first` procedure in Volume 1, it uses the same basic algorithm. Given a state as input, it processes that state and invokes itself recursively for all of the children of that state—the states reachable by arrows from the input state. Unlike `depth.first`, though, `nd.traverse` is an operation. It outputs a new list of moves (arrows) for the deterministic version of the machine.

What does it mean to process a state? `Nd.traverse` first checks whether this state has already been processed; if so, it outputs an empty list, because this state will contribute no new moves to the machine. Otherwise, it remembers this state number as having been processed, finds all the moves starting from this state, and calls `check.nd` to look for nondeterminism. `Check.nd` takes the first available arrow whose tail is at the state we're processing, and looks for all arrows with the same tail and with the same letter.* The local variable `heads` will contain a list of all the state numbers reachable by these arrows. (The state numbers are sorted into increasing order, and duplicates eliminated. If the machine has two completely identical arrows, that doesn't result in nondeterminism.)

There are three cases for what `check.nd` must do. First, if there is only one state number in `:heads`, then there is no nondeterminism for this letter, and `check.nd` includes the arrow from the original machine as part of the deterministic machine. Second, if there is more than one state number, `check.nd` looks to see if we've already seen the same combination of result states. If so, then we've already created a new state equivalent to that combination of old states, and `check.nd` creates a new arrow pointing to that existing new state. Finally, the third case is that this combination of states is one we haven't seen before. In that case, `check.nd` must create a new state, with arrows duplicating those from all of the original states.

In other words, if there are arrows

```
[[3 B 4] [3 B 7]]
```

then `check.nd` will invent a new state that is an "alias" for "four-and-seven." If the same machine also contains arrows

```
[[8 C 4] [8 C 7]]
```

then `check.nd` will use the *same* alias state for this pair, not inventing a new one. The new state is given arrows matching those of all its component states (4 and 7 in this

---

* By the way, `nondet` always creates arrows with only a single letter; if two or more letters lead from the same state to the same state, a separate arrow is created for each of them. This makes for a longer machine list, but makes steps like this one—looking for two arrows with the same letter—easier. Once the deterministic machine has been created, procedure `optimize` will combine such arrows into the abbreviated form with more than one letter per arrow.

example). The new state might itself contain a nondeterministic branch, but that's okay because the new state will eventually be processed as we continue to traverse the machine graph.

You might think that this process could go on forever: that each new state `check.nd` invents will turn out to include nondeterminism, which will require yet another new state to resolve. Fortunately, that doesn't happen; the process does always end eventually. (In the next chapter we'll see what the limit is on the number of necessary states for the deterministic machine.)

Because `determine` uses a graph traversal algorithm to examine the original machine's states, it will never find "orphan" states that can't be reached by arrows from some other state. That's why the process of making the machine deterministic also eliminates orphan states, with no extra effort.

Eliminating Redundant States

The machines produced by `determine` are runnable, but often ugly; they contain many more states than necessary. Procedure `optimize` eliminates many redundancies and also combines arrows with the same head and tail but with different letters. First it goes through the machine's arrow list, creating a list for each state representing the exits from that state:

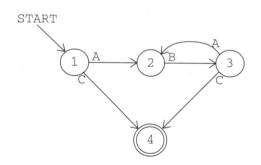

```
  [[* [A B]] C]
State 1: [[A 2] [C 4]]
State 2: [[B 3]]
State 3: [[A 2] [C 4]]
State 4: []
```

Chapter 1   Automata Theory

In this machine, states 1 and 3 have the same exit list. (In these lists, each arrow is represented with only two members; the arrow's tail is not included. That's because states 1 and 3 would *not* have identical lists if the tails were included. State 1's list would be

```
[[1 A 2] [1 C 4]]
```

and state 3's list would have arrows starting with 3. In the program, the two-member form of an arrow is called a *stub*.)

The program must be careful about the order in which it puts stubs in each state's list, so it doesn't end up with

```
[[C 4] [A 2]]
```

for one of the states. That's why `stub.add` takes trouble to insert each stub in a well-defined position, rather than just adding each new stub at the beginning or end of the list. It's also in `stub.add` that arrows connecting the same two states but with different letters are combined into a single arrow.

Since states 1 and 3 also agree in their acceptingness (namely they aren't accepting states), they can be combined into one state. `Optimize.state` can replace every reference to state 3 with a reference to state 1.

A Finite-State Adder

I promised earlier to show you a use for finite-state machines other than accepting or rejecting strings. In this section I'll fulfill that promise by designing a machine to add two numbers. We'll represent the numbers in binary notation, in which each digit represents a power of 2 instead of a power of 10.

If you've come across binary numbers before, you can skip this paragraph. Just as the ordinary notation for numbers is based on the ten digits 0 to 9, binary notation is based on *two* digits, 0 and 1. In ordinary ("decimal") notation, the amount that each digit contributes to the total depends on where it is in the number. For example, in the number 247, the digit 2 contributes two hundred, not just two, because it's in the third position counting from the right. Each digit's contribution is the value of the digit itself multiplied by a power of ten:

$$2 \times 10^2 + 4 \times 10^1 + 7 \times 10^0$$

(10^2 is 100; 10^1 is 10; 10^0 is just 1.) In binary, the contribution of each digit is multiplied by a power of *two,* so the binary number 10101 represents

$$1 \times 2^4 + 0 \times 2^3 + 1 \times 2^2 + 0 \times 2^1 + 1 \times 2^0$$

which is $16 + 4 + 1$ ($2^4 + 2^2 + 2^0$) or 21. Computers use binary notation because it's easy to build electrical circuits in which each wire is either on or off. In Chapter 2 we'll talk about an example. Right now I want to show something different—not an actual electronic machine but an abstract machine based on the ideas we've been using in this chapter.

The machine will add two binary numbers, one digit position at a time, just the way you add multi-digit numbers yourself. When you see a problem like

$$376$$
$$\underline{+572}$$

you start at the right and say, "6 plus 2 is 8; 7 plus 7 is 14, which is 4 carry 1; 1 plus 3 plus 5 is 9." The finite-state adder works the same way except that the digits are always 0 or 1.

The machine will add any numbers, but to explain how it works I want to consider a specific example. Let's say we want to add 52 and 21. (By the way, I didn't pick these numbers because they name card games, but because the pattern of digits in their binary forms is convenient for the explanation I want to give.) 52 in binary is 110100 ($32+16+4$) and 21 is 10101 ($16+4+1$). I'm going to write these one above the other, with a couple of extra zeros on the left to leave room for a possible carry:

```
0 0 1 1 0 1 0 0
0 0 0 1 0 1 0 1
```

Remember how a finite-state machine works: At a given moment it's in some *state,* then it reads some *input* symbol and goes to another state. In this problem, since we have two numbers to add, the most natural way to think about it would be to give the machine *two* inputs at a time. This idea doesn't quite fit in with the formal definition of a finite-state machine, but we can let the machine's "alphabet" consist of *pairs* of digits, so something like 01 would be a single input. (By the way, the word *bit* is commonly used as an abbreviation for "binary digit.") Just as you added vertical pairs of digits (first 6 and 2, then 7 and 7, and so on) in the earlier example, we'll use vertical pairs of bits as the inputs to the finite-state adder, starting from the right end. So the first input will be 01, then 00, then 11, then 00, then 11 again, then 10, and then 00 twice. From now on, in this section, when you see something like 10 you should remember that it is a *single* input to the finite-state machine, a single symbol, not two in a row. (In the diagram below, an arrow labeled 01/10 represents two arrows, one for the input 01 and one for the input 10. These two arrows will always go to the same state because 0 + 1 = 1 + 0.)

We need to make one change in the notation used in machine diagrams. We no longer want to mark each state as accepting (double circle) or rejecting (single circle). Instead, each state produces an *output* that can be any arbitrary symbol. In this machine the outputs will be 0 or 1, representing the binary digits of the sum. Inside each state circle, instead of just a state number you'll see something like "3/1"; this means that it's state number 3 and that the output from that state is 1.

Here is the machine:

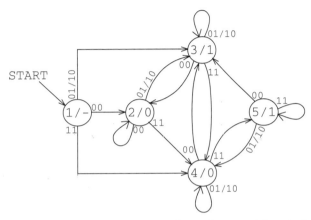

State 1, the start state, has no output. When the machine is in start state it hasn't seen any digits of the addends yet, so it can't compute a digit of the sum. States 2 and 4 output a zero digit, while states 3 and 5 output a one. (Like the inputs, the number that the machine outputs is presented with its rightmost bit first. The machine works this way for the same reason that *you* add numbers from right to left: That's the direction in which a "carry" digit moves from one column to another.)

Why are there *two* zero-output states and *two* one-output states? The reason is that the machine is in state 4 or 5 when there is a carry into the next digit of the sum.

Let's trace through my example. We start in state 1. The first input symbol is 01, representing a 0 in the rightmost (binary) digit of 52 and a 1 in the rightmost digit of 21. The machine enters state 3 and outputs a 1.

The next input is 00 because both numbers have zero as the second digit. The machine enters state 2 and outputs 0.

The next input is 11. The machine enters state 4 and outputs 0. Being in state 4 means that there is a carry from this position into the next.

You can finish the example yourself. The sum should be 01001001, or 73.

Counting and Finite-State Machines

Earlier we saw that you can't write a regular expression for a rule that requires balanced parentheses. Since regular expressions are equivalent to finite-state machines, you won't be surprised to learn that finite-state machines can't count.

Actually, they can count up to a point; it's just that each finite-state machine can only count up to a fixed limit. For example, here is a finite-state machine that accepts strings of balanced parentheses up to four deep:

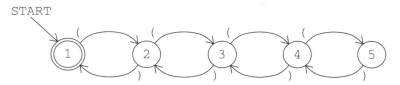

This machine will accept strings like these:

```
( )           ( ( ) )        ( ) ( )
( ( ) ( ) )   ( ( ( ( ) ) ) )  ( ( ( ( ) ) ) ) ( ( ) )
```

There is no limit to the *length* of the string this machine can handle. For example, it will accept this:

```
( ) ( ) ( ) ( ) ( ) ( ) ( ) ( ) ( ) ( ) ( ) ( ) ( ) ( )
```

But there can be no more than four parentheses open *at once*; the machine will reject

```
( ( ( ( ( ) ) ) ) )
```

Even this limited counting ability of finite-state machines is of great practical value. Real computers, after all, are finite-state machines. Any real computer has a finite amount of memory, and this memory can be in a finite number of states. But the number is quite huge. If a real computer includes a parenthesis-counting program that is limited to, say, 20,000 levels of parentheses, nobody will ever notice that the limit isn't infinite.

(The number of states in a real computer may be even larger than you're thinking. Each bit of computer memory isn't a state. Instead, if a computer has n bits of memory it has 2^n states! For example, a computer with three bits of memory can use those bits to represent *eight* states:

```
0  0  0
0  0  1
0  1  0
0  1  1
1  0  0
1  0  1
1  1  0
1  1  1
```

The number of possible states in a typical large computer is greater than the number of atoms in the galaxy.)

In a moment I'm going to talk about a theoretical model of a machine with infinite memory. You might wonder why it pays to study such machines, since any real machine has to be limited in memory. The answer has to do with my example about the 20,000 levels of parentheses. It is theoretically possible to write a regular expression for such strings. To show you how it's done, here is a regular expression for up to three levels:

[* [([* [([* [( )]])]])]]

(I've drawn boxes around the actual alphabet-rule symbols just to make it a little easier for you to distinguish between the parentheses, which are symbols in the input strings, and the brackets, which are part of the glue that holds a regular expression together.)

There is no theoretical problem about extending this regular expression to allow up to 20,000 parentheses. But a machine based on this technique would be very large and complicated. Instead, it makes more sense to *pretend* that the computer has an infinite amount of memory available and use a formal system (like the production rules I mentioned briefly) that depends on an infinite memory. Such a formal system leads to a shorter, more elegant expression of the balanced parentheses rule. In practice, we can provide enough memory for any of the strings our program will actually meet.

Turing Machines

One way we might explore infinite machines is to imagine that they're represented by state diagrams, like those of finite-state machines, but with an infinite number of states. For example, here is a picture of an infinite-capacity parenthesis counter:

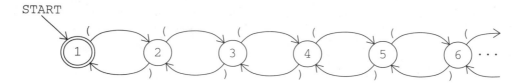

START

The trouble with this idea is that it's hard to model precisely what's meant by that row of dots on the right. There's no way we can have a *complete* formal description of an infinitely complex machine.

Instead, consider what *you* do when you have to solve a problem too complex to fit in your own memory. You don't build yourself a bigger brain; you get a pencil and some paper. That is, you use *external* storage. You can imagine that your brain is a finite-state machine but that it has access to an infinite supply of paper.

Of course, this division of a problem's necessary information into a finite *internal* state and an infinite *external* memory also models actual computers in an obvious way. The internal state in the model represents the internal memory of the computer, while the external memory in the model represents such storage devices as disks and tapes. To solve a bigger problem you don't have to buy a bigger computer; you just have to switch floppy disks occasionally.

You might think that the mathematical model I'm talking about was based on the analogy with real computers and that my story about the finite-state brain is just a coincidence. But in fact this model was invented by Alan M. Turing in 1936, before there were any computers! It was *human* problem-solving that Turing wanted to model with a machine.

What is a Turing machine? Start by imagining a finite-state machine with different possible outputs, like the adder we saw earlier. Attached to this machine is a tape of limitless length. Symbols from some alphabet, like the machine's input and output symbols, can be written on the tape. There is a reading and writing mechanism, like the heads of a magnetic tape recorder, that can travel along the tape.

Just as each state of the machine can have an output associated with it, each state can also take action to affect the tape: It can move the head by one symbol in either direction and it can change the symbol at the head's current position.

In fact, we simplify the formal description of the machine by using the tape as the input/output device as well as the storage device. That is, we can start with some sequence of symbols already written on the tape. That sequence serves as the input to the machine; state transitions are based on the symbol under the tape head, not a symbol from some other source. Likewise, the output from a state (if any) is written on the tape.

Somewhat analogous to the concept of an accepting state in our earlier examples, a Turing machine can have *halting* states. When the machine enters a halting state it stops its operation. There are no more state transitions. The output from the machine is whatever sequence of symbols it leaves written on the tape.

Turing's Thesis

Turing invented his abstract machine because he was trying to formalize the idea of an *effective procedure*. What does it mean to specify a technique for solving some problem well enough that we can be sure it will really work? As an analogy, think about directions for driving from here to somewhere. Someone can hand you a piece of paper with a list of instructions like "When you get to the gas station on the left, turn right." But sometimes you get directions that weren't careful enough. There may be a sharp right turn and a mild right turn available near the gas station. There may be a fork in the road before you even get to the gas station.

Turing's idea is that any problem for which there is *any* effective procedure can be modeled by a Turing machine. The phrase "any effective procedure" is taken to include the workings of the human mind. If Turing is right, any problem that a person can solve can be programmed for a computer.

This claim isn't something that can be proved or disproved mathematically because there is no prior formal definition of "effective procedure" to which Turing machines can be compared. Also, it may be that the idea of a procedure somehow doesn't cover all the different kinds of thinking that people do. Maybe it's true, for example, that computers are potentially as powerful as people at solving problems, but "solving problems" might not turn out to be an appropriate description of what's going on when we feel emotions. If that turned out to be true, we *should* expect a computer to become the world's chess champion someday, but we *shouldn't* expect one to become the world's champion poet.

But this possible conclusion has been attacked from both sides. Some people think that emotions really *are* a matter of computable procedures. Kenneth Colby's program called Parry attempts to model the behavior of a paranoid human being by manipulating variables for emotions like anger and fear. On the other hand, some people think that even chess doesn't fall within the realm of things that people do by carrying out effective procedures in Turing's sense. A chess master, these people say, doesn't analyze the chess board in a step-by-step fashion like a computer. He looks at the board as a single, whole entity, and the important features just spring to mind by some process that is still rather mysterious.

What *is* known is that several other mathematical models of effective procedures have been shown to be equivalent to Turing machines, in the same sense in which regular expressions are equivalent to finite-state machines. For example, all of the popular programming languages are Turing-equivalent. There's no such thing as a computation that can be done in Logo but not in Pascal, or vice versa. (Of course, one language may be more *convenient* than another for a given problem.)

The Halting Theorem

I'm not going to get into specific examples of Turing machine programming here. That would take too much space for a single chapter; if you're interested you should pursue the topic in a book on automata theory. But I want to give one example of the theoretical value of Turing machines.

You've undoubtedly had the experience of writing a Logo program with a bug that causes an "infinite loop"—you run the program and it just sits there forever, when instead it's supposed to compute and print some results. That's a frustrating kind of bug because you're never quite sure if the program is really broken or if it's just very slow. Maybe if you waited another minute it would come up with the answer. Wouldn't it be great if, when you started the program running, Logo could print an error message like `This program has an infinite loop`, just as it does for other errors?

It turns out that infinite loops can't, in general, be detected automatically. Certainly *some* infinite loops are very easy to spot, and we can write programs that catch certain categories of infinite loop. But we can't write a program that's *guaranteed* to catch infinite loops in programs, in Logo or any other Turing-equivalent language. The fact that it's impossible is called the *halting theorem*.

It's a little tricky understanding just what the halting theorem says because it involves Turing machines that manipulate Turing machines as data, which is a kind of self-reference akin to recursion. Self-reference is always hard to talk about and can lead to paradoxes like the classic "This statement is false." (Is the sentence in quotes true or false? If it's true, then it must be false, because it says so. But if it's false, and it *says* it's false, it must really be true!) So let's proceed carefully.

The data recorded on a Turing machine's tape is a string of symbols. Generally we choose the symbols to represent something meaningful; for example, a string of digits can represent a number. Earlier in this chapter we used strings of symbols like

```
[1 [[1 A 2] [2 B 3] [3 A 2]] [1 3]]
```

to represent a finite-state machine. There's no reason we couldn't put *that* string of symbols on the tape of a Turing machine as its input. For example, we could build a Turing machine that would work like my `fsm` program, simulating the finite-state machine that it found written on its tape when it started.

Letting a Turing machine simulate a finite-state machine doesn't raise questions of self-reference. But a Turing machine, too, is a formal structure; it, too, can be represented as a string of symbols.

Because a representation of a Turing machine can be the input to another Turing machine, we can design Turing machines that answer questions about Turing machines. For example, we can write a *universal* Turing machine, one that simulates any Turing machine the way `fsm` simulates any finite-state machine.

A universal Turing machine (a Turing machine simulator) sort of half-solves the halting problem. Suppose we want to know whether a given machine will halt after it is started with a given input. (This is like asking whether a certain Logo procedure will terminate if it's invoked with a particular input.) We can use the universal Turing machine to simulate the one we're interested in. If the machine *does* halt, we'll find out about it. But if the machine in question *doesn't* halt, then the simulator won't halt either. We'll still have the problem we had in the first place—how can we be sure it won't finally halt if we give it another minute?

To solve the halting problem, what we need is a Turing machine that accepts a representation of any Turing machine as input, just like the universal Turing machine. But this one has to be guaranteed to halt, even if the input machine wouldn't halt. That's what the halting theorem says we can't do.

Proving the Halting Theorem in Logo

What makes it possible to raise the question of whether a Turing machine can decide whether another Turing machine would halt for a given input tape is the fact that one Turing machine's "program" can be represented as data for another Turing machine. This is also true of Logo procedures. In particular, the higher-order procedures like `map` and `filter` manipulate other procedures by accepting their names as inputs. We can, therefore, use Logo procedures to illustrate the proof of the halting theorem.

We'll consider a Logo procedure with an input as analogous to a Turing machine with its input tape. We want to prove that there can't be a Logo procedure that could tell whether such a procedure stops for a given input. The technique we use is called *proof by contradiction.* In this technique we assume that there *is* such a procedure, then show that this assumption leads to a paradox.

So let's imagine that someone has written a Logo predicate `haltp` that takes two inputs: the name of a procedure and an input value for that procedure. `Haltp` will output `true` if the procedure it's testing would eventually stop, given the specified input; `haltp` outputs `false` if the procedure it's testing would get into an infinite loop, like a recursive procedure without a stop rule. (In practice, if you think about your own experience debugging programs, it's easy to tell if a procedure doesn't have a stop rule at all, but not so easy to be sure that the stop rule will always eventually be satisfied. Think about a Pig Latin program given a word of all consonants as input. We want

```
to piglatin :word
if memberp first :word [a e i o u] [output word :word "ay]
output piglatin word bf :word first :word
end

? print haltp "piglatin "salami
true
? print haltp "piglatin "mxyzptlk
false
```

Remember that `haltp` itself must *always* stop, even in the case where `piglatin` wouldn't stop.)

Now consider this Logo procedure:

```
to try :proc
if haltp :proc :proc [loop]
end

to loop
loop
end
```

Since `haltp` works, we're assuming, on *any* Logo procedure with one input, it must work on `try` in particular. What happens if we say

```
? try "try
```

Does this stop or loop? Suppose it stops. `try` begins its work by evaluating the expression

```
haltp "try "try
```

Since we've said `try` will stop, given `try` as input, `haltp` will output `true`. It follows, from the definition of `try`, that `try` will invoke `loop` and will *not* stop. Similarly, if we start with the assumption that `try` will loop, then `haltp` must output `false` and so, from the definition of `try`, you can see that `try` *will* stop. Whatever value `haltp` outputs turns out to be incorrect.

It was the assumption that we could write an infallible `haltp` that led us into this contradiction, so that assumption must be wrong. We can't write a Logo procedure that will automatically detect infinite loops in our programs. A similar proof could be made in any language in which one program can manipulate another program as data—that is, in any Turing-equivalent language.

Program Listing

```
;;; Finite State Machine Interpreter (FSM)

to game :which
fsm thing word "mach :which
end

to fsm :machine
cleartext
setcursor [0 3]
localmake "start startpart :machine
localmake "moves movepart :machine
localmake "accept acceptpart :machine
fsm1 :start
end

to fsm1 :here
ifelse memberp :here :accept [accept] [reject]
fsm1 (fsmnext :here readchar)
end

to fsmnext :here :input
blank
if memberp :input (list char 13 char 10) ~
   [print ifelse memberp :here :accept ["| ACCEPT|] ["| REJECT|] ~
    output :start]
type :input
catch "error [output last find [fsmtest :here :input ?] :moves]
output -1
end
```

```
to fsmtest :here :input :move
output and (equalp :here arrowtail :move) ~
         (memberp :input arrowtext :move)
end


;; Display machine state

to accept
display "accept
end

to reject
display "reject
end

to blank
display "|        |
end

to display :text
localmake "oldpos cursor
setcursor [15 1]
type :text
setcursor :oldpos
end


;; Data abstraction for machines

to startpart :machine
output first :machine
end

to movepart :machine
output first bf :machine
end

to acceptpart :machine
output last :machine
end

to make.machine :start :moves :accept
output (list :start :moves :accept)
end
```

```
;; Data abstraction for arrows

to arrowtail :arrow
output first :arrow
end

to arrowtext :arrow
output first butfirst :arrow
end

to arrowhead :arrow
output last :arrow
end

to make.arrow :tail :text :head
output (list :tail :text :head)
end


;; Machine descriptions for the guessing game

make "mach1 [1 [[1 AB 1]] [1]]
make "mach2 [1 [[1 ABC 2] [2 ABC 1]] [1]]
make "mach3 [1 [[1 A 2] [2 B 3] [3 ABC 3]] [3]]
make "mach4 [1 [[1 A 2] [1 B 3] [1 C 4] [2 A 1] [3 B 1] [4 C 1]] [1]]
make "mach5 [1 [[1 ABC 2] [2 B 1]] [1]]
make "mach6 [1 [[1 A 2] [2 AB 2] [2 C 3] [3 AB 2] [3 C 3]] [3]]
make "mach7 [1 [[1 AB 1] [1 C 2] [2 C 1]] [1]]
make "mach8 [1 [[1 A 2] [1 BC 1] [2 A 1] [2 BC 2]] [1]]
make "mach9 [1 [[1 AB 1] [1 C 2] [2 A 3] [2 B 1] [3 A 1]] [1]]
make "mach10 [1 [[1 A 2] [1 BC 1] [2 A 2] [2 B 3] [2 C 1]
                [3 A 2] [3 B 1] [3 C 4] [4 A 2] [4 B 5] [4 C 1]
                [5 A 6] [5 BC 1] [6 ABC 6]]
            [6]]


;;; Regular Expression to FSM Translation (MACHINE)

to machine :regexp
localmake "nextstate 0
output optimize determine nondet :regexp
end
```

```
;; First step: make a possibly nondeterministic machine

to nondet :regexp
if and (wordp :regexp) (equalp count :regexp 1) ~
   [output ndletter :regexp]
if wordp :regexp [output ndor reduce "sentence :regexp]
if equalp first :regexp "or [output ndor butfirst :regexp]
if equalp first :regexp "* [output ndmany last :regexp]
output ndconcat :regexp
end


;; Alphabet rule

to ndletter :letter
localmake "from newstate
localmake "to newstate
output (make.machine :from
                     (list (make.arrow :from :letter :to))
                     (list :to))
end


;; Concatenation rule

to ndconcat :exprs
output reduce "string (map "nondet :exprs)
end

to string :machine1 :machine2
output (make.machine (startpart :machine1)
                     (sentence (movepart :machine1)
                               (splice acceptpart :machine1 :machine2)
                               (movepart :machine2))
                     (stringa (acceptpart :machine1)
                              (startpart :machine2)
                              (acceptpart :machine2)))
end

to stringa :accept1 :start2 :accept2
if memberp :start2 :accept2 [output sentence :accept1 :accept2]
output :accept2
end
```

```
;; Alternatives rule

to ndor :exprs
localmake "newstart newstate
localmake "machines (map "nondet :exprs)
localmake "accepts map.se "acceptpart :machines
output (make.machine :newstart
                     (sentence map.se "movepart :machines
                               map.se "or.splice :machines)
                     ifelse not emptyp find [memberp (startpart ?)
                                                     (acceptpart ?)]
                                           :machines
                             [fput :newstart :accepts]
                             [:accepts])
end


to or.splice :machine
output map [newtail ? :newstart] (arrows.from.start :machine)
end


;; Repetition rule

to ndmany :regexp
localmake "machine nondet :regexp
output (make.machine (startpart :machine)
                     sentence (movepart :machine)
                              (splice (acceptpart :machine) :machine)
                     fput (startpart :machine) (acceptpart :machine))
end

;; Generate moves from a bunch of given states (:accepts) duplicating
;; the moves from the start state of some machine (:machine).
;; Used for concatenation rule to splice two formerly separate machines;
;; used for repetition rule to "splice" a machine to itself.

to splice :accepts :machine
output map.se [copy.to.accepts ?] (arrows.from.start :machine)
end

to arrows.from.start :machine
output filter [equalp startpart :machine arrowtail ?] movepart :machine
end
```

```
to copy.to.accepts :move
output map [newtail :move ?] :accepts
end


to newtail :arrow :tail
output make.arrow :tail (arrowtext :arrow) (arrowhead :arrow)
end


;; Make a new state number

to newstate
make "nextstate :nextstate+1
output :nextstate
end


;; Second step: Turn nondeterministic FSM into a deterministic one
;; Also eliminates "orphan" (unreachable) states.

to determine :machine
localmake "moves movepart :machine
localmake "accepts acceptpart :machine
localmake "states []
localmake "join.state.list []
localmake "newmoves nd.traverse (startpart :machine)
output make.machine (startpart :machine) ~
                    :newmoves ~
                    filter [memberp ? :states] :accepts
end


to nd.traverse :state
if memberp :state :states [output []]
make "states fput :state :states
localmake "newmoves (check.nd filter [equalp arrowtail ? :state] :moves)
output sentence :newmoves map.se "nd.traverse (map "arrowhead :newmoves)
end
```

```
to check.nd :movelist
if emptyp :movelist [output []]
localmake "letter arrowtext first :movelist
localmake "heads sort map "arrowhead ~
                        filter [equalp :letter arrowtext ?] :movelist
if emptyp butfirst :heads ~
   [output fput first :movelist
                   check.nd filter [not equalp :letter arrowtext ?]
                                   :movelist]
localmake "check.heads member :heads :join.state.list
if not emptyp :check.heads ~
   [output fput make.arrow :state :letter first butfirst :check.heads ~
                   check.nd filter [not equalp :letter arrowtext ?]
                                   :movelist]
localmake "join.state newstate
make "join.state.list fput :heads fput :join.state :join.state.list
make "moves sentence :moves ~
                   map [make.arrow :join.state
                                   arrowtext ?
                                   arrowhead ?] ~
                   filter [memberp arrowtail ? :heads] :moves
if not emptyp find [memberp ? :accepts] :heads ~
   [make "accepts sentence :accepts :join.state]
output fput make.arrow :state :letter :join.state ~
           check.nd filter [not equalp :letter arrowtext ?] :movelist
end

to sort :list
if emptyp :list [output []]
output insert first :list sort butfirst :list
end

to insert :value :sorted
if emptyp :sorted [output (list :value)]
if :value = first :sorted [output :sorted]
if :value < first :sorted [output fput :value :sorted]
output fput first :sorted insert :value butfirst :sorted
end
```

```
;; Third step: Combine redundant states.
;; Also combines arrows with same head and tail:
;;    [1 A 2] [1 B 2] -> [1 AB 2].

to optimize :machine
localmake "stubarray array :nextstate
foreach (movepart :machine) "array.save
localmake "states sort fput (startpart :machine) ~
                            map "arrowhead movepart :machine
localmake "start startpart :machine
foreach reverse :states [optimize.state ? ?rest]
output (make.machine :start
                        map.se [fix.arrows ? item ? :stubarray] :states
                        filter [memberp ? :states] acceptpart :machine)
end

to array.save :move
setitem (arrowtail :move) :stubarray ~
        stub.add (arrow.stub :move) (item (arrowtail :move) :stubarray)
end

to stub.add :stub :stublist
if emptyp :stublist [output (list :stub)]
if (stub.head :stub) < (stub.head first :stublist) ~
   [output fput :stub :stublist]
if (stub.head :stub) = (stub.head first :stublist) ~
   [output fput make.stub letter.join (stub.text :stub)
                                       (stub.text first :stublist)
                          stub.head :stub
                 butfirst :stublist]
output fput first :stublist (stub.add :stub butfirst :stublist)
end

to letter.join :this :those
if emptyp :those [output :this]
if beforep :this first :those [output word :this :those]
output word (first :those) (letter.join :this butfirst :those)
end
```

```
to optimize.state :state :others
localmake "candidates ~
          filter (ifelse memberp :state acceptpart :machine
                         [[memberp ? acceptpart :machine]]
                         [[not memberp ? acceptpart :machine]]) ~
                 :others
localmake "mymoves item :state :stubarray
localmake "twin find [equalp (item ? :stubarray) :mymoves] :candidates
if emptyp :twin [stop]
make "states remove :state :states
if equalp :start :state [make "start :twin]
foreach :states ~
        [setitem ? :stubarray
                   (cascade [emptyp ?2]
                            [stub.add (change.head :state :twin first ?2)
                                      ?1]
                            filter [not equalp stub.head ? :state]
                                   item ? :stubarray
                            [butfirst ?2]
                            filter [equalp stub.head ? :state]
                                   item ? :stubarray)]
end

to change.head :from :to :stub
if not equalp (stub.head :stub) :from [output :stub]
output list (stub.text :stub) :to
end

to fix.arrows :state :stublist
output map [stub.arrow :state ?] :stublist
end

;; Data abstraction for "stub" arrow (no tail)

to arrow.stub :arrow
output butfirst :arrow
end

to make.stub :text :head
output list :text :head
end

to stub.text :stub
output first :stub
end
```

```
to stub.head :stub
output last :stub
end

to stub.arrow :tail :stub
output fput :tail :stub
end
```

2   Discrete Mathematics

Program file for this chapter: `math`

Computer scientists often use mathematics as a tool in their work, but the mathematical problems that arise in computer science are of a special kind. Consider these examples:

Suppose you have a nondeterministic FSM with five states and you want to convert it to a deterministic one. What is the largest number of states that might be required for the new machine? Well, each state of the new machine corresponds to some *combination* of states of the old one, because the conversion works by finding multiple transitions (from some state via the same input character to multiple states) and creating a new state that combines all those resulting states. How many such combinations are possible? In other words, how many *subsets* does a five-element set have? The answer is 2^5 or 32 states. (31, really, because one of those is the empty subset and that will never be used.)

Suppose you want to write a program to translate telephone numbers into letters. A telephone number has seven digits, each of which corresponds to three letters. How many different strings of letters are possible? Well, there are three choices for the first digit, times three for the second, and so on...

These are typical of the kinds of mathematics problems that a computer scientist confronts in that they are *counting* problems—ones that involve integers. Another relevant kind of problem is the *logic* problem, in which the values under consideration are just `true` and `false`. These areas of mathematics are quite different from what is studied in the usual high school and college math courses: algebra, geometry, trig, calculus, differential equations. Those courses deal with *measurement* problems, in which the answer can be any number, including a fraction or an irrational number. This conventional mathematics curriculum, studying *continuous* functions, is dictated by the needs of physics and the physics-based engineering subjects. Computer scientists need a different kind of math, called *discrete* mathematics. ("Discrete" is the opposite of "continuous" and is not the same word as its homonym "discreet" meaning tactful.)

Propositional Logic

You already know that what in Logo is called an *operation* is the computer programming version of a mathematical *function*. The inputs and outputs of Logo operations may be numbers, or they may be other kinds of words or lists. In ordinary algebra the functions we use have numeric values. Certain Logo operations are identical to the ones used in algebra: `sin :x` is $\sin(x)$ and `sqrt :x` is $\sqrt{x}$. On the other hand, there is nothing in ordinary school mathematics quite like `first` or `sentence`. You may have been taught to use the word "function" only when you see a notation like $f(x)$, but in fact the ordinary arithmetic operations are functions, too. The addition in $a + b$ is a function with two arguments, just like `sum :a :b` in Logo.

In Logo there are also operations whose inputs and outputs are the words `true` and `false`. The primitive operations in this category are `and`, `or`, and `not`. Just as algebra deals with numeric functions, *logic* is the branch of mathematics that deals with these *truth-valued* functions. Instead of numbers, these functions combine *propositions*: statements that may be true or false. A Logo expression like `:x=0` represents a proposition. "Abraham Lincoln was the King of England" is a proposition; it happens to be false, but it's a perfectly valid one because it asserts something that's either true or false. "It will rain in Boston tomorrow" is a proposition whose truth value we don't know yet. "Chinese food is better than French food" is an example of a sentence whose validity as a proposition is open to question. If I say that, I'm expressing my personal taste, not an objective statement that could be proven true or false.*

Logical functions combine *simple* propositions into *compound* propositions. For example, "Either Abraham Lincoln was the King of England or he was the President of the United States" is a compound proposition. It's true even though one of the simple propositions within it is false. Just as in algebra we use letters like x to represent numbers and expressions like $x + y$ to indicate the use of functions to combine numbers, in logic we use letters to represent propositions and there are function symbols for the logical functions. If p is the proposition "Abraham Lincoln was the King of England," and q is the proposition "Abraham Lincoln was the President of the United States," then the expression $p \lor q$ represents the compound proposition above. The symbol $\lor$ represents the *or* function; $\land$ represents *and*; $\neg$ and $\sim$ are alternative representations for *not*. The symbol $\rightarrow$ represents "implies"; it turns out that $p \rightarrow q$ is equivalent to $\neg p \lor q$; in other words, the value of the function is true if either the "if" part is *false* or the "then" part is

---

* On the other hand, "The Beatles are better than Led Zeppelin" is a perfectly valid, obviously true proposition.

true. An example of the former is the classic "If wishes were horses then beggars would ride."

(Don't confuse the → function with the Logo `if` command. The latter isn't a function (an operation), but a command. It tells Logo to take some *action* if a given condition is met. The operation

```
to implies :p :q
output or (not :p) :q
end
```

is the Logo equivalent of the → function in logic.)

The most important use of logic in mathematics is in understanding the idea of *proof*. What is a valid reason for claiming that some proposition has been proven true? Many people come across the idea of proof for the first and last time in high school geometry. We are asked to prove some proposition like "the sum of the interior angles of a triangle is 180°." For each step in the proof we must give a *reason* such as "things equal to the same thing are equal to each other."

In logic there are certain rules that allow us to infer one proposition from one or more previously known propositions. These rules correspond roughly to the "reasons" in a geometry proof. They are called *rules of inference*. You use rules of inference informally all the time, whenever you try to convince someone of something by reasoning. "Is Jay here?" "Yes." "How do you know?" "I saw his car in the driveway, and if his car is here, he must be here too."

Suppose we use the letter p to represent the proposition "Jay's car is here" and the letter q to represent "Jay is here." Then the reasoning quoted in the last paragraph says "p is true and $p \to q$ is true, so q must be true." ("$p \to q$" is the proposition "If Jay's car is here, he must be here too.") The fact that p and $p \to q$ allow us to infer q is a rule of inference. (Of course the rule doesn't tell us about the truth of its component propositions. We have to determine that by some means outside of logic, such as observation of the world. I had to *see* Jay's car in the driveway to know that p is true.)

An Inference System

What does all this have to do with computer science? One application of logic is in *inference systems*: programs that deduce propositions from other ones. Such systems are important both in business applications where large data bases are used and in artificial intelligence programs that try to answer questions based on information implied by some text but not explicit in the text.

In this section I'll show you a special-purpose inference system that solves logic problems. Logic problems are the ones in which you're given certain propositions and asked to deduce others. Mr. Smith lives next to the carpenter; John likes classical music; who lives in the yellow house? Here is a typical problem taken from *Mind Benders,* Book B–2, by Anita Harnadek.

> A cub reporter interviewed four people. He was very careless, however. Each statement he wrote was half right and half wrong. He went back and interviewed the people again. And again, each statement he wrote was half right and half wrong. From the information below, can you straighten out the mess?

> The first names were Jane, Larry, Opal, and Perry. The last names were Irving, King, Mendle, and Nathan. The ages were 32, 38, 45, and 55. The occupations were drafter, pilot, police sergeant, and test car driver.

> On the first interview, he wrote these statements, one from each person:

> 1. Jane: "My name is Irving, and I'm 45."
> 2. King: "I'm Perry and I drive test cars."
> 3. Larry: "I'm a police sergeant and I'm 45."
> 4. Nathan: "I'm a drafter, and I'm 38."

> On the second interview, he wrote these statements, one from each person:

> 5. Mendle: "I'm a pilot, and my name is Larry."
> 6. Jane: "I'm a pilot, and I'm 45."
> 7. Opal: "I'm 55 and I drive test cars."
> 8. Nathan: "I'm 38 and I drive test cars."

The chart provided with the problem is a guide to its solution. Each square in the chart represents a proposition. For example, the box where the "Larry" row meets the "pilot" column represents the proposition "Larry is the pilot." In solving the problem, you can put marks in the boxes to indicate what you know about the propositions. The status of a proposition need not be only true or false. Initially the status of each proposition is *unknown*; we have no idea whether it's true or false. The structure of this particular problem also allows the status of a proposition to be that it is linked with another proposition in an *exclusive-or* relationship; that is, if one of the linked propositions turns out to be true, then the other must be false, and vice versa. You can use whatever notation

	Irving	King	Mendle	Nathan	draft	pol ser	pilot	test dr	32	38	45	55
Jane												
Larry												
Perry												
Opal												
draft												
pol ser												
pilot												
test dr												
32												
38												
45												
55												

you find convenient to express these possibilities. After experimenting with T and F and with check marks and crosses, I found that circles for true propositions and crosses for false ones made it easiest for me to see quickly the pattern of known truths. For the linked propositions, I used the statement numbers (1 to 8) in the boxes; two boxes with the same number represent linked statements.

You should probably solve this problem by hand before we go on to discuss the computer solution. Stop reading now and work on the problem if you want to do it without any hints from me.

Let me introduce a little new terminology to help in the following discussion. I'll call something like "last name" or "occupation" a *category*; something like "Mendle" or "pilot" I'll call an *individual*. As I'm using this terminology, "Mendle" and "pilot" are two different individuals even if they turn out, when we solve the problem, to be the same person.

It's important that each group of four statements contains one from each person, because the names of the speakers include first and last names. That is, from the first group of statements we know that Jane, King, Larry, and Nathan are four distinct people. This falsifies such propositions as "Jane is King." After noting the first group of statements my chart looks like this:

	Irving	King	Mendle	Nathan	draft	pol ser	pilot	test dr	32	38	45	55
Jane	|	X		X							|	
Larry		X		X	3						3	
Perry		2										
Opal												
draft				4								
pol ser												
pilot												
test dr		2										
32												
38				4								
45												
55												

From the second group of statements we learn that Mendle, Jane, Opal, and Nathan are all distinct people. When I marked an X in the "Jane is Mendle" box, I noticed that all but one last name for Jane had been eliminated. I therefore put a circle in the "Jane is Irving" box. This illustrates a special rule of inference for problems of this kind: If, for a given individual *x*, all but one proposition "*x* is *y*" have been falsified for a certain *category* of *y* individuals, then the remaining proposition in that category must be true. (The reason I'm going through this analysis is that the rules of inference I discover while working the problem by hand are going to end up in the design of the computer program.) I'm going to call this the *elimination* rule.

Since Jane is Irving, nobody else can be Irving. This falsifies three propositions whose status was formerly unknown: "Larry is Irving," "Opal is Irving," and "Perry is Irving." (The truth of "Jane is Irving" would also falsify "Jane is King" and so on, but we already knew those to be false.) The general rule is that if "*x* is *y*" is true then "*x* is *z*" must be false for all other *z* in the same category as *y*, and likewise "*w* is *y*" is false for all other *w* in the same category as *x*. I'll call this the *uniqueness* rule.

The proposition "Jane is Irving" was linked with the proposition "Jane is 45" earlier. That latter proposition must therefore be false. This is another rule of inference, the *link falsification* rule. There is also a *link verification* rule that comes into play when a linked proposition is found to be false; the other linked proposition must then be true.

Since we know that "Jane is 45" is false, and that "Jane is Irving" is true, it follows that "Irving is 45" must be false. The general rule is that if "*x* is *y*" is true and "*x* is *z*" is false, then "*y* is *z*" must also be false. Similarly, if "*x* is *y*" is true and "*x* is *z*" is true, then "*y* is *z*" must be true. I'll call these the *transitive* rules.

You should be following along with your own copy of the chart. By the elimination rule, "Opal is King" must be true. Then, by the uniqueness rule, "Perry is King" is false. Then, by the link verification rule, "King is test driver" must be true. By the transitive rule, "Opal is test driver" is true also. Here is my chart after making all possible deductions from the fact that Mendle, Jane, Opal, and Nathan are distinct people:

	Irving	King	Mendle	Nathan	draft	pol ser	pilot	test dr	32	38	45	55
Jane	O	X	X	X				X			X	
Larry	X	X	O	X		3		X			3	
Perry	X	X	X	O				X				
Opal	X	O	X	X	X	X	X	O				
draft		X		4								
pol ser		X										
pilot		X										
test dr	X	O	X	X								
32												
38			4									
45	X											
55												

Looking at statement number 5, we see that "Mendle is pilot" is linked to "Mendle is Larry." But we already know that the latter is true, so the former must be false. We can just put an X in that box and not bother marking the number 5 anywhere. The same is true for statements 6 and 7; my chart after statement 7 is on the next page. I haven't marked anything in the age vs. occupation section of the chart, even though I can deduce some propositions for that section. For example, I know that "Jane is pilot" is true and that "Jane is 45" is false. By the transitive rule, "pilot is 45" must be false. I just haven't bothered making *all* possible deductions; I can always fill in that section of the chart if I get to the end of the problem and still don't know who's who.

	Irving	King	Mendle	Nathan	draft	pol ser	pilot	test dr	32	38	45	55
Jane	O	X	X	X	X	X	O	X			X	
Larry	X	X	O	X		3	X	X			3	
Perry	X	X	X	O			X	X				
Opal	X	O	X	X	X	X	X	O				X
draft	X	X		4				
pol ser	X	X						
pilot	O	X	X	X				
test dr	X	O	X	X				
32								
38				4				
45	X							
55		X						

Before dealing with the final statement we know all the pairings of first and last names, but we don't know any ages and we only know half the jobs. The last statement lets loose a flurry of deductions. The critical one is that if Nathan is 38, he or she (Perry is an ambiguous first name) can't be the drafter because of the link from statement 4. Here is my final chart:

	Irving	King	Mendle	Nathan	draft	pol ser	pilot	test dr	32	38	45	55
Jane	O	X	X	X	X	X	O	X	X	X	X	O
Larry	X	X	O	X	O	X	X	X	X	X	O	X
Perry	X	X	X	O	X	O	X	X	X	O	X	X
Opal	X	O	X	X	X	X	X	O	O	X	X	X
draft	X	X	O	X				
pol ser	X	X	X	O				
pilot	O	X	X	X				
test dr	X	O	X	X				
32								
38				O				
45	X		O					
55		X						

Chapter 2   Discrete Mathematics

Once it was clear that I was in the final steps of the solution, I didn't bother maintaining the age vs. last name section. The results can be found by reading just the three sections at the top; for example, Jane is Irving, the pilot, and 55.

Problems with Ordering

The elimination, uniqueness, and transitive rules are useful in just about all logic problems, but the link falsification and link verification rules depend on this specific problem's gimmick that we are given pairs of propositions and told that exactly one of them is true. To solve other problems, a more flexible kind of linkage is needed; we must be able to say "if p is true, then q is true also" or "if p is false, then q must be true," and so on.

A very common kind of linkage is an *ordering*, in which we are told a sequence of events, or a row of houses on a street, for example. In the cub reporter problem, the ages form an ordering, but aren't used as such—that is, the problem doesn't include clues such as "the test driver is younger than Jane." Suppose we did see that clue; what could we conclude from it? Certain propositions would be settled for sure:

- The test driver must not be Jane.
- The test driver isn't the oldest age (55).
- Jane isn't the youngest age (32).

Other propositions would be linked by *implications:*

- **If** Jane is 38, **then** the driver is 32.
- **If** Jane is 45, **then** the driver is 32 or 38.

and so on. (Actually, the second of these isn't directly representable on the chart, because there's no notation for a single proposition with two alternatives, like "32 or 38." So instead we'd represent this using propositions about what *can't* be true:

- **If** Jane is 45, **then** the driver is not 55.

We already know that the driver isn't Jane, so there's no need to record the implication that if Jane is 45 the driver isn't 45.)

Here is another problem, called "Forgetful Footes," by Diane C. Baldwin. It is taken from *The Dell Book of Logic Problems #4.*

> The forgetful Foote family fairly flew from their flat up Fleet Street to the freeway for a fling in Florida. Before they passed five intersections, Felix

and the other four Footes found they each had forgotten something (including the food) and were forced back to their flat to fetch it. Each turnaround was made at a different street intersection, one of them at Field Street. From the following clues, can you figure out who forgot what and in what order, and find the order of the intersections on Fleet Street from the Foote's flat to the freeway?

1. The second turnaround began at the street following Flag Street and the street before Fred had to return to the flat.
2. The men were responsible for the return for the film, the turnaround at Fig Street, and the fifth trip back.
3. Fork Street followed the one where they returned to fetch the flashlight and preceded the one where a woman had them make their first turnaround.
4. The final trip back didn't begin at Frond Street, nor was it the one to fetch the fan.
5. Frank's forgetfulness turned them back one block and one return trip following Francine's.
6. One woman was the third to forget, while the other woman turned them back at Flag Street.
7. They returned for the fiddle just before the trip back that began at Frond Street and just following the one requested by Flo.

This problem includes *two* orderings. The order of the intersections with cross streets is not necessarily the same as the time order of the return trips. That is, the Footes might have gone four blocks before making their first turnaround, then gone only one block before the second return, and so on. In making a chart for this problem, I used the numbers 1–5 to represent the order of streets, and the ordinals 1st–5th to represent the time order of return trips. Clue 1, then, gives us this series of implications:

- **If** Flag Street is 1, **then** 2nd is 2.
- **If** Flag Street is 2, **then** 2nd is 3.
- **If** Flag Street is 3, **then** 2nd is 4.

- **If** 2nd is 2, **then** Flag Street is 1.
- **If** 2nd is 3, **then** Flag Street is 2.
- **If** 2nd is 4, **then** Flag Street is 3.

- **If** 2nd is 2, **then** Fred is 3.
- **If** 2nd is 3, **then** Fred is 4.
- **If** 2nd is 4, **then** Fred is 5.

- **If** Fred is 3, **then** 2nd is 2.
- **If** Fred is 3, **then** 2nd is 3.
- **If** Fred is 5, **then** 2nd is 4.

It may seem that there are some missing from this list. What if Flag Street is 4? But that can't happen (and I so marked the chart) because then 2nd would have to be 5, and that would make Fred 6, which is too far. But notice that we do have to include both directions of implication between any two propositions. The clue tells us that if Flag Street is 1, then 2nd is 2, and also that if 2nd is 2, then Flag Street is 1.

See if you can solve this problem, and then we'll talk about the Logo-based inference system.

Data Structure

In addition to the status of the "*x* is *y*" propositions, the program needs to keep track of the categories, like "first name," and the individuals within each category. This information is needed for the sake of the elimination and uniqueness rules. I chose to have a global variable named `categories` containing (for the cub reporter problem) the list

```
[first last age job]
```

Each of the elements of that list is the name of a variable containing the individuals in that category; for example, `:age` is the list

```
[32 38 45 55]
```

The status of the "is" propositions is kept in property lists associated with the names of individuals. For example, to indicate that the proposition "Jane is King" is false, the program carries out these two instructions:

```
pprop "Jane "King "false
pprop "King "Jane "false
```

Both are necessary because we can't predict whether we're going to be figuring out something about Jane or something about King when we next need this information. Actually, the fact that the proposition is stored twice reflects another inference rule, one that's so obvious we don't think about it at all when solving these problems without using a computer: the *symmetric* rule says that if *x* is *y*, then *y* is *x*.

If a given property's value is the empty list, that means that the truth of the proposition is unknown. (Remember that Logo property lists give the empty list as the value of a property that you haven't defined explicitly, so I don't have to predefine all possible properties.) The word `true` means that the proposition is known to be true; the word `false` means that it's known to be false. If the proposition is linked to other propositions by implication, then the value of the property is a list containing four-element implication lists. The first member of each implication is `true` or `false` to indicate which value of this proposition implies something about the other proposition. The next two members are names of individuals, indicating which other proposition is determined by this one. The fourth member is again `true` or `false`, indicating whether that other proposition is implied to be true or implied to be false.

For example, the statement "My name is Irving, and I'm 45" attributed to Jane is stored as the following two implications:

- Under `Jane` and `Irving`, the list `[true Jane 45 false]`.
- Under `Jane` and `45`, the list `[true Jane Irving false]`.

Although the data structure as described so far contains all the necessary information, it turned out to be convenient to include some redundant forms of the same information. For example, the elimination rule and the uniqueness rule require the program to find all the *peers* of an individual—the other individuals in the same category. It would be possible to start with `:categories` and search for the known individual in a category list, but it was easier to give each individual a `category` property whose value is the name of the category to which it belongs.

Similarly, the transitive rule needs to know all of the propositions involving a particular individual that are known to be true, and all those that are known to be false. This information is implicit in the properties already described, but to simplify the program each individual has a `true` property whose value is a list of the other individuals known to be equal to this one, and a `false` property whose value is a list of the others known to be different from this one. For example, after processing statement 7 we know that Jane is Irving and that Jane is the pilot, but we don't know Jane's age. Therefore the property list for `Jane` has a property whose name is `true` and whose value is the list

```
[Irving pilot]
```

and one whose name is `false` and whose value is

```
[King Mendle Nathan drafter sergeant driver]
```

Finally, it turned out that at the end of the program, in order to print out the solutions, it was convenient to have, for each individual, properties with a category as the name and an individual in that category as the value. For example, since Jane's last name is Irving, `Jane` has a property whose name is `last` and whose value is `Irving`.

Program Structure: Recording Simple Propositions

I wanted to enter the problem as a series of assertions, each represented by a Logo instruction. That is, I wrote this procedure:

```
to cub.reporter
cleanup
category "first [Jane Larry Opal Perry]
category "last [Irving King Mendle Nathan]
category "age [32 38 45 55]
category "job [drafter pilot sergeant driver]
differ [Jane King Larry Nathan]
says "Jane "Irving 45
says "King "Perry "driver
says "Larry "sergeant 45
says "Nathan "drafter 38
differ [Mendle Jane Opal Nathan]
says "Mendle "pilot "Larry
says "Jane "pilot 45
says "Opal 55 "driver
says "Nathan 38 "driver
print []
solution
end
```

(The first instruction erases any old property lists left over from a previous logic problem; the last prints out the results.) I made `category`, `differ`, and `says` print out their inputs when invoked, so that you can watch the progress of the solution while it's being computed.

The procedures `differ` and `says` were designed to reflect the terms in which this problem is presented, rather than the internal workings of the inference system. That is, if you compare the problem statement with this procedure, it's easy to see which instructions represent which clues, even if you have no idea how the program will actually solve the problem! Our task is to implement `differ` and `says` using propositional logic.

There's an important difference between `differ` and `says`. `Differ` gives us direct information about the truth or falsehood of some simple propositions; specifically, we learn that several "*x* is *y*" propositions are false. `Says`, on the other hand, gives us no direct information about simple propositions; it tells us about implications linking two such propositions.

First let's consider how `differ` works. The instruction

```
differ [Jane King Larry Nathan]
```

tells us that Jane is not King, Jane is not Larry, Jane is not Nathan, King is not Larry, King is not Nathan, and Larry is not Nathan. In effect, `differ` will carry out the instructions

```
falsify "Jane "King
falsify "Jane "Larry
falsify "Jane "Nathan
falsify "King "Larry
falsify "King "Nathan
falsify "Larry "Nathan
```

There's no need to invoke `falsify` for the six cases with inputs in the opposite order (such as the proposition that King is not Jane) because, as we'll see, `falsify` knows about the symmetric rule and will record those automatically. By the way, some of these six are unnecessary because the two individuals have the same category and therefore couldn't possibly be the same, such as Jane and Larry, both first names. But `falsify` will catch these cases and return without doing anything.

Here's how `differ` actually carries out all those `falsify` instructions:

```
to differ :list
print (list "differ :list)
foreach :list [differ1 ? ?rest]
end

to differ1 :a :them
foreach :them [falsify :a ?]
end
```

`Falsify`, and a similar procedure `verify` to assert the truth of a proposition, are implemented in terms of the central procedure about propositions, `settruth`:

```
to verify :a :b
settruth :a :b "true
end
```

```
to falsify :a :b
settruth :a :b "false
end
```

`Settruth` takes three inputs, two individuals and a truth value. It records the truth or falsehood of the proposition that `:a` is `:b`, and uses the rules of inference I've described to derive other propositions when possible.

```
to settruth :a :b :truth.value
if equalp (gprop :a "category) (gprop :b "category) [stop]
localmake "oldvalue get :a :b
if equalp :oldvalue :truth.value [stop]
if equalp :oldvalue (not :truth.value) ~
   [(throw "error (sentence [inconsistency in settruth]
                            :a :b :truth.value))]
print (list :a :b "-> :truth.value)
store :a :b :truth.value
settruth1 :a :b :truth.value
settruth1 :b :a :truth.value
if not emptyp :oldvalue ~
   [foreach (filter [equalp first ? :truth.value] :oldvalue)
           [apply "settruth butfirst ?]]
end
```

```
to settruth1 :a :b :truth.value
apply (word "find not :truth.value) (list :a :b)
foreach (gprop :a "true) [settruth ? :b :truth.value]
if :truth.value [foreach (gprop :a "false) [falsify ? :b]
                 pprop :a (gprop :b "category) :b]
pprop :a :truth.value (fput :b gprop :a :truth.value)
end
```

If the two individuals are in the same category, `settruth` does nothing. This is to allow for cases such as the example

```
falsify "Jane "Larry
```

as explained earlier. If the individuals are in different categories, the next step is to find what information was previously available about this proposition. If it was already known to be true or false, and the truth value input in this call agrees with what was known, then the program has merely generated some redundant information and `settruth` stops. If the known value disagrees with the input value, then something is wrong; the program has proven two contradictory propositions. Generally this means that some clue has been represented incorrectly in the program.

If the proposition was not already known to be true or false, then we have some new information. After notifying the user by printing a message, `settruth` must store that fact. (Procedures `get` and `store` are an interface to the property list primitives that implement the symmetric rule.) The next step is to make any possible inferences using the elimination, uniqueness, and transitive rules; this is done separately for ":a is :b" and for ":b is :a" by two calls to the subprocedure `settruth1`.

Settruth1 invokes either `findtrue` or `findfalse` depending on the truth value. Because of the `not` in the first instruction of `settruth1`, `findtrue` is called when we are falsifying a proposition, and vice versa. This makes sense because of the tasks of these procedures. If we are falsifying a proposition, then the elimination rule comes into play, and we try to find a true proposition. If we are verifying a proposition, then the uniqueness rule lets us find several false propositions on the same row or column of the chart. The next instructions in `settruth1` implement the transitive rule, looking at other individuals known to be the same as, or different from, :a. The last two instructions maintain the redundant information used for printing the results and for carrying out the transitive rule.

The final instruction in `settruth` deals with implications. If we already knew that $p \rightarrow q$ and now we're learning that p is true, we can infer that q is true. (This is another rule of inference, which I'll call the *implication* rule.)

Program Structure: Recording Implications

Speaking of implications, we can now explore how the `says` procedure produces and records implications. The instruction

```
says "Jane "Irving 45
```

establishes a relationship between the two propositions "Jane is Irving" and "Jane is 45." The relationship is that exactly one of them must be true; the name for this is *exclusive or.*

```
to says :who :what1 :what2
print (list "says :who :what1 :what2)
xor :who :what1 :who :what2
end

to xor :who1 :what1 :who2 :what2
implies :who1 :what1 "true :who2 :what2 "false
implies :who1 :what1 "false :who2 :what2 "true
end
```

Says is a special case of **xor** (a common abbreviation for exclusive or) in which the two propositions are about a common individual, Jane in the example. The **xor** procedure establishes two implications, $p \rightarrow \neg q$ and $\neg p \rightarrow q$. In other words, if we learn that Jane is Irving, then we can infer that Jane is not 45; if we learn that Jane is not Irving, we can infer that Jane is 45. (These two implications are *not* equivalent to each other; in general, one might be true and the other false. But the exclusive or relationship means that both are true.)

The **implies** procedure takes six inputs. The first three are for one proposition and the others for the second proposition. For each proposition, two inputs are individuals (call them x and y) and the third is **true** or **false**. If **true**, then the proposition is "x is y"; if **false**, the proposition is "x is not y."

Yet another rule of inference comes into play here, the *contrapositive* rule. It says that if $p \rightarrow q$ is true, then so is $\neg q \rightarrow \neg p$. Although these two implications are mathematically equivalent, we must enter both of them into our data structure because we might happen to discover that $\neg q$ is true, and we'll look for relevant implications filed under q rather than under p.

```
to implies :who1 :what1 :truth1 :who2 :what2 :truth2
implies1 :who1 :what1 :truth1 :who2 :what2 :truth2
implies1 :who2 :what2 (not :truth2) :who1 :what1 (not :truth1)
end
```

The first call to **implies1** stores the implication in the form given to us; the second call stores its contrapositive.

```
to implies1 :who1 :what1 :truth1 :who2 :what2 :truth2
localmake "old1 get :who1 :what1
if equalp :old1 :truth1 [settruth :who2 :what2 :truth2  stop]
if equalp :old1 (not :truth1) [stop]
if memberp (list :truth1 :who2 :what2 (not :truth2)) :old1 ~
    [settruth :who1 :what1 (not :truth1)  stop]
if memberp (list :truth1 :what2 :who2 (not :truth2)) :old1 ~
    [settruth :who1 :what1 (not :truth1)  stop]
store :who1 :what1 ~
     fput (list :truth1 :who2 :what2 :truth2) :old1
end
```

The first three instructions in **implies1** check for the case in which we are told that $p \rightarrow q$ but we already know either p or $\neg p$. If we already know p, then we can derive that q is true. There's no need to store the implication, because it is already serving its purpose, which is to allow us to infer q. If we already know $\neg p$, then we can forget about this implication, because it isn't going to do us any good. We can't infer anything about *q* from this situation.

The next two instructions check for the situation in which we are told $p \rightarrow q$ but we already know that $p \rightarrow \neg q$. In that case, *p* must not be true, because if it were, we could infer two contradictory conclusions. Therefore, we can falsify the proposition *p*.

Finally, if none of these conditions is met, we add this implication to the (possibly empty) list of already known implications about *p*.

Using Implications to Represent Orderings

For another example of implications at work, here's the Logo program for the Foote problem:

```
to foote.family
cleanup
category "when [1st 2nd 3rd 4th 5th]
category "name [Felix Fred Frank Francine Flo]
category "street [Field Flag Fig Fork Frond]
category "item [food film flashlight fan fiddle]
category "position [1 2 3 4 5]
print [Clue 1]
justbefore "Flag "2nd :position
justbefore "2nd "Fred :position
print [Clue 2]
male [film Fig 5th]
print [Clue 3]
justbefore "flashlight "Fork :position
justbefore "Fork "1st :position
female [1st]
print [Clue 4]
falsify "5th "Frond
falsify "5th "fan
print [Clue 5]
justbefore "Francine "Frank :position
justbefore "Francine "Frank :when
print [Clue 6]
female [3rd Flag]
print [Clue 7]
justbefore "fiddle "Frond :when
justbefore "Flo "fiddle :when
print []
solution
end
```

I've included `print` instructions to let the user know when the program reaches each of the seven numbered clues. Clue 4 tells us directly that two possible pairings of individuals are false, and the program reflects this with two invocations of `falsify`. But the other clues either tell us about the sex of the family members or tell us that certain individuals are next to each other in an ordering. The procedures `male`, `female`, and `justbefore` reflect the language of the problem in the same way that `says` reflected the language of the other problem.

```
to male :stuff
differ sentence :stuff [Francine Flo]
end

to female :stuff
differ sentence :stuff [Felix Fred Frank]
end
```

Needless to say, this implementation of `male` and `female` works only for this specific logic problem! It's tempting to try to use the more general category mechanism this way:

```
category "sex [male female]
verify "Francine "female
verify "Flo "female
verify "Felix "male
verify "Fred "male
verify "Frank "male
```

but unfortunately the structure of this inference system requires that each individual can only match one individual in another category; once we've verified that Francine is female, the uniqueness rule will deduce that Flo isn't female!

On the other hand, I've tried to write `justbefore` in a way that will work for future problems.

```
to justbefore :this :that :lineup
falsify :this :that
falsify :this last :lineup
falsify :that first :lineup
justbefore1 :this :that :lineup
end
```

```
to justbefore1 :this :that :slotlist
if emptyp butfirst :slotlist [stop]
equiv :this (first :slotlist) :that (first butfirst :slotlist)
justbefore1 :this :that (butfirst :slotlist)
end

to equiv :who1 :what1 :who2 :what2
implies :who1 :what1 "true :who2 :what2 "true
implies :who2 :what2 "true :who1 :what1 "true
end
```

The input named `lineup` is a list of individuals from an ordering, in the correct order. In this problem, it will be the list

```
[1 2 3 4 5]
```

if the clue is about street position, or

```
[1st 2nd 3rd 4th 5th]
```

if the clue is about the order of events in time. As I explained when talking about orderings earlier, the instruction

```
justbefore "Flag "2nd :position
```

results in falsifying some propositions:

```
falsify "Flag "2nd
falsify "Flag 5
falsify "2nd 1
```

and also asserts some implications:

```
implies "Flag 1 "true "2nd 2 "true
implies "2nd 2 "true "Flag 1 "true
implies "Flag 2 "true "2nd 3 "true
implies "2nd 3 "true "Flag 2 "true
implies "Flag 3 "true "2nd 4 "true
implies "2nd 4 "true "Flag 3 "true
implies "Flag 4 "true "2nd 5 "true
implies "2nd 5 "true "Flag 4 "true
```

Backtracking

This inference system can solve many logic problems, but sometimes it runs into trouble. I've already mentioned, while discussing the `male` and `female` procedures, that the program insists that each individual in a category must appear exactly once in the solution. Suppose you have a problem about five people living in five houses; they have five distinct first names, five last names, five occupations—but two of the houses are yellow. It's sometimes possible to get around this, but the technique is a little awkward. You can set up a category like this:

```
category "color [yellow1 yellow2 blue brown green]
```

then you find *one* clue that mentions a yellow house and use `yellow1` for that one:

```
verify "Fred "yellow1
```

but for any other mention of something being yellow in the problem, you represent that by saying that the individual is *not* one of the other colors:

```
differ "architect [blue brown green]
```

You never explicitly mention `yellow2` except in setting up the category.

That technique works if you know that yellow is the color that appears twice. What if the problem tells you only that there are five houses and four colors? Or what if some individuals are *not* in the solution? For example, a problem might discuss the activities of five people, each doing something on a different day of the week, but you don't know until you solve the problem which of the seven weekdays are involved.

An entirely different approach to solving logic problems by computer is *backtracking*. Instead of starting from the clues and making deductions, a program can start by making arbitrary guesses about who goes with what, and then use the clues to look for contradictions. If a contradiction is found, the program systematically makes a different guess until every possible arrangement has been tried. (Presumably before every possibility has been tried, one of them will *not* lead to a contradiction, and that's the solution.)

In practice, backtracking is a more flexible technique than the inference system I wrote, because it's easy to let a backtracking program try multiple appearances of an individual if the problem allows that. But I thought the inference system would be more interesting to study, for two reasons. First, the inference system more closely models the way people solve logic problems. In the cub reporter problem, with four people to keep straight, there are $(4!)^3$ or 13,824 possible solutions. In the Foote problem, with five people, there are $(5!)^4$ or just over 200 million possibilities. A computer can try them all, but a person couldn't.* (If multiple appearances were allowed, the numbers would be even higher.) Second, backtracking doesn't work at all unless the problem deals with a finite set of individuals, as in a logic problem. Inference systems can be generalized to deal with potentially unbounded problems.

Generalized Inference Systems and Predicate Logic

The rules of inference in this program are specially designed for problems like the ones we've just solved. The implication rule is applicable to any propositional logic situation, but the ones based on categories, such as the uniqueness and elimination rules, are not. The idea of a "category" as we've used it isn't a general principle of logic; instead, that idea should really be expressed as a series of propositions. For example, to say "there is a category called 'last name' whose members are Irving, King, Mendle, and Nathan" is really to make several statements of the form "Jane has exactly one last name," or, in terms of the basic "x is y" propositions,

$$(\text{Jane is Irving}) \vee (\text{Jane is King})$$
$$\vee (\text{Jane is Mendle}) \vee (\text{Jane is Nathan})$$

(i.e., Jane has at least one last name)

$$\neg((\text{Jane is Irving}) \wedge (\text{Jane is King}))$$

(i.e., Jane isn't named both Irving and King)

$$\neg((\text{Jane is Irving}) \wedge (\text{Jane is Mendle}))$$

and so on. If we wanted to solve this problem in a general inference system we'd assert the truth of all those propositions at the beginning. Then if the program discovers that Jane is Irving, it would have the two propositions

$$\neg((\text{Jane is Irving}) \wedge (\text{Jane is King}))$$

---

* People do sometimes use a combination of inference and backtracking. If, by inference, you've established that Jane must be either the pilot or the drafter, but you can't settle which, you might decide to *assume* that Jane is the pilot and hope that you can then infer either a complete solution to the problem or a contradiction. In the latter case, you'd know that Jane must be the drafter.

and

(Jane is Irving)

and from these it could infer

¬(Jane is King)

using the standard inference rules of propositional logic.

The "and so on" just above includes quite a large number of propositions. And yet this small problem concerns a mere 16 individual names divided into four categories. For a larger problem it would be nearly impossible to list all the relevant propositions, and for a problem involving an infinite set of individuals, such as the integers, it would be literally impossible. What would make the representation of a problem easier is if we could use, in a formal system, the same kind of language I used in describing (in English) the inference rules earlier: "for all other z in the same category as y..." There are two parts to such a formal notation. First, in addition to the *propositional* variables like p used in propositional logic, we need variables like x and y that can represent objects in the system we want to describe. Second, we need a notation for "for all." The formal system including these additions to propositional logic is called *predicate* logic. The name is like that used in Logo to refer to operations with `true` or `false` outputs because the statements in predicate logic involve truth-valued functions of objects analogous to the Logo predicates. For example, the formula we've been representing informally as "x is y" is represented formally using the predicate function $\underline{is(x, y)}$. This is much like the Logo expression

```
equalp :x :y
```

A predicate function of two arguments ("inputs" in Logo) is also called a *relation* in mathematics. Algebraic relations include ones like = (equal) and < (less than).

We are almost ready to show how the uniqueness rule can be expressed as a formula in predicate logic. If you're not accustomed to mathematical formalism, this formula is a little scary—perhaps the scariest thing in this book. But I want you to see it so that you'll appreciate the fact that just *one* formula of predicate logic can sum up a rule that would require *many* formulas in propositional logic. I'm going to introduce a new relation called "isa" that's true if its first argument is a member of its second argument. The first must be an individual and the second a category. For example, isa(pilot, job) is true. And the symbol $\forall$ means "for all." The uniqueness rule says that if x is y then x can't also be z for any z in the same category as y. Here's how to say that formally:

$$is(x, y) \rightarrow \forall z((isa(y, a) \wedge isa(z, a) \wedge \neg(y = z)) \rightarrow \neg is(x, z))$$

To indicate the linking of two propositions in the general inference system, no special rules of inference are required. To say "the reporter wrote down these two statements; one is true and the other false" is just to say $p \otimes q$; I'm using the symbol $\otimes$ to represent the *exclusive or* function. This formula is equivalent to

$$(p \vee q) \wedge \neg(p \wedge q)$$

A general inference system will know that if it's been told $p \otimes q$ and then later it learns, say, p then it can infer $\neg q$.

The cub reporter problem is simpler than some of its type in that the only relevant relation among individuals is "is," which is an *equivalence* relation. This means that if Jane is Irving then also Irving is Jane (the technical name for a relation with that property is *symmetric*), and also that if Jane is Irving, and Irving is the pilot, then Jane is the pilot (so the relation is *transitive*). It's relatively easy to work out all the implications of a proposition about equivalence relations.

By contrast, the Foote problem contains *ordering* relations like "is later than" that are transitive but not symmetric. To handle such problems the inference system must have a way to represent "x is the last." Other problems contain relations like "lives in the house next to" that are symmetric but not transitive. A statement like "Mr. Smith lives in the house at the end" has to be represented formally as something like "there is only one person x such that x lives in the house next to Mr. Smith."

One reason a general inference system is harder to program than the special-purpose one I've written in this chapter is that my system makes all possible inferences from any newly verified or falsified proposition. This is possible only because there is a finite, fairly small number of such inferences. Once you introduce variables and predicates, the number of possible inferences is potentially infinite. A general inference system must take care not to infer infinitely many useless results. One solution is to defer the making of inferences until the user of the system asks a question, and then infer only what's needed to answer that particular question. But it isn't always easy to know exactly what's needed.

An inference system like the one I'm vaguely describing is a central part of the programming language Prolog. In that language, you program not by issuing instructions that tell the computer what to do, but rather by making *assertions* that some proposition is true. You can then ask questions like "for what values of x is this formula true?"

Logic and Computer Hardware

Besides inference systems, another area in which logic is important in computer science is in the design of the computers themselves. In a computer, information is represented as electrical signals flowing through wires. (These days, a "wire" is likely to be a microscopic conducting region on a silicon chip rather than a visible strand of metal, but the principle is the same.) In almost all computers, each wire may be carrying one of two voltage levels at any moment. (It is the restriction to two possible voltages that makes them *binary* computers. It would be possible to build *ternary* computer circuits using three voltages, but I know of no practical application of that idea.) A computer is built out of small circuit elements called *gates* that combine or rearrange binary signals in various ways. Perhaps the simplest example of a gate is an *inverter*; it has one input signal and provides one output signal that is the opposite of the input. That is, if you have a high voltage coming into the inverter you get a low voltage out, and vice versa.

The voltages inside the computer can be thought of as representing numbers (zeros and ones) or truth values (false and true). From now on I'll use the symbols 0 and 1 to represent the voltages, but you can mentally replace 0 with `false` and 1 with `true` to see how what I'm saying here ties in with what's gone before.

Suppose you have a gate with two input wires and one output. What are the possibilities for how that output is determined by the inputs? Each of the two inputs can have two possible values; that means that a gate has four different possible input configurations. For each of those four, the gate can output 0 or 1. As you can see from the chart below, this means that there are 16 possible kinds of two-input gates:

input p:	0	0	1	1	
input q:	0	1	0	1	
outputs:	0	0	0	0	
	0	0	0	1	and $(p \wedge q)$
	0	0	1	0	
	0	0	1	1	
	0	1	0	0	
	0	1	0	1	
	0	1	1	0	exclusive or $(p \otimes q)$
	0	1	1	1	or $(p \vee q)$
	1	0	0	0	nor (not-or, $\neg(p \vee q)$)
	1	0	0	1	equivalence $(p \leftrightarrow q)$
	1	0	1	0	
	1	0	1	1	

```
1   1   0   0
1   1   0   1     implies $(p \rightarrow q)$
1   1   1   0     nand (not-and, $\neg(p \wedge q)$)
1   1   1   1
```

The table indicates, for example, that a gate whose output is 1 only when both inputs are 1 is an *and* gate, implementing the usual logical and operation. The 16 possibilities include all the standard logic functions as well as several less obviously useful ones. Two gate types called *nand* and *nor* represent functions rarely used in mathematical logic but common in computer design because it is sometimes helpful to have the opposite of the signal you're logically interested in.

Numbers other than 0 and 1 can't be represented as a single signal in a single wire. That's why there isn't a "plus gate" along with the and gates, or gates, and so on; if both inputs to a plus gate were 1, the output would have to be 2. To add two zero-or-one numbers we need a more complicated device with *two* output wires, one of which is the "carry" to the next binary digit:

A input:	0	0	1	1
B input:	0	1	0	1
sum out:	0	1	1	0
carry out:	0	0	0	1

These sum and carry outputs can be defined in terms of logical operations:

$$\text{Sum} = A \otimes B$$

$$\text{Carry} = A \wedge B$$

Exclusive or gates are, in fact, not generally used as basic hardware components, so this device is traditionally represented in terms of and gates, or gates, and inverters:

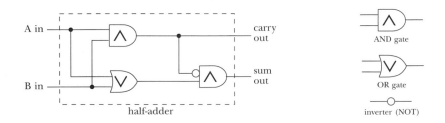

The device we've just built is called a *half-adder* for reasons that should become clear in a moment.

To represent numbers larger than 1 we have to use more than one signal wire. Each signal represents a binary digit, or *bit,* that is implicitly multiplied by a power of 2 just as in the ordinary decimal representation of numbers each digit is implicitly multiplied by a power of 10. For example, if we have three signal wires for a number, they have multipliers of 1, 2, and 4; with these signals we can represent the eight numbers from 0 (all signals 0) to 7 (all signals 1). When we want to add two such three-bit numbers, the sum for all but the rightmost bit can involve a carry *in* as well as a carry out. The circuit for each bit position must have *three* inputs, including one for the carry from the next bit over as well as the two external inputs. The outputs are found using these formulas:

$$\text{Sum} = (A \otimes B) \otimes \text{CarryIn}$$

$$\text{CarryOut} = (A \wedge B) \vee ((A \otimes B) \wedge \text{CarryIn})$$

This circuit can be built using two half-adders:

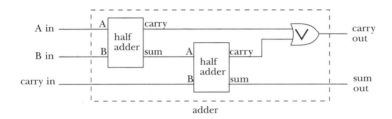

To add two three-bit numbers we connect three adders together this way:

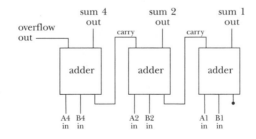

The carry out signal from the leftmost adder (the one representing the largest power of 2) is the *overflow* signal; if it's true, the sum didn't fit in the number of bits provided. Many computers use this signal to *interrupt* the execution of their programs so that people don't end up seeing incorrect results.

The phrase "computer logic" is widely used, even by non-experts, to refer to the inner workings of a computer. Many people, though, think that the phrase describes the *personality* of the computer, which they imagine to be like that of Mr. Spock. "Computers may be able to play chess, but they can't write poetry, because that isn't logical." Here you've seen the real meaning of the phrase: Just as a Logo program has procedures defined in terms of subprocedures and ultimately in terms of primitive procedures, the capabilities of a computer itself are built out of smaller pieces, and the primitive hardware components compute logical, rather than arithmetic, functions. (For a computer to exhibit Mr. Spock's sense of purpose, understanding of cause and effect, drive for self-preservation, loyalty to his species and his government, and so on, would be no less miraculous than for it to write a love poem or throw a temper tantrum. Later we'll discuss the efforts of artificial intelligence researchers to produce such miracles.)

Combinatorics

Earlier I listed the 16 possible logical functions of two logical arguments. I could have figured out that there are 16 without actually listing them this way: If a function has two arguments, and each argument has two possible values, that makes 2^2 possible combinations of argument values. A logical function is determined by its result for each of those four possible argument combinations. (The four are $f(0,0), f(0,1), f(1,0)$, and $f(1,1)$.) There are two possible results for $f(0,0)$, two for $f(0,1)$, and so on; the number of possible functions is the product of all these twos, 2^{2^2} or 16.

The mathematics of counting how things can be combined is called *combinatorics*. The problem we've just done illustrates a fundamental rule of combinatorics, namely that the number of possibilities for a choice with several components is the product of the number of possibilities for each component choice. This may be easier to understand with an example in which not all the relevant numbers are 2. Here's a classic: Suppose you have a group of four men and three women, and you want to form a committee of one man and one woman chosen from this group. How many such committees are possible? There are 4 choices for the male member of the committee and 3 choices for the female member; that means 4×3 or 12 committees.

(The multiplication rule only works if the component choices are *independent*; that is, the possible outcomes of one choice can't be affected by the outcome of any of the others. For example, if our committees are to have a chairperson who can be of either sex and then two other members, one man and one woman, you can't say "there are 7 choices for the chairperson, times 4 for the man, times 3 for the woman" because after choosing the chairperson the number of choices for the other members is changed depending on the sex of the chair. There are two correct ways to solve this problem. One is to say "The chairperson is either male or female. If male, there are 4 possible chairs, times 3 possible other male members, times 3 possible female members, for 36 possible committees. If female, there are 3 possible chairs, times 4 possible male members, times 2 possible other female members, for 24 committees. The total is 36 + 24 or 60 committees." The second solution is to pick the chairperson *last*; then you say "There are 4 possible male members, times 3 possible females, times 5 possible chairs (7 people in the original group minus 2 already chosen)." Apart from arithmetic errors, almost all the mistakes people make in solving combinatorics problems come from forgetting that events have to be independent to allow you to multiply the choices.)

Let's return to logical functions for a moment. Suppose we experiment with a ternary logic in which the possible values are yes, no, and maybe. (You can represent these using the numbers 0, 1, and 2.) How many three-argument ternary logic functions are there? Is it $3^{(3^3)}$ or is it $(3^3)^3$? (It doesn't matter which way you group the twos for the binary logic version because the two groupings have the same value, 16, but this isn't true with threes.) How many two-argument ternary logic functions are there? $2^{(3^2)}$? $3^{(2^3)}$? $(3^3)^2$? How many three-argument binary logic functions? The virtue of these problems is that you can check your own answers by listing all the possible functions as I did for the two-argument binary logic functions.

Most people are introduced to combinatorics by way of *probability*, the mathematics of gambling. Given a number of equally likely possible situations, some of which win a bet and the rest of which lose it, the probability of winning is a ratio:

$$\text{probability} = \frac{\text{number of possible winning situations}}{\text{total number of possible situations}}$$

The role of combinatorics is to help in computing the numerator and denominator of that fraction.

For example, suppose you have six brown socks and four blue socks in a drawer, and you pull out two socks without looking. What is the probability of getting a matching pair? I'm going to give each sock a name like *brown₃* for the third brown sock so that we can talk about individual socks even if they're the same color. How many possible pairs of socks are there? That is, given the set

$$\{\ brown_1,\ brown_2, \ldots, brown_6,\ blue_1, \ldots, blue_4\ \}$$

containing ten socks, how many two-sock subsets are there?

The first step in answering this question is to notice that we have 10 choices for the first sock and then 9 choices for the second. So there are 10×9 ways to make the two choices. (There is a subtle point here that some textbooks don't bother explaining. The choice of the second sock is *not* independent of the first choice, since we can't choose the same sock twice. However, the *number* of second choices is always 9, even though the particular nine available socks depend on the first choice. So we can get away with multiplying in this example.)

This isn't quite the answer we want, though. We've shown that there are 90 *ordered pairs* of socks. But once we get the socks out of the drawer, it doesn't matter which we picked first. In other words, if we say there are 90 possible choices, we are counting { *brown₂, brown₅* } and { *brown₅, brown₂* } as two different choices. Since we don't care which sock came out of the drawer first, we are really counting every pair twice, so there are only $90/2$ or 45 possible pairs.

An ordered subset of a set is called a *permutation;* a subset without a particular order is a *combination*. We say that there are 90 permutations of ten things taken two at a time; there are 45 combinations of ten things taken two at a time.

It turns out that combinations are what matters most of the time; it's relatively rare for permutations to turn up in a math problem. An exception is the device wrongly called a "combination lock"; to open one, you must know a particular permutation of the possible numbers. My high school locker "combination" was 18–24–14. If I tried the same numbers in a different order, like 24–18–14, the lock wouldn't open. (Actually it's misleading for me to use this example because the same number can appear twice in most locks of this type, so the "combination" is not a subset of the available numbers. If there are 50 numbers available, the total number of possibilities is not $50 \times 49 \times 48$ but rather $50 \times 50 \times 50$. These lock-opening patterns are therefore neither permutations nor combinations but something else that we might call "permutations with repetition allowed.")

We haven't finished solving the sock problem. How many of the possible pairs of socks are matching pairs? One way to find out would be to list all the possible pairs and actually count how many of them match. This is the sort of thing computers do well. First we have to write a procedure that takes as input a list and a number, and outputs a list of lists, each of which is a subset of the input list whose length is the input number. That is, we want to take

```
combs [brown1 brown2 ... brown6 blue1 ... blue4] 2
```

and this should output a list of pairs:

```
[[brown1 brown2] [brown1 brown3] ... [brown4 blue3] ... [blue3 blue4]]
```

This is a fairly tricky program to write. Try it before you read further. Can you reduce the problem to a smaller, similar problem? Don't forget that we want combinations, not permutations, so the output can't have two sublists containing the same elements.

To make sure that each combination appears in the result in only one order, we can decide explicitly what that order will be. The most convenient thing is to say that the elements will appear in each sublist in the same order in which they appear in the original list. That is, since the input list has `brown2` before `blue3`, the output will contain the list

```
[brown2 blue3]
```

but not the list

```
[blue3 brown2]
```

It follows that the very first element of the input list, `brown1`, can only appear as the first element of any output sublist. In other words, there are two kinds of sublists: ones with `brown1` as their first element and ones that don't include `brown1` at all. This is a way to divide the problem into smaller pieces.

If we are looking for n-element subsets, the first kind consists of `brown1` stuck in front of a smaller subset of $n-1$ elements chosen from the remainder (the `butfirst`) of the input list. The second kind of subset is an n-element subset of the `butfirst`. We can collect all of each kind by a recursive invocation of the procedure we're going to write, then append the two collections and output the result. So the procedure will look like this:

```
to combs :list :howmany
... <stop rule> ...
output sentence (map [fput first :list ?]
                    combs (butfirst :list) (:howmany-1)) ~
             (combs (butfirst :list) :howmany)
end
```

By now you've had a lot of experience writing recursive procedures, but I'm going over this one in detail for two reasons: It's tricky and it's a model for solving many other combinatorial problems. What makes it tricky is a combination of two things. One is that it's recursive twice; that is, there are two recursive invocations of `combs` within `combs`. This makes the control structure very different from the

```
to blah :list
output fput (something first :list) (blah butfirst :list)
end
```

sort of recursion that may be more familiar. The second tricky part is that there are two input variables, each of which may be made smaller (by butfirsting or by subtracting 1) but need not be in a particular recursive call.

One implication of these complicating factors is that we need *two* stop rules. It may be obvious that we need one for the situation of counting :howmany down to zero, but we also need one for :list getting too small. Ordinarily this latter would be an emptyp test, but in fact any list whose length is less than :howmany is too small, not just the empty list. Here is the finished procedure:

```
to combs :list :howmany
if equalp :howmany 0 [output [[]]]
if equalp :howmany count :list [output (list :list)]
output sentence (map [fput first :list ?]
                 combs (butfirst :list) (:howmany-1)) ~
           (combs (butfirst :list) :howmany)
end
```

```
? show combs [a b c d e] 3
[[a b c] [a b d] [a b e] [a c d] [a c e] [a d e]
       [b c d] [b c e] [b d e] [c d e]]
```

Now we can use combs on the sock problem. (Note: The procedure socks shown here is not the one in the program file; there will be a modified version a few paragraphs down the road.)

```
to socks :list
localmake "total combs :list 2
localmake "matching filter [equalp butlast first ? butlast last ?] ~
                        :total
print (sentence [There are] count :total [possible pairs of socks.])
print (sentence [Of these,] count :matching [are matching pairs.])
print sentence [Probability of match =] ~
             word (100*(count :matching)/(count :total)) "%
end
```

Chapter 2   Discrete Mathematics

```
? socks [brown1 brown2 brown3 brown4 brown5 brown6
        blue1 blue2 blue3 blue4]
There are 45 possible pairs of socks.
Of these, 21 are matching pairs.
Probability of match = 46.6666667%
```

The answer is that the probability of a matching pair is just under half. The template used in the invocation of `filter` in `socks` depends on the fact that two socks match if their names are equal except for the last character, such as `brown3` and `brown4`.

I've numbered the socks because it's easier for us to talk about how the program works (and about how the underlying mathematics works, too) if we can identify an individual sock. But it's worth noting that the program doesn't really need individual sock names. We could instead use the list

```
[brown brown brown brown brown brown blue blue blue blue]
```

and change the `filter` template to

```
[equalp first ? last ?]
```

The program will generate some `[brown brown]` pairs, some `[brown blue]` pairs, and some `[blue blue]` pairs. The number of pairs will still be 45 and the number of matching pairs will still be 21.

Having come to that realization, we can make the "user interface" a little smoother by having `socks` accept an input list like

```
[6 brown 4 blue]
```

and expand that into the desired list of ten socks itself. Here is the final program:

```
to socks :list
localmake "total combs (expand :list) 2
localmake "matching filter [equalp first ? last ?] :total
print (sentence [There are] count :total [possible pairs of socks.])
print (sentence [Of these,] count :matching [are matching pairs.])
print sentence [Probability of match =] ~
              word (100*(count :matching)/(count :total)) "%
end
```

```
to expand :list
if emptyp :list [output []]
if numberp first :list ~
   [output cascade (first :list)
                    [fput first butfirst :list ?]
                    (expand butfirst butfirst :list)]
output fput first :list expand butfirst :list
end
```

? socks [6 brown 4 blue]
There are 45 possible pairs of socks.
Of these, 21 are matching pairs.
Probability of match = 46.6666667%

My reason for presenting this refinement of the program is that it offers a concrete opportunity for reflection on how you can tell which differences are important in a combinatorics problem. In discussing the first version of the program, I said that the two lists

`[brown2 brown5]` and `[brown5 brown2]`

represent the same pair of socks, so both shouldn't be included in the list of lists output by `combs`. Now I'm saying that several lists that look identical like

`[brown brown]`

represent *different* pairs of socks and must all be counted. It would be a mistake to say, "There are three possibilities: brown-brown, brown-blue, and blue-blue. So the probability of a match is 2/3." It's true that there are three *kinds* of pairs of socks, but the three kinds are not equally represented in the list of 45 possible pairs.

Inductive and Closed-Form Definition

The usual approach to problems like the one about the socks is not to enumerate the actual combinations, but rather to compute the *number* of combinations directly. There are formulas for both number of combinations and number of permutations. Usually the latter is derived first because it's easier to understand.

With 10 socks in the drawer, the number of two-sock permutations is 10×9. If we'd wanted three socks for a visiting extraterrestrial friend, the number of permutations would be $10 \times 9 \times 8$. In general, if we have n things and we want to select r of them, the number of permutations is

$$_nP_r = \underbrace{n \cdot (n-1) \cdot \;\cdots\; \cdot (n-r+1)}_{r \text{ factors}}$$

Mathematicians don't like messy formulas full of dots, so this is usually abbreviated using the factorial function. The notation "$n!$" is pronounced "n factorial" and represents the product of all the integers from 1 to n. Using this notation we can write

$$_nP_r = \frac{n!}{(n-r)!}$$

This is an elegant formula, but you should resist the temptation to use it as the basis for a computer program. If you write

```
to perms :n :r
output (fact :n)/(fact (:n-:r))
end

to fact :n
output cascade :n [# * ?] 1
end
```

then you're doing more multiplications than necessary, plus an unnecessary division. Instead, go back to the earlier version in which r terms are multiplied:

```
to perms :n :r
if :r=0 [output 1]
output :n * perms :n-1 :r-1
end
```

The set of all permutations of n things taken r at a time includes several rearrangements of each *combination* of n things r at a time. How many rearrangements of each? Each combination is a set of r things, so the number of possible orderings of those r things is the number of permutations of r things r at a time, $_rP_r$ or $r!$. $_nP_r$ is greater than $_nC_r$, the number of combinations of n things taken r at a time, by this factor. In other words, if each combination corresponds to $r!$ permutations, then the number of permutations is $r!$ times the number of combinations. So we have

$$\binom{n}{r} = {}_nC_r = \frac{_nP_r}{_rP_r} = \frac{n!}{r!\,(n-r)!}$$

The notation $\binom{n}{r}$ is much more commonly used in mathematics and computer science texts than $_nC_r$. It's pronounced "n choose r."

The traditional way to do the sock problem is this: The total number of possible pairs of socks is $\binom{10}{2}$. The number of matching pairs is equal to the number of brown pairs plus the number of blue pairs. The number of brown pairs is the number of combinations of 6 brown socks chosen 2 at a time, or $\binom{6}{2}$. Similarly, the number of pairs of blue socks is $\binom{4}{2}$. So

$$\text{probability of match} = \frac{\binom{6}{2} + \binom{4}{2}}{\binom{10}{2}} = \frac{15 + 6}{45} = \frac{21}{45}$$

which is the same answer we got by enumerating and testing all the possible pairs.

A formula like

$$\binom{n}{r} = \frac{n!}{r!\,(n-r)!}$$

defines a mathematical function in terms of other, more elementary functions. It is comparable to a Logo procedure defined in terms of primitives, like

```
to second :thing
output first butfirst :thing
end
```

The "primitives" of mathematics are addition, subtraction, and so on, along with a few more advanced ones like the trigonometric and exponential functions. These are called "elementary functions" and a formula that defines some new function in terms of those is called a *closed form definition*.

The function $\binom{n}{r}$ could also be defined in a different way based on the ideas in the `combs` program we used to enumerate combinations. The combinations fall into two categories, those that include the first element and those that don't. So the number of combinations is the sum of the numbers in each category:

$$\binom{n}{r} = \begin{cases} 1, & \text{if } r = 0; \\ 1, & \text{if } r = n; \\ \binom{n-1}{r-1} + \binom{n-1}{r}, & \text{otherwise.} \end{cases}$$

This is called an *inductive definition*. It is analogous to a recursive procedure in Logo.

These two formulas provide alternative definitions for the *same* function, just as two Logo procedures can employ different algorithms but have the same input-output behavior. How do we know that the two definitions of $\binom{n}{r}$ really do define the same function? Each definition was derived from the fundamental definition of "the number of combinations of n things taken r at a time" by different arguments. If those arguments are correct, the two versions must define the same function because there is just one correct number of combinations. It is also possible to prove the two definitions equivalent by algebraic manipulation; start with the closed form definition and see if it does, in fact, obey the requirements of the inductive definition. For example, if $r = 0$ we have

$$\binom{n}{0} = \frac{n!}{0!\,(n-0)!} = \frac{n!}{n!} = 1$$

(It may not be obvious that $0!$ should be equal to 1, but mathematicians define the factorial function that way so that the formula $n! = n \cdot (n-1)!$ remains true when $n = 1$.) See if you can verify the other two parts of the inductive definition. Here's a hint:

$$\binom{n-1}{r-1} + \binom{n-1}{r} = \frac{(n-1)!}{(r-1)!\,((n-1)-(r-1))!} + \frac{(n-1)!}{r!\,(n-1-r)!} = \cdots$$

Why would anyone be interested in an inductive definition when the closed form definition is mathematically simpler and also generally faster to compute? There are two reasons. First, some functions don't have closed form definitions in terms of elementary functions. For those functions, there is no choice but to use an inductive definition. Second, sometimes when you start with a non-formal definition of a function in terms of its purpose, like "the number of combinations..." for $\binom{n}{r}$, it may be easier to see how to translate that into an inductive definition as a first step, even if it later turns out that there is also a less obvious closed form. In fact, that's what I did in presenting the idea of combinations. I found it more straightforward to understand the inductive definition because it made sense to think about the actual combinations and not merely how many of them there are. (In fact there is a mathematical technique called *generating functions* that can sometimes be used to transform an inductive definition into a closed form definition, but that technique requires calculus and is beyond the scope of this book.)

Pascal's Triangle

In addition to closed form and inductive definitions, it's often helpful to present a sort of partial definition of a function in the form of a table of values. (For logic functions, with only a finite number of possible values for the arguments of the function, such a table is actually a complete definition.) Partial definitions in a table of values can be particularly useful when the function displays some regularity that allows values outside the table to be computed easily based on the values in the table. For example, the sine function is *periodic;* its values repeat in cycles of 360 degrees. If you need to know the sine of 380 degrees, you can look up the sine of 20 degrees and that's the answer.

For functions of two variables, like addition and multiplication, these function tables are often presented as square arrays of numbers. In elementary school you learned the addition and multiplication tables for numbers up to 10, along with algorithms for reducing the addition and multiplication of larger numbers to a sequence of operations on single digits.

The function $\binom{n}{r}$ is a function of two variables, so it would ordinarily be presented as a square table like the multiplication table, except for the fact that this particular function is meaningfully defined only when $r \leq n$. (There are no combinations of three things taken five at a time, for example, so $\binom{3}{5}$ is 0.) So instead of a square format like this:

$r\backslash^n$	0	1	2	3	4	5
0	1	1	1	1	1	1
1	0	1	2	3	4	5
2	0	0	1	3	6	10
3	0	0	0	1	4	10
4	0	0	0	0	1	5
5	0	0	0	0	0	1

this function is traditionally presented in a triangular form called "Pascal's Triangle" after Blaise Pascal (1623–1662), who invented the mathematical theory of probability along with Pierre de Fermat (1601–1665). Pascal didn't invent the triangle, but he did pioneer its use in combinatorics. Each row of the triangle contains the nonzero values of $\binom{n}{r}$ for a particular n:

$$
\begin{array}{ccccccccccc}
 & & & & & 1 & & & & & \\
 & & & & 1 & & 1 & & & & \\
 & & & 1 & & 2 & & 1 & & & \\
 & & 1 & & 3 & & 3 & & 1 & & \\
 & 1 & & 4 & & 6 & & 4 & & 1 & \\
1 & & 5 & & 10 & & 10 & & 5 & & 1 \\
\end{array}
$$

Pascal's Triangle is often introduced in algebra because the numbers in row n (counting from zero) are the *binomial coefficients*, the constant factors in the terms in the expansion of $(a + b)^n$. For example,

$$(a + b)^4 = 1a^4 + 4a^3b + 6a^2b^2 + 4ab^3 + 1b^4$$

$$= \binom{4}{0} a^4 + \binom{4}{1} a^3b + \binom{4}{2} a^2b^2 + \binom{4}{3} ab^3 + \binom{4}{4} b^4$$

Do you see why the binomial coefficients are related to combinations? An expression like $(a + b)^4$ is a sum of products of four as and bs. (How many such products? Each term involves four choices between a and b; there are 2 ways to make each choice, and the choices are independent, so there are 2^4 possible products.) These products are combined into terms based on the fact that some are equal to each other, such as $aaab$ and $abaa$, both of which contribute to the $a^3 b$ term. How many arrangements of three as and one b are there? That's like asking how many ways there are to choose one slot for a b out of four possible slots, which is $\binom{4}{1}$.

Can you predict what the coefficients will be in the expansion of $(a + b + c)^4$? For example, what is the coefficient of $ab^2 c$? Try to multiply it out and see if your formula is right.

Everyone is taught in school that each number in Pascal's Triangle, except for the 1s at the ends, is the sum of the two numbers above it. But this is usually presented as a piece of magic with no explanation. It's not obvious how that fact is connected to the formula expressing $\binom{n}{r}$ in terms of factorials. But the technique I used in writing the `combs` procedure to enumerate the actual combinations explains how Pascal's Triangle works. The set of all combinations of n things taken r at a time can be divided into those combinations that include the first of the n things and those that don't. How many of the former are there? Each such combination must be completed by adjoining to that first thing $r - 1$ out of the remaining $n - 1$ available things, so there are $\binom{n-1}{r-1}$ such combinations. The second category, those not containing the first thing in the list, requires us to choose r things out of the remaining $n - 1$, so there are $\binom{n-1}{r}$ of them. So $\binom{n}{r}$ must be the sum of those two numbers, which are indeed the ones above it in the triangle.

Thinking about the triangle may also help you to understand why `combs` needs two stop rules; each row contains *two* numbers, the ones (pun) at each end, that can't be computed as the sum of two other numbers.

Simulation

Yet another approach to solving the sock problem would be the experimental method: Load a drawer with six brown and four blue socks, pull out pairs of socks a few thousand times, and see how many of the pairs match. The actual experiment would be time-consuming and rather boring, but we can *simulate* the experiment with a computer program. The idea is to use random numbers to represent the random choice of a sock.

```
to socktest
localmake "first ~
          pick [brown brown brown brown brown brown blue blue blue blue]
localmake "second ~
          pick (if equalp :first "brown
                  [[brown brown brown brown brown blue blue blue blue]]
                  [[brown brown brown brown brown brown blue blue blue]] )
output equalp :first :second
end
```

Socktest is a predicate that simulates one trial of picking a pair of socks and outputs true if the socks match. Notice how the available choices for the second sock depend on which color sock was chosen first. (It's a little unaesthetic that this particular selection of six brown and four blue socks is built into the program, with three slightly different lists explicitly present inside socktest. It would be both more elegant and more flexible if socktest could take a list like [6 brown 4 blue] as input, like socks, and compute the list of possibilities for the second sock itself. But right now I'm more interested in showing how a simulation works than in programming style; you can make that change yourself if you like.)

What we want to do is invoke socktest repeatedly and keep track of how many times the output is true. That can be done with an instruction like

```
print (cascade 1000 [? + if socktest [1] [0]] 0) / 10
```

I divide by 10 so that the result will be expressed as a percent probability. (If I made 100 trials instead of 1000 the output from cascade would already be a percentage.) Your results will depend on the random number generator of your computer. I tried it three times and got results of 50.1%, 50.8%, and 45.5%. I then did 10,000 trials at once with a result of 48.78%. The result expected on theoretical grounds was $46\frac{2}{3}\%$.

Simulation is generally much slower than either of the techniques we used earlier (enumeration of possibilities and direct computation of the number of possibilities), and it gives results that are only approximately correct. So why would anyone want to use this method? For a simple problem like this, you probably wouldn't. But some combinatorics problems are too complicated to be captured by a simple formula. For example, what is the probability of winning a game of solitaire? (To make this a sensible question, you'd have to decide on a particular set of strategy rules to determine which card to play next when there are several possibilities. The rule could be "play the higher ranking card" or "choose a card at random," for example.) In principle this question could be answered exactly, since there are only a finite number of ways a deck of cards can be arranged and we could analyze each of them. But in practice the most reasonable approach is probably to write a solitaire simulator and have it play out a few thousand randomly ordered hands.

Solitaire is a rather complicated game; even a simulator for it would be quite a large project. A more manageable one, if you'd like something to program, would be a craps simulator. Remember that the 11 possible results of rolling two dice (2 to 12) are not equally likely! You have to simulate each die separately.

The Simplex Lock Problem

This is a picture of a Simplex lock, so called because it's manufactured by Simplex Security Systems, Inc. It is a five-button mechanical (i.e., no electricity) combination lock with an unusual set of possible combinations. As an example of a challenging problem in combinatorics, I'd like you to figure out how many possible combinations there are.

What makes this lock unusual is that a combination can include more than one button pushed at the same time. For example, one possible combination is "2, then 1 and 4 at the same time, then 3." Here are the precise rules:

1. Each button may be used at most once. For example, "2, then 2 and 3 at the same time" is not allowed.
2. Each push may include any number of buttons, from one to five. For example, one legal combination is "hit all five buttons at once with your fist." (But hitting all five buttons can't be part of a larger combination because of rule 1.)

It follows from these rules that there can be at most five distinct pushes. (Do you see why?) The rules also allow for the null combination, in which you don't have to push any buttons at all.

When working on this problem, don't forget that when two or more buttons are pushed at the same time, their order doesn't matter. That is, you shouldn't count "2 and 3 together, then 5" and "3 and 2 together, then 5" as two distinct combinations. (For this reason, the Simplex lock *is* entitled, at least in part, to the name "combination lock"!)

Try to figure out how many combinations there are before reading further. You can enumerate all the possibilities or you can derive a formula for the number of possibilities. You might want to start with a smaller number of buttons. (As a slight hint, when you buy one of these locks, the box it comes in says "thousands of combinations.")

I first attacked this problem by trying to enumerate all the possible combinations, but that turns out to be quite messy. The trouble is that it isn't obvious how to *order* the combinations, so it's hard to be sure you haven't missed any. Here is how I finally decided to do it. First of all, divide the possible combinations into six categories depending on how many buttons (zero to five) they use. There is exactly one combination using zero buttons, and there are five using one button each. After that it gets tricky because there are different *patterns* of simultaneous pushes within each category. For example, for combinations using two buttons there are two patterns: the one in which they're pressed together (**x-x**) and the one in which they're pressed separately (**x x**). (I'm introducing a notation for patterns in which hyphens connect buttons that are pressed together and spaces connect the separate pushes.) How many distinct combinations are there in each of those patterns? Figure it out before reading on.

In the **x x** pattern there are $_5P_2$ "combinations" because the order in which you push the buttons matters. In the **x-x** pattern there are only $\binom{5}{2}$ combinations because the two buttons are pushed together; 1-4 and 4-1 are the same combination. Altogether there are 20 + 10 or 30 combinations usng two of the five buttons.

Beyond this point it gets harder to keep track of the different patterns. Among the three-button patterns are **x-x x**, **x x x**, and **x-x-x**. How many more are there? How many four-button patterns? You might, at this point, like to see if you can finish enumerating all the possibilities for the five-button lock.

My solution is to notice that in a three-button pattern, for example, there are two slots between the xs, and each slot has a space or a hyphen. If I think of those slots as binary digits, with 0 for space and 1 for hyphen, then each pattern corresponds to a 2-bit number. There are four such numbers, 00 to 11 (or 0 to 3 in ordinary decimal notation).

number	pattern
00	x x x
01	x x-x
10	x-x x
11	x-x-x

Similarly, there are eight four-button patterns:

number	pattern
000	x x x x
001	x x x-x
010	x x-x x
011	x x-x-x
100	x-x x x
101	x-x x-x
110	x-x-x x
111	x-x-x-x

And there are 16 five-button patterns, from 0000 to 1111.

How many combinations are there within each pattern? There are two different ways to go about calculating that number. To be specific, let's consider four-button patterns. The way I chose to do the calculation was to start with the idea that there are $_5P_4$ ways to choose four buttons in order. For the x x x x pattern, this is the answer. For the other patterns, this number (120) has to be divided by various factors to account for the fact that the order is *partially* immaterial, just as in deriving the formula for combinations from the formula for permutations we divided by r! because the order is completely immaterial. Consider the pattern x-x x x. In this pattern the order of the first two numbers is immaterial, but the choice of the first two numbers as a pair matters, and so does the order of the last two numbers. So 1-2 3 4 is the same combination as 2-1 3 4 but different from 1-3 2 4 or 1-2 4 3. That means the number 120 is too big by a factor of 2, because every significant choice of combination is represented twice. For this pattern the number of different combinations is 60. Of course the same argument applies to the patterns x x-x x and x x x-x.

What about `x-x x-x`? In this pattern there are two pairs of positions within which order doesn't matter. Each combination appears *four* times in the list of 120; `1-2 3-4` is the same as `1-2 4-3`, `2-1 3-4`, and `2-1 4-3`. So there are 30 significantly different combinations in this pattern. What about `x-x-x x`? In this pattern, the order of the first three numbers is irrelevant; this means that there are 3! or 6 appearances of each combination in the 120, so there are 20 significantly different combinations in this pattern. The general rule is that for each group of m consecutive hyphens in the pattern you must divide by $(m+1)!$ to eliminate duplicates.

(My approach was to start with permutations and then divide out redundant ones. Another approach would be to build up the pattern using combinations. The pattern `x-x x x` contains three groups of numbers representing three "pushes": a group of two and two groups of one. Since this is a five-button lock, for the first group of two there are $\binom{5}{2}$ choices. (Order doesn't matter within a group.) For the second group there are only three buttons remaining from which we can choose, so there are $\binom{3}{1}$ choices for that button. Finally, there are $\binom{2}{1}$ choices for the fourth button (the third group). This makes $10 \times 3 \times 2$ possible combinations for this pattern, the same as the 60 we computed the other way. For the `x-x x-x` pattern this method gives $\binom{5}{2}\binom{3}{2}$ or 30 combinations.)

Having worked all this out, I was ready to write a computer program to count the total number of combinations. The trickiest part was deciding how to deal with the binary numbers that represent the patterns. In the end I used plain old numbers. The expression

```
remainder :number 2
```

yields the rightmost bit of a number, and then `:number/2` gives all but the rightmost bit (with a little extra effort for odd numbers). To help you read the program, here is a description of the most important procedures:

> `lock 5` outputs the total number of combinations for the 5-button lock.
>
> `lock1 5 4` outputs the number of combinations that use 4 out of the 5 buttons.
>
> `lock2 120 5 1` outputs the number of combinations for the 4-button pattern corresponding to the binary form of the number 5 (101 or x-x x-x). The 120 is $_5P_4$ and the 1 is always used as the third input except in recursive calls.

Here is the program:

```
to lock :buttons
output cascade :buttons [? + lock1 :buttons #] 1
end
```

```
to lock1 :total :buttons
localmake "perms perms :total :buttons
output cascade (twoto (:buttons-1)) ~
               [? + lock2 :perms #-1 1] ~
               0
end

to twoto :power
output cascade :power [2 * ?] 1
end

to lock2 :perms :links :factor
if equalp :links 0 [output :perms/(fact :factor)]
if equalp (remainder :links 2) 0 ~
   [output lock2 :perms/(fact :factor) :links/2 1]
output lock2 :perms (:links-1)/2 :factor+1
end
```

One slight subtlety is that in lock the third input to cascade is 1 rather than 0 to include the one 0-button combination that would not otherwise be added in.

An Inductive Solution

When I wrote that program, I was pleased with myself for managing to turn such a messy solution into executable form, but I wasn't satisfied with the underlying approach. I wanted something mathematically more elegant.

What made it possible for me to find the approach I wanted was the chance discovery that the number of combinations that use all five buttons (541) is half of the total number of combinations (1082). Could this possibly be a coincidence, or would that have to be true for any number of buttons? To see that it has to be true, I used an idea from another branch of mathematics, *set theory*. A *set* is any collection of things, in no particular order. One can speak of the set of all the fingers on my left hand, or the set of all the integers, or the set of all the universities in cities named Cambridge. Much of the interesting part of set theory has to do with the properties of infinite sets; for example, it turns out that the set of all the integers is the same size as the set of all the rational numbers, but both of these are smaller than the set of irrational numbers. What does it mean for one infinite set to be the same size as, or to be larger than, another? The same definition works equally well for finite sets: Two sets are the same size if they can be placed in *one-to-one correspondence*. This means that you must exhibit a way to pair the elements of one set with the elements of the other so that each element of one has exactly one partner in the other. (A set is larger than another if they aren't the same size, but a subset of the first is the same size as the second.)

To prove that my observation about the lock combinations has to be true regardless of the number of buttons, I have to exhibit a one-to-one correspondence between two sets: the set of all combinations using all the buttons of an n-button lock and the set of all combinations using fewer than n of the buttons. But that's easy. Starting with a combination that uses all the buttons, just eliminate the last push (one or more buttons pushed at the same time) to get a combination using fewer than all the buttons. For example, for a five-button lock, the five-button combination 2 3-4 1-5 is paired with the three-button combination 2 3-4. (We have to eliminate the last *push* and not merely the last *button* for two reasons. First, if we always eliminated exactly one button, we'd always get a four-button combination, and we want to pair five-button combinations with all the fewer-than-five ones. Second, which is the "last" button if the last push involves more than one? Remember, 2 3-4 1-5 is the *same* combination as 2 3-4 5-1. But writing this combination in two different forms seems to pair it with two different smaller ones. The rules of one-to-one correspondence say that each element of a set must have exactly one partner in the other set.)

To show that the correspondence works in both directions, start with a combination that doesn't use all the buttons; its partner is formed by adding one push at the end that contains all the missing buttons. For example, if we start with 1 2-5 then its partner is 1 2-5 3-4.

I've just proved that the number of all-n combinations must be equal to the number of fewer-than-n combinations. So it's not a coincidence that 541 is half of 1082. In order to be able to talk about these numbers more succinctly, I want to define

$$f(n) = \text{number of } n\text{-button combinations of an } n\text{-button lock}$$

We've just proved that it's also true that

$$f(n) = \text{number of fewer-than-}n\text{-button combinations}$$

Now, what does "fewer than n buttons" mean? Well, there are combinations using no buttons, one button, two buttons, and so on up to $n-1$ buttons. Let's define

$$g(n, i) = \text{number of } i\text{-button combinations in an } n\text{-button lock}$$

So we can formalize the phrase "fewer than n" by saying

$$f(n) = g(n, 0) + g(n, 1) + g(n, 2) + \cdots + g(n, n-1)$$

Instead of using those dots in the middle, mathematicians have another notation for a sum of several terms like this.

$$f(n) = \sum_{i=0}^{n-1} g(n, i)$$

If you haven't seen this notation before, the Σ (*sigma*) symbol is the Greek letter S, and is used to represent a *S*um. It works a little like the `for` iteration tool; the variable below the Σ (in this case, i) takes on values from the lower limit (0) to the upper limit $(n-1)$, and for each of those values the expression following the Σ is added into the sum. The Logo equivalent would be

```
for [i 0 [:n-1]] [make "sum :sum + (g :n :i)]
```

The Σ-expression is pronounced "the sum from i equals zero to n minus one of g of n comma i."

So far, what I've done is like what I did before: dividing the set of all possible combinations into subsets based on the number of buttons used in each combination. This is like the definition of `lock` in terms of `lock1`. The next step is to see if we can find a formula for $g(n, i)$. How many 3-button combinations, for example, can we make using a 5-button lock? (That's $g(5, 3)$.) There are many different ways in which I might try to derive a formula, but I think it will be helpful at this point to step back and consider my overall goal. I started this line of reasoning because I'm trying to express the solution for the five-button lock in terms of easier solutions for smaller numbers of buttons. That is, I'm looking for an inductive definition of $f(n)$ in terms of values of f for smaller arguments. I'd like to end up with a formula like

$$f(n) = \ldots f(0) \ldots f(1) \ldots f(n-1) \ldots$$

but I don't yet know exactly what form it will take. So far I've written a formula for $f(n)$ in terms of $g(n, i)$ for values of i less than n. It would be great, therefore, if I could express $g(n, i)$ in terms of $f(i)$; that would give me exactly what I want.

To put that last sentence into words, it would be great if I could express the number of i-button combinations of an n-button lock in terms of the number of i-button combinations of an i-button lock. For example, can I express the number of combinations using 3 out of 5 buttons in terms of the number of combinations of 3 out of 3 buttons? Yes, I can. The latter is the number of rearrangements of three buttons once we've selected the three buttons. If we start with five buttons, there are $\binom{5}{3}$ possible sets of three buttons to choose. For each of those $\binom{5}{3}$ sets of three buttons, there arc $f(3)$ ways to arrange those three buttons in a combination.

$$g(n, i) = \binom{n}{i} \cdot f(i)$$

It may not be obvious why this is so. Suppose you list all the 3-button combinations of a 3-button lock. There are 13 of them, consisting of the numbers from 1 to 3 in various orders and with various groups connected by hyphens. Those 13 combinations are also some of the 3-button combinations of a 5-button lock, namely, the ones in which the particular three buttons we chose are 1, 2, and 3. If instead we choose a different set of three (out of five) buttons, that gives rise to a different set of 13 combinations. For example, if we choose the buttons 2, 3, and 4, we can take the original 13 combinations and change all the 1s to 2s, all the 2s to 3s, and all the 3s to 4s:

```
buttons:        1,2,3          2,3,4          1,4,5

                1 2 3          2 3 4          1 4 5
                1 3 2          2 4 3          1 5 4
                2 1 3          3 2 4          4 1 5
                2 3 1          3 4 2          4 5 1
                3 1 2          4 2 3          5 1 4
                3 2 1          4 3 2          5 4 1
                1 2-3          2 3-4          1 4-5
                2 1-3          3 2-4          4 1-5
                3 1-2          4 2-3          5 1-4
                1-2 3          2-3 4          1-4 5
                1-3 2          2-4 3          1-5 4
                2-3 1          3-4 2          4-5 1
                1-2-3          2-3-4          1-4-5
```

This table has a column for each of three possible combinations of five numbers three at a time. The table could be extended to have a column for *every* such combination of numbers, and then it would contain all the lock combinations using three out of five buttons. The total number of entries in the extended table is therefore $g(5, 3)$; the table has $f(3)$ rows and $\binom{5}{3}$ columns. So

$$g(5, 3) = \binom{5}{3} \cdot f(3)$$

which is a particular case of the general formula above.

We now have a formula for $f(n)$ in terms of all the $g(n, i)$ and a formula for $g(n, i)$ in terms of $f(i)$. Combining these we have

$$f(n) = \binom{n}{0} \cdot f(0) + \binom{n}{1} \cdot f(1) + \cdots + \binom{n}{n-1} \cdot f(n-1)$$

or

$$f(n) = \sum_{i=0}^{n-1} \binom{n}{i} \cdot f(i) \qquad \text{for } n > 0$$

Like any inductive definition, this one needs a special rule for the smallest case, from which all the others are computed:

$$f(0) = 1$$

The total number of combinations for an n-button lock is $2 \times f(n)$. I find this much more elegant than my original solution. (So why didn't I just show you this one to begin with? Because I never would have figured this one out had I not first done the enumeration of cases. I want you to see how a combinatorics problem is solved, not just what the beautiful solution looks like.) This formula can also be turned into a computer program:

```
to simplex :buttons
output 2 * f :buttons
end

to f :n
if equalp :n 0 [output 1]
output cascade :n [? + ((choose :n (#-1)) * f (#-1))] 0
end

to choose :n :r
output (perms :n :r)/(fact :r)
end
```

This program is faster as well as simpler than the other; on my home computer, `lock 5` takes about 4 seconds, `simplex 5` about 2 seconds.

The `simplex` function has no exact closed form equivalent, but it turns out that there is (amazingly!) a closed form definition that, when rounded to the nearest integer, gives the desired value:

```
to simp :n
output round (fact :n)/(power (ln 2) (:n+1))
end
```

The `ln` function, a Logo primitive, computes the "natural logarithm" of its input; `ln 2` has the approximate value 0.69314718056. The `power` function of two inputs takes the first input to the power of the second input. `Fact` is the factorial function as defined earlier in this chapter.

An Inductive Solution

Another related programming problem is to list the actual combinations, rather than merely count them. Probably the simplest way to do that is to use an approach similar to the one I used in the `combs` procedure that lists combinations of members of a list: First use recursion to find the lock combinations using only the `butfirst` of the available buttons, then find the ways in which the `first` button can be added to each of them.

Multinomial Coefficients

Earlier, in talking about Pascal's Triangle, I showed how binomial coefficients are related to combinations and asked you to think about *trinomial* coefficients. What, for example, is the coefficient of ab^2c in the expansion of $(a + b + c)^4$?

The expansion is a sum of products; each of those products contains four variables (*aaaa*, *aaab*, etc.). The ones that contribute to the ab^2c term are the ones with one *a*, two *b*s, and one *c*; these include *abbc*, *bcab*, *cabb*, and so on. Out of the four slots for variables in one of those products, how many ways can we choose a slot for one *a*? The answer is $\binom{4}{1}$. Having chosen one, we are left with three slots and we want to choose two of them for *b*s. There are $\binom{3}{2}$ ways to do that. Then we have one slot left, just enough for the one *c*, which makes a trivial contribution of $\binom{1}{1}$ to the overall number of possibilities. The total is $\binom{4}{1} \cdot \binom{3}{2} \cdot \binom{1}{1}$ or $4 \times 3 \times 1$ or 12, and that is the coefficient of ab^2c. Similarly, the coefficient of ac^3 is $\binom{4}{1} \cdot \binom{3}{3}$ or 4.

The same sort of argument can be used for even more complicated cases. In the expansion of $(a + b + c + d + e)^{14}$ what is the coefficient of $a^2b^3cd^5e^3$? It's

$$\binom{14}{2} \cdot \binom{12}{3} \cdot \binom{9}{1} \cdot \binom{8}{5} \cdot \binom{3}{3} = 91 \times 220 \times 9 \times 56 \times 1 = 10,090,080$$

Here is a harder question: How many terms are there in, say, $(a + b + c + d)^7$? It's easy to see that there are 4^7 products of four variables, but after the ones that are equal to each other have been combined into terms, how many distinct terms are there?

Like the Simplex lock problem, this one can probably be solved most easily by reducing the problem to a smaller subproblem—in other words, by an inductive definition. This problem also has something in common with the earlier problem of listing all the combinations of a given size from a given list, as we did in the `combs` procedure. Try to solve the problem before reading further. (It's hard to say how another person will find a problem, but I think this one is easier than the Simplex one.)

In order to be able to express the original problem in terms of a smaller version, we have to generalize it. I posed a specific problem, about the seventh power of the sum of four variables. I'd like to be able to give the answer to that problem the name $t(4, 7)$ and try to find a way to express that in terms of, let's say, $t(4, 6)$. So I'm going to define the function t as

$$t(n, k) = \text{number of terms in } (a_1 + a_2 + \cdots + a_n)^k$$

(If this were a "straight" math book I'd cheerfully recycle the name f for the function, even though we had a different f in the last section, but I'm anticipating wanting to write a Logo program for this problem and I can't have two procedures named f in the same workspace.)

In writing `combs` I used the trick of dividing all possible combinations into two groups: those including the first member of the list and those not including that member. A similar trick will be useful here; we can divide all the terms in an expansion into two groups. One group will contain those terms that include the first variable (a_1) and the other will contain the rest. For example, in the original problem, $a^2 b^3 d^2$ is a term in the first group, while c^7 is a term in the second group.

A term in the first group can be divided by a_1; the result must be a term in the expansion of $(a_1 + a_2 + \cdots + a_n)^{k-1}$. How many such terms are there? There are $t(n, k-1)$ of them. So that's how many terms there are in the first group.

A term in the second group is a product of k variables *not* including a_1. That means that such a term is also part of the expansion of $(a_2 + \cdots + a_n)^k$. How many such terms are there? There are $t(n-1, k)$ of them. Notice the difference between the two groups. In the first case, we associate a term with a similar term in the expansion of an expression involving a *smaller power* of the *same number* of variables. In the second case, we associate a term with an equal term in the expansion of an expression involving *fewer variables* taken to the *same power*.

Combining these two results, we see that

$$t(n, k) = t(n, k-1) + t(n-1, k)$$

Since this is a function of two variables, it needs two "stop rules," just like the function $\binom{n}{r}$. Picking these limiting cases seems much simpler than inventing the induction rule, but even so, it may repay some attention. For the rule

$$\binom{n}{r} = \binom{n-1}{r-1} + \binom{n-1}{r}$$

we ended up considering the limiting cases $r = 0$ and $r = n$. I didn't say anything about it at the time because I didn't want to get distracted, but it's not obvious why there is the asymmetry between the two variables in those limiting cases. That is, why didn't I pick

$r = 0$ and $n = 0$ as the limiting cases? That would be more like what you're accustomed to in recursive Logo procedures, where stop rules almost always involve a comparison of something with zero or with the empty list.

The funny limiting cases for $\binom{n}{r}$ (and the corresponding funny stop rules in **combs**) are related to the fact that this function is meaningful only when $n \geq r$. The two arguments can't be chosen independently. If we didn't have the $r = n$ limiting case, the inductive formula would have us compute

$$\binom{5}{5} = \binom{4}{4} + \binom{4}{5}$$

If we define $\binom{4}{5}$ as zero, this equation does turn out to be true, but it isn't a very sensible way to compute $\binom{5}{5}$.

In the case of the function t, the two arguments *are* independent. Both $t(4, 7)$ and $t(7, 4)$ are sensible things to ask for. Therefore, we should use the more obvious limiting cases $n = 0$ and $k = 0$. The trouble is that it's not obvious what the value of $t(0, k)$ or $t(n, 0)$ should be. The first of these, $t(0, k)$, represents the number of terms in the expansion of $()^k$—nothing to the kth power! That seems meaningless. On the other hand, $t(n, 0)$ represents the number of terms in $(\sum a_i)^0$, which is 1. Anything to the zeroth power is 1. Does "1" count as a term? It doesn't have any variables in it.

One solution would be to take as limiting cases $n = 1$ and $k = 1$. It's much easier to see what those values should be. $(a_1)^k$ has one term, so $t(1, k) = 1$. And $(a_1 + \cdots + a_n)^1$ has n terms, so $t(n, 1) = n$. We could, then, define the function t as

$$t(n, k) = \begin{cases} 1, & \text{if } n = 1; \\ n, & \text{if } k = 1; \\ t(n, k - 1) + t(n - 1, k), & \text{otherwise.} \end{cases}$$

But it is possible to figure out appropriate values for zero arguments by working backwards from the cases we already understand. For example, we know that $t(2, 1)$ must equal 2. But

$$t(2, 1) = t(2, 0) + t(1, 1) = t(2, 0) + 1$$

It follows that $t(2, 0)$ must be 1. So it's reasonable to guess that $t(n, 0) = 1$ will work in general. Similarly, we know that $t(1, 2) = 1$, but

$$t(1, 2) = t(1, 1) + t(0, 2) = 1 + t(0, 2)$$

Therefore $t(0, 2)$ must be 0. We can define t as

$$t(n, k) = \begin{cases} 0, & \text{if } n = 0; \\ 1, & \text{if } k = 0; \\ t(n, k-1) + t(n-1, k), & \text{otherwise.} \end{cases}$$

What is $t(0, 0)$? The definition above contradicts itself about this. The answer should be 0 because $n = 0$ but also 1 because $k = 0$. This reminds me of the similar problem about powers of integers. What is 0^0? In general $0^x = 0$ but $x^0 = 1$, for nonzero x. There is really no "right" answer, but mathematicians have adopted the convention that $0^0 = 1$. To make our definition of t truly correct I have to choose a convention for $t(0, 0)$ and modify the definition to reflect it:

$$t(n, k) = \begin{cases} 1, & \text{if } k = 0; \\ 0, & \text{if } n = 0 \text{ and } k > 0; \\ t(n, k-1) + t(n-1, k), & \text{otherwise.} \end{cases}$$

It's straightforward to translate this mathematical function definition into a Logo procedure:

```
to t :n :k
if equalp :k 0 [output 1]
if equalp :n 0 [output 0]
output (t :n :k-1)+(t :n-1 :k)
end
```

Using this function we can compute t 4 7 and find that the answer to the original problem is 120.

(Can you write a program to display the actual expansion? That is, it should print something like

```
(A+B+C+D)^7 =
   1 A^7 +
   7 A^6 B +
   21 A^5 B^2 +
   ...
```

There are two parts to this problem. One is to figure out the combinations of variables in the 120 terms, which can be done with a procedure like combs, and the other is to figure out the coefficients, which I discussed at the beginning of this section.)

I was introduced to this problem as a student teacher in a high school probability class. The teacher gave "how many terms are there in the expansion of $(a + b + c + d)^7$" as a quiz problem, and nobody answered it. In the ensuing class discussion, it turned out that she meant the students to answer the much easier question of how many products of seven variables there are. As I noted earlier, the answer to *that* question is just 4^7. But all the students interpreted the question as meaning the harder one we've been exploring here. I took the problem home that evening and reached the point we've reached in this chapter. I didn't think I could get a better answer than that until my housemate taught me about generating functions. It turns out that there *is* a closed form definition for this function:

$$t(n, k) = \binom{k + n - 1}{n - 1}$$

This definition is faster to compute as well as more beautiful.

Once armed with the formula, it wasn't hard to invent a way to demonstrate that it must be correct without going through the inductive definition and the use of calculus. The trick is that we must be choosing $n - 1$ somethings out of a possible $k + n - 1$ for each term. What does a term look like? Ignoring the constant coefficient, it is the product of k (seven, in the specific problem given) variables, some of which may be equal. Furthermore, when the terms are written in the usual way, the variables come in alphabetical order. A term like $a^2 b^4 d$ represents *aabbbbd*; there won't be a different term with the same letters in another order. In general, the k variables will be some number (zero or more) of a_1s, then some number of a_2s, and so on.

Now comes the trick. Suppose we write the string of variables with a "wall" for each change to the next letter. So instead of *aabbbbd* I want to write *aa | bbb | | d*. (There are two walls before the final d to reflect the fact that we skipped over c.) In this notation there are always exactly $n - 1$ walls. (That's why I chose to put the walls in; remember, we're looking for $n - 1$ of something.) The term includes k variables and $n - 1$ walls, for a total of $k + n - 1$ symbols.

Once the walls are there, it really is no longer necessary to preserve the individual variable letters. The sample term we've been using could just as well be written *xx | xxx | | x*. What comes before the first wall is the first variable letter, and so on. So *| | xxx | xxxx* represents $c^3 d^4$. But now we're finished. We have found a way to represent each possible term as a string of k copies of the letter x interspersed with $n - 1$ walls. How many such arrangements are there? How many ways are there to choose $n - 1$ positions for walls in a string of $k + n - 1$ symbols?

Earlier, in talking about the difference between closed form and inductive definitions, I suggested that the an inductive definition might be much easier to discover even if a closed form definition also exists. This is a clear example. If I'd given the demonstration just above, with *xs* and walls, without first showing you the more roundabout way I really discovered the definition, you'd rightly complain about rabbits out of hats.

Program Listing

```
;;; Logic problem inference system

;; Establish categories

to category :category.name :members
print (list "category :category.name :members)
if not namep "categories [make "categories []]
make "categories lput :category.name :categories
make :category.name :members
foreach :members [pprop ? "category :category.name]
end


;; Verify and falsify matches

to verify :a :b
settruth :a :b "true
end


to falsify :a :b
settruth :a :b "false
end


to settruth :a :b :truth.value
if equalp (gprop :a "category) (gprop :b "category) [stop]
localmake "oldvalue get :a :b
if equalp :oldvalue :truth.value [stop]
if equalp :oldvalue (not :truth.value) ~
   [(throw "error (sentence [inconsistency in settruth]
                            :a :b :truth.value))]
print (list :a :b "-> :truth.value)
store :a :b :truth.value
settruth1 :a :b :truth.value
settruth1 :b :a :truth.value
if not emptyp :oldvalue ~
   [foreach (filter [equalp first ? :truth.value] :oldvalue)
            [apply "settruth butfirst ?]]
end
```

```
to settruth1 :a :b :truth.value
apply (word "find not :truth.value) (list :a :b)
foreach (gprop :a "true) [settruth ? :b :truth.value]
if :truth.value [foreach (gprop :a "false) [falsify ? :b]
                 pprop :a (gprop :b "category) :b]
pprop :a :truth.value (fput :b gprop :a :truth.value)
end


to findfalse :a :b
foreach (filter [not equalp get ? :b "true] peers :a) ~
        [falsify ? :b]
end


to findtrue :a :b
if equalp (count peers :a) (1+falses :a :b) ~
   [verify (find [not equalp get ? :b "false] peers :a)
           :b]
end


to falses :a :b
output count filter [equalp "false get ? :b] peers :a
end


to peers :a
output thing gprop :a "category
end


;; Common types of clues

to differ :list
print (list "differ :list)
foreach :list [differ1 ? ?rest]
end


to differ1 :a :them
foreach :them [falsify :a ?]
end


to justbefore :this :that :lineup
falsify :this :that
falsify :this last :lineup
falsify :that first :lineup
justbefore1 :this :that :lineup
end
```

Chapter 2   Discrete Mathematics

```
to justbefore1 :this :that :slotlist
if emptyp butfirst :slotlist [stop]
equiv :this (first :slotlist) :that (first butfirst :slotlist)
justbefore1 :this :that (butfirst :slotlist)
end


;; Remember conditional linkages

to implies :who1 :what1 :truth1 :who2 :what2 :truth2
implies1 :who1 :what1 :truth1 :who2 :what2 :truth2
implies1 :who2 :what2 (not :truth2) :who1 :what1 (not :truth1)
end

to implies1 :who1 :what1 :truth1 :who2 :what2 :truth2
localmake "old1 get :who1 :what1
if equalp :old1 :truth1 [settruth :who2 :what2 :truth2  stop]
if equalp :old1 (not :truth1) [stop]
if memberp (list :truth1 :who2 :what2 (not :truth2)) :old1 ~
   [settruth :who1 :what1 (not :truth1)  stop]
if memberp (list :truth1 :what2 :who2 (not :truth2)) :old1 ~
   [settruth :who1 :what1 (not :truth1)  stop]
store :who1 :what1 ~
      fput (list :truth1 :who2 :what2 :truth2) :old1
end


to equiv :who1 :what1 :who2 :what2
implies :who1 :what1 "true :who2 :what2 "true
implies :who2 :what2 "true :who1 :what1 "true
end


to xor :who1 :what1 :who2 :what2
implies :who1 :what1 "true :who2 :what2 "false
implies :who1 :what1 "false :who2 :what2 "true
end

;; Interface to property list mechanism

to get :a :b
output gprop :a :b
end

to store :a :b :val
pprop :a :b :val
pprop :b :a :val
end
```

```
;; Print the solution

to solution
foreach thing first :categories [solve1 ? butfirst :categories]
end

to solve1 :who :order
type :who
foreach :order [type "|  |    type gprop :who ?]
print []
end

;; Get rid of old problem data

to cleanup
if not namep "categories [stop]
ern :categories
ern "categories
erpls
end

;; Anita Harnadek's problem

to cub.reporter
cleanup
category "first [Jane Larry Opal Perry]
category "last [Irving King Mendle Nathan]
category "age [32 38 45 55]
category "job [drafter pilot sergeant driver]
differ [Jane King Larry Nathan]
says "Jane "Irving 45
says "King "Perry "driver
says "Larry "sergeant 45
says "Nathan "drafter 38
differ [Mendle Jane Opal Nathan]
says "Mendle "pilot "Larry
says "Jane "pilot 45
says "Opal 55 "driver
says "Nathan 38 "driver
print []
solution
end
```

```
to says :who :what1 :what2
print (list "says :who :what1 :what2)
xor :who :what1 :who :what2
end

;; Diane Baldwin's problem

to foote.family
cleanup
category "when [1st 2nd 3rd 4th 5th]
category "name [Felix Fred Frank Francine Flo]
category "street [Field Flag Fig Fork Frond]
category "item [food film flashlight fan fiddle]
category "position [1 2 3 4 5]
print [Clue 1]
justbefore "Flag "2nd :position
justbefore "2nd "Fred :position
print [Clue 2]
male [film Fig 5th]
print [Clue 3]
justbefore "flashlight "Fork :position
justbefore "Fork "1st :position
female [1st]
print [Clue 4]
falsify "5th "Frond
falsify "5th "fan
print [Clue 5]
justbefore "Francine "Frank :position
justbefore "Francine "Frank :when
print [Clue 6]
female [3rd Flag]
print [Clue 7]
justbefore "fiddle "Frond :when
justbefore "Flo "fiddle :when
print []
solution
end

to male :stuff
differ sentence :stuff [Francine Flo]
end

to female :stuff
differ sentence :stuff [Felix Fred Frank]
end
```

```
;;; Combinatorics toolkit

to combs :list :howmany
if equalp :howmany 0 [output [[]]]
if equalp :howmany count :list [output (list :list)]
output sentence (map [fput first :list ?]
                     combs (butfirst :list) (:howmany-1)) ~
     (combs (butfirst :list) :howmany)
end


to fact :n
output cascade :n [# * ?] 1
end


to perms :n :r
if equalp :r 0 [output 1]
output :n * perms :n-1 :r-1
end


to choose :n :r
output (perms :n :r)/(fact :r)
end


;; The socks problem

to socks :list
localmake "total combs (expand :list) 2
localmake "matching filter [equalp first ? last ?] :total
print (sentence [there are] count :total [possible pairs of socks.])
print (sentence [of these,] count :matching [are matching pairs.])
print sentence [probability of match =] ~
     word (100 * (count :matching)/(count :total)) "%
end


to expand :list
if emptyp :list [output []]
if numberp first :list ~
   [output cascade (first :list)
                   [fput first butfirst :list ?]
                   (expand butfirst butfirst :list)]
output fput first :list expand butfirst :list
end
```

```
to socktest
localmake "first pick [brown brown brown brown brown brown
                       blue blue blue blue]
localmake "second ~
          pick (ifelse equalp :first "brown ~
                              [[brown brown brown brown brown
                                blue blue blue blue]] ~
                              [[brown brown brown brown brown brown
                                blue blue blue]])
output equalp :first :second
end


;; The Simplex lock problem

to lock :buttons
output cascade :buttons [? + lock1 :buttons #] 1
end

to lock1 :total :buttons
localmake "perms perms :total :buttons
output cascade (twoto (:buttons-1)) [? + lock2 :perms #-1 1] 0
end

to lock2 :perms :links :factor
if equalp :links 0 [output :perms/(fact :factor)]
if equalp (remainder :links 2) 0 ~
   [output lock2 :perms/(fact :factor) :links/2 1]
output lock2 :perms (:links-1)/2 :factor+1
end

to twoto :power
output cascade :power [2 * ?] 1
end

to simplex :buttons
output 2 * f :buttons
end

to f :n
if equalp :n 0 [output 1]
output cascade :n [? + ((choose :n (#-1)) * f (#-1))] 0
end
```

```
to simp :n
output round (fact :n)/(power (ln 2) (:n+1))
end

;; The multinomial expansion problem

to t :n :k
if equalp :k 0 [output 1]
if equalp :n 0 [output 0]
output (t :n :k-1)+(t :n-1 :k)
end
```

3   Algorithms and Data Structures

Program file for this chapter: `algs`

What's wrong with this procedure?

```
to process.sentence :sent
output fput (process.word first :sent) (process.sentence bf :sent)
end
```

If you said "It's a recursive procedure without a stop rule," you've solved a simple problem in *analysis of algorithms.* This branch of computer science is concerned with the *correctness* and the *efficiency* of programs.

The field is called analysis of *algorithms* rather than analysis of *programs* because the emphasis is on the meaning of a program (how you might express the program in English) and not on the details of its expression in a particular language. For example, the error in the procedure

```
to process.sentence :sent
if emptyp :sent [output []]
output fput (process.word first :sent) (process.snetence bf :sent)
end
```

is just as fatal as the error in the first example, but there isn't much of theoretical interest to say about a misspelled procedure name. On the other hand, another branch of computer science, *program verification,* is concerned with developing techniques to ensure that a computer program really does correctly express the algorithm it is meant to express.

The examples I've given so far are atypical, it's worth noting, in that you were able to see the errors in the procedures without having any real idea of what they do! Without seeing `process.word` you can tell that this program is doing something or other to each word of a sentence, but you don't know whether the words are being translated to another language, converted from upper case to lower case letters, translated into a string of phoneme codes to be sent to a speech synthesizer, or what. (Even what I just said about doing something to the words of a sentence is an inference based on the names of procedures and variables, which might not really reflect the results of the program.) More interesting problems in analysis of algorithms have to do with the specific properties of particular algorithms.

In this chapter I discuss algorithms along with *data structures,* the different ways in which information can be represented in a computer program, because these two aspects of a program interact strongly. That is, the choices you make as a programmer about data representation have a profound effect on the algorithms you can use to solve your problem. Similarly, once you have chosen an algorithm, that choice determines the particular kinds of information your program will need to do its work. Algorithms and data structures are the central concerns of software engineering, the overall name for the study of how to turn a problem statement into a working program in a way that uses both the computer and the programming staff effectively.

Local Optimization vs. Efficient Algorithms

When you're trying to make a computer program run as fast as possible, the most obvious place to start is with the details of the instructions in the program. But that's generally *not* the most effective approach. Rethinking the big picture can give much more dramatic improvements. To show you what I mean, I'll give some examples of both. Later I'll talk about *order of growth,* a more formal way to understand this same idea.

Consider the following procedure that implements the *quadratic formula*

$$x = \frac{-b \pm \sqrt{b^2 - 4ac}}{2a}$$

This formula gives the two values of x that solve the equation

$$ax^2 + bx + c = 0$$

```
to quadratic :a :b :c
localmake "x1 (-:b + sqrt (:b*:b - 4*:a*:c))/2*:a
localmake "x2 (-:b - sqrt (:b*:b - 4*:a*:c))/2*:a
print (sentence [The solutions are] :x1 "and :x2)
end
```

Before we talk about the efficiency of this program, is it correct? This is not a simple yes-or-no question. The procedure gives the correct results for those quadratic equations that have two real solutions. For example, the equation $2x^2 + 5x - 3 = 0$ has the solutions $x = -3$ and $x = \frac{1}{2}$; the instruction `quadratic 2 5 -3` will print those solutions. Some quadratic equations, like $x^2 - 8x + 16 = 0$, have only one solution; for these equations, `quadratic` prints the same solution twice, which is not exactly incorrect but still a little embarrassing. Other equations, like $x^2 + 1 = 0$, have solutions that are complex numbers. Depending on our purposes, we might want `quadratic` to print the solutions i and $-i$ for this equation, or we might want it to print "This equation has no real solutions." But since most versions of Logo do not provide complex arithmetic, what will really happen is that we'll get the error message

```
sqrt doesn't like -1 as input.
```

If `quadratic` is used as part of a larger project, getting the Logo error message means that the program dies altogether in this case without a chance to recover. If we have several equations to solve, it would be better if the program could continue to the remaining equations even if no solution is found for one of them. A program that operates correctly for the kinds of inputs that the programmer had in mind, but blows up when given unanticipated inputs, is said not to be *robust;* a robust program should do something appropriate even if there are errors in its input data.

But my real reason for displaying this example is to discuss its efficiency. It computes the expression

```
sqrt (:b*:b - 4*:a*:c)
```

twice. Multiplication is slower than addition on most computers; this expression involves three multiplications as well as the even slower square root extraction. The program would be faster if it were written this way:

```
to quadratic :a :b :c
localmake "sqrt sqrt (:b*:b - 4*:a*:c)
localmake "x1 (-:b + :sqrt)/2*:a
localmake "x2 (-:b - :sqrt)/2*:a
print (sentence [The solutions are] :x1 "and :x2)
end
```

This kind of change to a program is called *common subexpression elimination*. It's a pretty easy way to speed up a program; so easy, in fact, that some "optimizing compilers" for large computers do it automatically. In other words, an optimizing compiler for Logo would treat the first version of `quadratic` as if it were written like the second version. (As far as I know, nobody has actually written such a compiler for Logo.)

Common subexpression elimination is an example of *local* optimization. This means that we improved the program by paying attention to one small piece of it at a time. (A less elegant name for local optimization is "code bumming.") Is it worth the effort? It depends how many times this procedure will be run. When I say that multiplication is slow, I mean that it takes a few millionths of a second. If you are writing a `quadratic` procedure to do the dozen problems in your high school algebra homework, the extra time you spend thinking up the second version and typing it into the editor probably outweighs the saving of time in running the procedure. But if you are trying to predict the weather and need to solve tens of thousands of equations, the saving may be significant.

If you want to write locally optimized Logo programs, it's important to know that `first`, `butfirst`, and `fput` take a constant amount of time regardless of the length of the input list, whereas `last`, `butlast`, and `lput` take an amount of time proportional to the length of the list. If you add n items to a list, one by one, using `fput`, the length of time required is n times the constant amount of time for each item. But if you add the same n items using `lput`, if the first item takes t microseconds, the last takes nt. On the average, each `lput` takes something like $nt/2$ microseconds, so the total time is $n^2t/2$. The gain in efficiency from using `fput` instead of `lput` isn't significant if your list has only a few items, but the gain gets more and more significant as the size of the list increases. Suppose you want to create a list of the numbers from 1 to 1000. One straightforward way would be

```
print cascade 1000 [lput # ?] []
```

On my home computer this instruction takes about 26 seconds.* If you just use `fput` in place of `lput` the list will come out in the wrong order, but it's possible to reverse the order of that list to get the same result as the first version:

```
print reverse cascade 1000 [fput # ?] []
```

You might think this would be slower, because it has the extra `reverse` step. But in fact this instruction took about 12 seconds. (It's important that the `reverse` tool in the Berkeley Logo library uses `first` and `fput` to do its work. If we used the more obvious

```
to reverse :list
if emptyp :list [output []]
output lput first :list reverse bf :list
end
```

---

* The actual time depends not only on what model of computer you have but also on how much memory and what else is in it.

then the elimination of `lput` in the `cascade` template would be offset by the `lput` in the reversal.)

At the other extreme, the broadest possible *global* optimization of a program is to think of an entirely new algorithm based on a different way of thinking about the original problem. As an example, in Chapter 2 there are three different programs to solve the Simplex lock problem. The first program, `lock`, works by enumerating explicitly all the different patterns of possible combinations. That algorithm is not fundamentally recursive; although my Logo implementation includes recursive subprocedures, the number of combinations for a five-button lock is not determined on the basis of the number for a four-button lock. (The program does compute the number of combinations that use four out of the five available buttons, but that isn't the same thing.) The second program, `simplex`, is based on a mathematical argument relating the number of combinations to a fairly simple *recursive function*—that is, a mathematical function with an inductive definition. Because the function is computationally simple, the intellectual energy I invested in doing the mathematics paid off with a significantly faster program. The third version, `simp`, uses a closed form formula that solves the problem in no time!

To illustrate more sharply the differences among these three programs, I tried each of them on a ten-button version of the Simplex lock. To compute `lock 10` took 260 seconds on my computer; `simplex 10` took 80 seconds; and `simp 10` took less than half a second. For this size lock, understanding the mathematical idea of a recursive function sped up the program by a factor of three, and using the mathematical technique called generating functions achieved an additional speedup by a factor of almost 200! What's important to understand about this example is that it wasn't better *programming* skill that made the difference, but greater knowledge of *mathematics*. (In the next section, though, you'll learn a programming trick that can sometimes achieve similar speedups.)

Many "trick" math problems involve a similar shift in thinking about the fundamental algorithm to be used. For example, in Chapter 2 we computed the probability of picking a matching pair of socks out of a drawer containing six brown and four blue socks this way:

$$\frac{\text{pairs of 2 browns} + \text{pairs of 2 blues}}{\text{total pairs}} = \frac{\binom{6}{2} + \binom{4}{2}}{\binom{10}{2}} = \frac{21}{45}$$

Suppose we ask this question: Out of the same drawer of six browns and two blues, we pick *three* socks at random; what is the probability that at least two of the socks match?

The number of triples of socks in which at least two are brown is the number in which all three are brown, $\binom{6}{3}$, plus the number in which two are brown and one is blue, $\binom{6}{2} \cdot \binom{4}{1}$. The number in which at least two are blue is, similarly, $\binom{4}{3} + \binom{4}{2} \cdot \binom{6}{1}$. The total number of triples is of course $\binom{10}{3}$. So the probability of a matching pair within the chosen triple is

$$\frac{\binom{6}{3} + \binom{6}{2} \cdot \binom{4}{1} + \binom{4}{3} + \binom{4}{2} \cdot \binom{6}{1}}{\binom{10}{3}} = \frac{20 + 15 \cdot 4 + 4 + 6 \cdot 6}{120} = \frac{120}{120} = 1$$

which is 100% probability. We could modify the socks procedure to get the same result by listing all the possible triples and then filtering all the ones containing a matching pair, using a filter like

```
to haspair :triple
output or (memberp first :triple butfirst :triple) ~
         (equalp (item 2 :triple) last :triple)
end
```

But the problem becomes entirely trivial if you notice that there are only two possible colors, so obviously there is no way that three randomly chosen socks can have three distinct colors! Of course there has to be a matching pair within any possible triple. A problem like this, that invites a messy arithmetic solution but is obvious if properly understood, is the mathematician's idea of a joke. (Did you get it?)

Memoization

Some efficiency tricks are applicable to a number of different problems and become part of the "toolkit" of any professional programmer. One example is relevant to many inductively defined functions; the trick is to have the program remember the result of each invocation of the function. For example, in Chapter 2 we defined the number of terms in a multinomial expansion to be

```
to t :n :k
if equalp :k 0 [output 1]
if equalp :n 0 [output 0]
output (t :n :k-1)+(t :n-1 :k)
end
```

What happens when we compute `t 4 7`?

$$t(4,7)\begin{cases}t(4,6)\begin{cases}t(4,5)\begin{cases}t(4,4)\ \dots\\[4pt]\underline{t(3,5)}\begin{cases}t(3,4)\ \dots\\t(2,5)\ \dots\end{cases}\end{cases}\\[14pt]t(3,6)\begin{cases}\underline{t(3,5)}\begin{cases}t(3,4)\ \dots\\t(2,5)\ \dots\end{cases}\\[4pt]t(2,6)\ \dots\end{cases}\end{cases}\\[40pt]t(3,7)\begin{cases}t(3,6)\begin{cases}\underline{t(3,5)}\begin{cases}t(3,4)\ \dots\\t(2,5)\ \dots\end{cases}\\[4pt]t(2,6)\ \dots\end{cases}\\[14pt]t(2,7)\begin{cases}t(2,6)\ \dots\\t(1,7)\ \dots\end{cases}\end{cases}\end{cases}$$

Many calculations are performed repeatedly. In the chart above I've underlined three places where $t(3,5)$ is computed. Each of those in turn involves repeated computation of $t(3,4)$ and so on. This computation took me about 18 seconds.

Here is a version of `t` that uses property lists to remember all the values it's already computed. This version will calculate $t(3,5)$ only the first time it's needed; a second request for $t(3,5)$ will instantly output the remembered value.

```
to t :n :k
localmake "result gprop :n :k
if not emptyp :result [output :result]
make "result realt :n :k
pprop :n :k :result
output :result
end

to realt :n :k
if equalp :k 0 [output 1]
if equalp :n 0 [output 0]
output (t :n :k-1)+(t :n-1 :k)
end
```

Computing `t 4 7` isn't really a big enough problem to show off how much faster this version is; even the original program takes only $2\frac{1}{2}$ seconds on my home computer. But the amount of time needed grows quickly as you try larger inputs. Using the original procedure from Chapter 2, my computer took just under five *minutes* to compute `t 8 10`; the program shown here took less than two *seconds*. This program computed `t 12 12` in about three seconds; I estimate that the original procedure would take five *hours* to solve that problem! (As you can imagine, I didn't try it.)

The memoized version of t has the same structure as the original. That is, in order to compute t 4 7, the program must first carry out the two subtasks t 4 6 and t 3 7. The only difference between the original version and the memoized version is that in the latter, whenever a second invocation is made with inputs that have already been seen, the result is output immediately without repeating that subtask. Any recursive function can be memoized in the same way.*

Sometimes, though, the same general idea—remembering the results of past computations—can be used more effectively by changing the program structure so that just the right subproblems are solved as they're needed to work toward the overall solution. Rearranging the program structure isn't called memoization, but we're still using the same idea. For example, the Simplex lock function

$$ f(n) = \sum_{i=0}^{n-1} \binom{n}{i} \cdot f(i) $$

from Chapter 2 is a combination (sorry about the pun) of values of two functions. It isn't exactly helpful to remember every possible value of $\binom{n}{i}$ because each value is used only once. But the calculation of $f(n)$ uses the entire nth row of Pascal's Triangle, and it's easy to compute that if we remember the row above it. The values of $f(i)$ are used repeatedly, so it makes sense to keep a list of them. So my plan is to have two lists, the first of which is a list of values of $f(i)$ and the second a row of Pascal's Triangle:

```
round                    ?1                    ?2

  0                        [1]               [1 1]
  1                      [1 1]             [1 2 1]
  2                    [3 1 1]           [1 3 3 1]
  3                 [13 3 1 1]         [1 4 6 4 1]
  4              [75 13 3 1 1]      [1 5 10 10 5 1]
  5          [541 75 13 3 1 1]   [1 6 15 20 15 6 1]
```

---

* I've used property lists of numbers to hold the remembered values of the t function. If I wanted to use the same technique for some other function in the same workspace, I'd have to find a way to keep the values for the two functions from getting in each other's way. For example, if $t(4, 7) = 120$ and some other function $h(4, 7) = 83$, then I might store the value

[t 120 h 83]

on the appropriate property list.

The solution to the problem is twice the first member of the last value of ?1.

Instead of starting with a request for $f(5)$ and carrying out subtasks as needed, the new program will begin with $f(0)$ and will work its way up to larger input values until the desired result is found. This technique is called *dynamic programming:*

```
to simplex :buttons
output 2 * first (cascade :buttons
                          [fput (sumprods bf ?2 ?1) ?1] [1]
                          [fput 1 nextrow ?2] [1 1])
end

to sumprods :a :b
output reduce "sum (map "product :a :b)
end

to nextrow :combs
if emptyp butfirst :combs [output :combs]
output fput (sum first :combs first butfirst :combs) ~
            nextrow butfirst :combs
end
```

I tried both versions of simplex for a 12-button lock. The version in Chapter 2 took about $5\frac{1}{2}$ minutes to get the answer (which is that there are about 56 billion combinations); this version took about one second, comparable to the closed form simp procedure.

If you just read this program with no prior idea of what algorithm it's using, it must be hard to see how it reflects the original problem. But if you think of it as a quasi-memoization of the earlier version it should make sense to you.

Sorting Algorithms

Every textbook on algorithms uses sorting as one of its main examples. There are several reasons for this. First of all, sorting is one of the most useful things to do with a computer, in a wide variety of settings. There are many different known sorting algorithms, ranging from obvious to subtle. These algorithms have been analyzed with great care, so a lot is known about their behavior. (What does that mean? It means we can answer questions like "How long does this algorithm take, on the average?" "How long does it take, at worst?" "If the things we're sorting are mostly in order to begin with, does that make it faster?") And all this effort pays off, in that the cleverest algorithms really are much faster than the more obvious ones.

The problem we want to solve is to take a list in unknown order and rearrange it to get a new list of the same members in some standard order. This might be alphabetical order if the members of the list are words, or size order if they're numbers, or something else. For the most part, the exact ordering relation isn't very important. As long as we have a way to compare two items and find out which comes first (or that they're equal, sometimes) it doesn't matter what the details of the comparison are. To make things simple, in this chapter I'll assume we're always sorting numbers.

Because the length of time per comparison depends on the nature of the things being compared, and because that length isn't really part of what distinguishes one sorting algorithm from another, analyses of the time taken by a sorting program are usually expressed not in terms of seconds but in terms of number of comparisons. This measure also eliminates the effect of one computer being faster than another. To help make such measurements, we'll compare two numbers using this procedure:

```
to lessthanp :a :b
if not namep "comparisons [make "comparisons 0]
make "comparisons :comparisons+1
output :a < :b
end
```

Of course, if we want to use > or = comparisons in a sorting algorithm, we should write analogous procedures for those. But in fact I'll only need lessthanp for the algorithms I'm going to show you. After trying out a sort program, we can find out how many comparisons it made using this convenient little tool:

```
to howmany
print :comparisons
ern "comparisons
end
```

After telling us the number of comparisons, this procedure erases the counter variable to prepare for the next experiment.

If you haven't studied sort algorithms before, it will be a good exercise for you to invent one yourself before you continue. Your procedure sort should take a list of numbers as input, and should output a list of the same numbers in order from smallest to largest.

```
? show sort [5 20 3 5 18 9]
[3 5 5 9 18 20]
```

Notice that it's allowable for two (or more) equal numbers to appear in the input.

So that we can compare different algorithms fairly, we should try them on the same input data. You can make a list of 100 random numbers this way:

```
make "list cascade 100 [fput random 100 ?] []
```

You should try out both your sort procedures and mine on your random list. In case you want to try your algorithm on my data, to compare the exact numbers of comparisons needed, here is the list I used:

```
[11 41 50 66 41 61 73 38  2 94 43 55 24  1 77 77 13  2 93 35
 43 69  9 46 88 20 43 73 11 74 69 33 28  4  5  1 15 17 13 94
 88 42 12 31 67 42 30 30 13 91 31  8 55  6 31 84 57 50 50 31
 36 52  5 12 10 19 69  0  9 81 62 14 39 54 45 72 18 47 48 35
 76 44 77 34 75 52 61 86 34 44 64 53 25 39  4 55 55 54 53 64]
```

Notice in passing that this is a list of 100 random numbers, but not a list of the first 100 numbers in random order. Some numbers, like 43, appear more than once in the list, while others don't appear at all. This is perfectly realistic for numbers that occur in real life, although of course some situations give rise to lists of *unique* items.

Sorting by Selection

Although there are many known sorting algorithms, most fall into two main groups. There are the ones that order the input items one at a time and there are the ones that divide the problem into roughly equal-sized smaller problems. I'll show you one of each. Within a group, the differences between algorithms have to do with details of exactly how the problem is divided into pieces, what's where in computer memory, and so on. But these details are generally much less important than the basic division between the two categories. If you took my advice and wrote your own sort procedure, and if you hadn't studied sorting before, the one you wrote is almost certainly in the first category.

My sample algorithm in the first group is a *selection* sort. Expressed in words, the algorithm is this: First find the smallest number, then find the next smallest, and so on. This idea can be put in recursive form; the output from the procedure should be a list whose first member is the smallest number and whose remaining elements are the sorted version of the other numbers. I'll show you two versions of this algorithm: first a straightforward but inefficient one, and then a version that's improved in speed but not quite so obvious. Here's the first version:

```
to ssort :list
if emptyp :list [output []]
localmake "smallest reduce "min :list
output fput :smallest (ssort remove.once :smallest :list)
end

to remove.once :item :list
if equalp :item first :list [output butfirst :list]
output fput first :list (remove.once :item butfirst :list)
end
```

In this version of **ssort**, we start by finding the smallest number in the list. Then we remove that number from the list, sort what's left, and put the smallest number back at the front of the sorted list. The only slight complication is that I had to write my own variant of **remove** that, unlike the standard Berkeley Logo library version, removes only one copy of the chosen number from the list, just in case the same number appears more than once.

By using **min** to find the smallest number, I've interfered with my goal of counting the number of comparisons, but I didn't worry about that because I'm about to rewrite **ssort** anyway. The problem is that this version goes through the list of numbers twice for each invocation, first to find the smallest number and then again to remove that number from the list that will be used as input to the recursive call. The program will be much faster if it does the finding and the removing all at once. The resulting procedure is a little harder to read, but it should help if you remember that it's trying to do the same job as the original version.

```
to ssort :list
if emptyp :list [output []]
output ssort1 (first :list) (butfirst :list) []
end

to ssort1 :min :in :out
if emptyp :in [output fput :min ssort :out]
if lessthanp :min (first :in) ~
   [output ssort1 :min (butfirst :in) (fput first :in :out)]
output ssort1 (first :in) (butfirst :in) (fput :min :out)
end
```

Ssort is invoked once for each time a smallest number must be found. For each of those iterations, **ssort1** is invoked once for each member of the still-unsorted list; the numbers in the list are moved from **:in** to **:out** except that the smallest-so-far is singled out in **:min**.

Chapter 3   Algorithms and Data Structures

Suppose we try out `ssort` on our list of 100 numbers. How many comparisons will be needed? To find the smallest of 100 numbers we have to make 99 comparisons; the smallest-so-far must be compared against each of the remaining ones. To find the next smallest requires 98 comparisons, and so on. Finally we have two numbers remaining to be sorted and it takes one comparison to get them in order. The total number of comparisons is

$$99 + 98 + 97 + \cdots + 2 + 1 = 4950$$

It makes no difference what order the numbers were in to begin with, or whether some of them are equal, or anything else about the input data. It takes 4950 comparisons for `ssort` to sort 100 numbers, period. You can try out the program on various lists of 100 numbers to make sure I'm right.

In general, if we want to sort a list of length n with `ssort` the number of comparisons required is the sum of the integers from 1 to $n-1$. It turns out that there is a closed form definition for this sum:

$$\frac{n(n-1)}{2}$$

Selection sort uses these three steps:

- Pull out the smallest value.
- Sort the other values.
- Put the smallest one at the front.

It's the first of those steps that does the comparisons. A similar but different algorithm is *insertion sort,* which defers the comparisons until the last step:

- Pull out any old value (such as the `first`).
- Sort the other values.
- Put the chosen one where it belongs, in order.

Try writing a procedure `isort` to implement this algorithm. How many comparisons does it require? You'll find that for this algorithm the answer depends on the input data. What is the smallest possible number of comparisons? The largest number? What kinds of input data give rise to these extreme values?

Sorting by Partition

There is one fundamental insight behind all methods for sorting with fewer comparisons: Two small sorting jobs are faster than one large one. Specifically, suppose we have 100 numbers to sort. Using `ssort` requires 4950 comparisons. Instead, suppose we split up the 100 numbers into two groups of 50. If we use `ssort` on each group, each will require 1225 comparisons; the two groups together require twice that, or 2450 comparisons. That's about half as many comparisons as the straight `ssort` of 100 numbers.

But this calculation underestimates how much time we can save using this insight, because the same reasoning applies to each of those groups of 50. We can split each into two groups of 25. Then how many comparisons will be required altogether?

The basic idea we'll use is to pick some number that we think is likely to be a median value for the entire list; that is, we'd like half the numbers to be less than this partition value and half to be greater. There are many possible ways to choose this partition value; I'm going to take the average of the first and last numbers of the (not yet sorted!) input. Then we run through the input list, dividing it into two smaller pieces by comparing each number against the partition value. (Notice that `ssort` compares pairs of numbers within the input list; the partition sort compares one number from the list against another number that might or might not itself be in the list.) We use the same technique recursively to sort each of the two sublists, then append the results.

Note the similarities and differences between this selection sort algorithm:

- Pull out the smallest value.
- Sort the other values.
- Put the smallest one at the front.

and the following *partition sort* algorithm:

- Divide the input into the small-value half and the large-value half.
- Sort each half separately.
- Put the sorted small values in front of the sorted large ones.

Again, I'll write this program more than once, first in an overly simple version and then more realistically. Here's the simple one:

```
to psort :list
if (count :list) < 2 [output :list]
localmake "split guess.middle.value :list
output sentence psort filter [? < :split] :list
                psort filter [not (? < :split)] :list
end

to guess.middle.value :list
output ((first :list) + (last :list)) / 2
end
```

To minimize the number of comparisons, we want to split the input list into two equal-size halves. It's important to note that this program is only guessing about which value of :split would achieve that balanced splitting. You may wonder why I didn't take the average of all the numbers in the list. There are two reasons. One is that that would add a lot of time to the sorting process; we'd have to look at every number to find the average, then look at every number again to do the actual splitting. But a more interesting reason is that the average isn't quite what we want anyway. Suppose we are asked to sort this list of numbers:

```
[3 2 1000 5 1 4]
```

The average of these numbers is about 169. But if we use that value as the split point, we'll divide the list into these two pieces:

```
[3 2 5 1 4]   and   [1000]
```

Not a very even division! To divide this list of six values into two equal pieces, we'd need a split point of $3\frac{1}{2}$. In general, what we want is the *median* value rather than the *average* value. And if you think about it, you pretty much have to have the numbers already sorted in order to find the median.* So we just try to make a good guess that doesn't take long to compute.

Just as in the case of selection sort, one problem with this simple program is that it goes through the input list twice, once for each of the calls to `filter`. And the call to `count` in the end test adds a third walk through the entire list. Here's a version that fixes those inefficiencies:

```
to psort :list
if emptyp :list [output []]
if emptyp butfirst :list [output :list]
localmake "split ((first :list) + (last :list)) / 2
output psort1 :split :list [] []
end
```

---

* That isn't quite true; there is a clever algorithm that can find the median after only a partial sorting of the values. But it's true enough that we can't use a sorting algorithm whose first step requires that we've already done some sorting.

```
to psort1 :split :in :low :high
if emptyp :in [output sentence (psort :low) (psort :high)]
if lessthanp first :in :split ~
   [output psort1 :split (butfirst :in) (fput first :in :low) :high]
output psort1 :split (butfirst :in) :low (fput first :in :high)
end
```

This version of psort has one good attribute and one bad attribute. The good attribute is that it's very cleanly organized. You can see that it's the job of psort to choose the partition value and the job of psort1 to divide the list in two parts based on comparisons with that value. The bad attribute is that it doesn't *quite* work as it stands.

As for any recursive procedure, it's important that the input get smaller for each recursive invocation. If not, psort could end up invoking itself over and over with the same input. It's very easy to see that ssort avoids that danger, because the input list is shorter by exactly one member for each recursive invocation. But psort divides its input into two pieces, each of which ought to be about half the length of the original if we're lucky. We're lucky if the partition value we choose is, in fact, the median value of the input list. If we're less lucky, the two parts might be imbalanced, say 1/4 of the members below the partition and 3/4 of them above it. Can we be *so* unlucky that *all* of the input numbers are on the same side of the partition? See if you can think of a case in which this will happen.

The partition value is chosen as the average of two members of the input list. If those two members (the first and last) are unequal, then one of them must be less than the partition value and the other greater. So there will be at least one number on each side of the partition. But if the two averaged numbers are equal, then the partition value will be equal to both of them. Each of them will be put in the high bucket. If all the other numbers in the list are also greater than or equal to the partition, then they'll all end up in the high bucket, and nothing will be accomplished in the recursion step. The simplest failing example is trying to sort a list of numbers all of which are equal, like

? show psort [4 4 4 4 4]

We could take various approaches to eliminating this bug. See how many ways you can think of, and decide which you like best, before reading further.

Since the problem has to do with the choice of partition value, you could imagine using a more complicated means to select that value. For example, you could start with the first member of the input list, then look through the list for another member not equal to the first. When you find one, average the two of them and that's the partition value. If you get all the way to the end of the list without finding two unequal members, declare the list sorted and output it as is. The trouble with this technique is that many extra comparisons are needed to find the partition value. Those comparisons don't really help in ordering the input, but they do add to the time taken just as much as the "real" comparisons done later.

Another approach is to say that since the problem only arises if the first and last input members are equal, we should treat that situation as a special case. That is, we'll add an instruction like

```
if equalp first :list last :list [...]
```

Again, this approach adds a comparison that doesn't really help to sort the file, although it's better than the first idea because it only adds one extra comparison per invocation instead of perhaps several.

A more straightforward approach that might seem to make the program more efficient, rather than less, is to divide the list into *three* buckets, `low`, `high`, and `equal`. This way, the problem gets shorter faster, since the `equal` bucket doesn't have to be sorted recursively; it's already in order. The trouble is that it takes two comparisons, one for equality and one for `lessthanp`, to know how to direct each list member into a three-way split. Some computers can compare numbers once and branch in different directions for less, equal, or greater; one programming language, Fortran, includes that kind of three-way branching through an "arithmetic IF" statement that accepts different instructions for the cases of a given quantity being less than, equal to, or greater than zero. But in Logo we'd have to say

```
if lessthanp first :in :split [...]
if equaltop first :in :split [...]
```

with two comparisons for each list member. (I'm imagining that `equaltop` would keep track of the number of comparisons just as `lessthanp` does.)

What I chose was to do the first `lessthanp` test for the list in `psort` instead of `psort1`, and use it to ensure that either the first or the last member of the list starts out the `low` bucket.

```
to psort :list
if emptyp :list [output []]
if emptyp butfirst :list [output :list]
localmake "split ((first :list) + (last :list)) / 2
if lessthanp first :list :split ~
   [output psort1 :split (butfirst :list) (list first :list) []]
output psort1 :split (butlast :list) (list last :list) []
end
```

`Psort1` is unchanged.

How many comparisons should `psort` require to sort 100 numbers? Unlike `ssort`, its exact performance depends on the particular list of numbers given as input. But we can get a general idea. The first step is to divide the 100 numbers into two buckets, using 100 comparisons against the partition value. The second step divides each of the buckets in two again. We can't say, in general, how big each bucket is; but we do know that each of the original 100 numbers has to be in one bucket or the other. So each of 100 numbers will participate in a comparison in this second round also. The same argument applies to the third round, and so on. Each round involves 100 comparisons. (This isn't quite true toward the end of the process. When a bucket only contains one number, it is considered sorted without doing any comparisons. So as the buckets get smaller, eventually some of the numbers "drop out" of the comparison process, while others are still not in their final position.)

Each round involves 100 comparisons, more or less. How many rounds are there? This is where the original ordering of the input data makes itself most strongly felt. If we're lucky, each round divides each bucket exactly in half. In that case the size of the buckets decreases uniformly:

```
round     size

  1        100
  2         50
  3         25
  4         12,13
  5          6,7
  6          3,4
  7          1,2
```

There is no round 8, because by then all of the buckets would be of length 1 and there is no work left to do. So if all goes well we'd expect to make about 700 comparisons, really a little less because by round 7 some of the numbers are already in length-1 buckets. Maybe 650?

What is the *worst* case? That would be if each round divides the numbers into buckets as unevenly as possible, with one number in one bucket and all the rest in the other. In that case it'll take 99 rounds to get all the numbers into length-1 buckets. You may be tempted to estimate 9900 comparisons for that situation, but in fact it isn't quite so bad, because at each round one number falls into a length-1 bucket and drops out of the sorting process. So the first round requires 100 comparisons, but the second round only 99, the third 98, and so on. This situation is very much like the way `ssort` works, and so we'd expect about 5000 comparisons.

Now try some experiments. Try `psort` on your random list, then try to find input lists that give the best and worst possible results.

`Psort` required 725 comparisons for my random list. That's somewhat more than we predicted for the best case, but not too much more. `Psort` seems to have done pretty well with this list. The simplest worst-case input is one in which all the numbers are the same; I said

```
make "bad cascade 100 [fput 20 ?] []
```

to make such a list. `Psort` required 5049 comparisons to sort this list, slightly *worse* than `ssort` at 4950 comparisons.

What would a best-case input look like? It would divide evenly at each stage; that is, the median value at each stage would be the average of the first and last values. The simplest list that should meet that criterion is a list of all the numbers from 1 to 100 in order:

```
make "inorder cascade 100 [lput # ?] []
```

(Or you could use the `reverse` trick discussed earlier, but for only 100 numbers it didn't seem worth the extra typing to me.) Using `psort` to sort this list should require, we said, somewhere around 650 to 700 comparisons. In fact it took 734 comparisons when I tried it, slightly *more* than my randomly ordered list (725 comparisons).

Even 734 comparisons isn't terrible by any means, but when an algorithm performs worse than expected, a true algorithm lover wants to know why. Test cases like these can uncover either inefficiencies in the fundamental algorithm or else ways in which the actual computer program doesn't live up to the algorithm as described in theoretical language. If we could "tune up" this program to sort `:inorder` in fewer than 700 comparisons, the change might well improve the program's performance for any input. See if you can figure out what the problem is before reading further. You can try having `psort` print out its inputs each time it's called, as a way to help gather information.

Here's a very large hint. I tried using the original version of `psort`, before fixing the bug about the recursion sometimes leaving all the numbers in one basket, and it sorted `:inorder` in only 672 comparisons. (I knew the bug wouldn't make trouble in this case because none of the numbers in this particular input list are equal.) Can you devise a better `psort` that both works all the time and performs optimally for the best-case input?

This partition sorting scheme is essentially similar to a very well-known algorithm named quicksort, invented by C. A. R. Hoare. Quicksort includes many improvements over this algorithm, not primarily in reducing the number of comparisons but in decreasing the overhead time by, for example, exchanging pairs of input items in their original memory locations instead of making copies of sublists. Quicksort also switches to a more straightforward `ssort`-like algorithm for very small input lists, because the benefit of halving the problem is outweighed by the greater complexity. (In fact, for a two-item input, `ssort` makes one comparison and `psort` two.)

Here's the partition sort algorithm again:

- Divide the input into the small-value half and the large-value half.
- Sort each half separately.
- Put the sorted small values in front of the sorted large ones.

The idea of cutting the problem in half is also used in the following algorithm, called *mergesort:*

- Divide the input arbitrarily into two equal size pieces.
- Sort each half separately.
- *Merge* the two sorted pieces by comparing values.

In a way, mergesort is to partition sort as insertion sort is to selection sort. Both insertion sort and mergesort defer the comparisons of numbers until the final step of the algorithm.

There is one important way in which mergesort is better than partition sort. Since mergesort doesn't care how the input values are separated, we can ensure that the two pieces are each exactly half the size of the input. Therefore, the number of comparisons needed is always as small as possible; there are no bad inputs. Nevertheless, quicksort is more widely used than mergesort, because the very best implementations of quicksort seem to require less overhead time, for the average input, than the best implementations of mergesort.

If you want to write a mergesort program, the easiest way to divide a list into two equal pieces is to select every other member, so the odd-position members are in one half and the even-position members in the other half.

Order of Growth

I've mentioned that the complete quicksort algorithm includes several optimization strategies to improve upon the partition sort I've presented here. How important are these strategies? How much does overhead contribute to the cost of a program? I did some experiments to investigate this question.

First I timed `psort` and `ssort` with inputs of length 300. Here are the results:

program	comparisons	time	comparisons per second
psort	2940	29 seconds	100
ssort	44850	313 seconds	143

Ssort seems to have much less overhead, since it can do more comparisons per second than psort. Nevertheless, psort always seems to be faster, for every size input I tried. The number of comparisons outweighs the overhead. (By the way, these numbers don't measure how fast the computer can compare two numbers! A typical computer could perform more than a million comparisons per second, if only comparisons were involved. Most of the time in these experiments is actually going into the process by which the Logo interpreter figures out what the instructions in the program mean. Because Berkeley Logo is an interpreter, this figuring-out process happens every time an instruction is executed. By contrast, I tried ssort on a list of length 300 in Object Logo, a compiled version in which each instruction is figured out only once, and the total time was 3.6 seconds.)

I wanted to give local optimization the best possible chance to win the race, and so I decided to make selection sort as fast as I could, and partition sort as slow as I could. I modified ssort to use the Logo primitive lessp for comparison instead of doing the extra bookkeeping of lessthanp, and I replaced psort with this implementation:

```
to slowsort :list
if (count :list) < 2 [output :list]
localmake "split (reduce "sum :list)/(count :list)
output (sentence slowsort filter [? < :split] :list
                filter [? = :split] :list
                slowsort filter [? > :split] :list)
end
```

This version examines every member of the input list six times on each recursive call! (Count is invoked twice; reduce looks at every list member once; and filter is called three times to do the actual partition.) Under these conditions I was able to get ssort to win the race, but only for very small inputs:

program	20 numbers	100 numbers	300 numbers
slowsort	2.7 seconds	18 seconds	63 seconds
ssort	1.2 seconds	20 seconds	182 seconds

Ssort wins when sorting 20 numbers, but both programs take less than three seconds. For 100 numbers, slowsort is already winning the race, and its lead grows as the input list grows. This is a common pattern: For small amounts of data, when the program is fast enough no matter how you write it, local optimization can win the race, but once the problem is large enough so that you actually care about efficiency, choosing a better overall algorithm is always more important. (Of course the very best results will come from choosing a good algorithm *and* optimizing the program locally.)

What does "a better algorithm" actually mean? How do we measure the quality of an algorithm? We've made a good start by counting the number of comparisons required for our two sorting algorithms, but there is a formal notation that can make the issues clearer.

Earlier I said that for a list of n numbers, `ssort` makes

$$\frac{n(n-1)}{2}$$

comparisons. But in a sense this tells us more than we want to know, like saying that a certain program took 1,243,825 microseconds instead of saying that it took somewhat over a second. The important thing to say about `ssort` is that the number of comparisons is roughly proportional to n^2; that is, doubling the size of the input list will quadruple the time needed to sort the list. More formally, we say that the time required for selection sorting is $O(n^2)$, pronounced "big-oh of n^2" or "order n^2." This is an abbreviation for the statement, "for large enough n, the time is bounded by n^2 times a constant." The part about "for large enough n" is important because the running time for some algorithm might, for example, involve a large constant setup time. For small n that setup time might contribute more to the overall time required than the part of the algorithm proportional* to n^2, but once n becomes large enough, the n^2 part will overtake any constant.

I'd like to have a similar representation, $O(\text{something})$, for the number of comparisons used by `psort` in the typical case. We said that for 100 numbers, each round of sorting involves about 100 comparisons, and the number of rounds required is the number of times you have to divide 100 by 2 before you get down to 1, namely between 6 and 7. The number of comparisons expected is the product of these numbers. In the general case, the first number is just n. But what is the general formula for the number of times you have to divide n by 2 to get 1? The answer is $\log_2 n$. For example, if we had 128 numbers in the list instead of 100, we would require exactly 7 rounds (in the best

---

* Strictly speaking, the fact that an algorithm's time requirement is $O(n^2)$ doesn't mean that it's even approximately proportional to n^2, because $O(\ldots)$ only establishes an upper bound. The time requirement could be proportional to n, which would be better than n^2, and still be $O(n^2)$. But usually people use $O(\ldots)$ notation to mean that no smaller order of growth would work, even though there's an official notation with that meaning, $\Theta(n^2)$, pronounced "big theta."

case) because $2^7 = 128$ and so $\log_2 128 = 7$. (By the way, $\log_2 100 \approx 6.65$, so the theoretical best case for 100 numbers is 665 comparisons.)

In general, all the obvious sorting algorithms are $O(n^2)$ and all the clever ones are $O(n \log n)$.* (I don't have to say $O(n \log_2 n)$ because the difference between logarithms to different bases is just multiplication by a constant factor, which doesn't count in $O(\ldots)$ notation, just as I don't have to worry about the fact that the formula for ssort comparisons is nearer $n^2/2$ than n^2.) By the way, I haven't really *proven* that psort is $O(n \log n)$ in the *typical* case, only that it is in the best case. It's much harder to prove things about the typical (or average) performance of any sorting algorithm, because what is an "average" input list? For some algorithms there is no proven formula for the average run time, but only the results of experiments with many randomly chosen lists.

An $O(n)$ algorithm is called *linear* and an $O(n^2)$ one *quadratic*. $O(n \log n)$ is in between those, better than quadratic but not as good as linear. What other orders of growth are commonly found? As one example, the pre-memoized procedures for the t and simplex functions in Chapter 2 have time requirements that are $O(2^n)$; these are called *exponential* algorithms. This means that just adding one to n makes the program take twice as long! The experimental results I gave earlier agree with this formula: simplex 10 took 80 seconds, while simplex 12 took $5\frac{1}{2}$ minutes, about four times as long. Simplex 16 would take over an hour. (Start with 80 seconds, and double it six times.) The memoized versions in this chapter are $O(n^2)$ (can you prove that?), which is much more manageable. But for some *really* hard problems there is no known way to make them any faster than $O(2^n)$; problems like that are called *intractable*, while ones that are merely polynomial—$O(n^i)$ for any constant i—are called *tractable*.

Data Structures

One of the reasons computers are so useful is that they can contain a tremendous amount of information. An important part of writing a large computer program is figuring out how to organize the information used in the program. Most of the time, a program doesn't have to deal with a bunch of unrelated facts, like "Tomatoes are red" and "7 times 8 is 56." Instead there will be some kind of uniformity, or natural grouping, in the information a program uses.

---

* Don Knuth has written an $O(n^3)$ sort program, just as an example of especially bad programming.

We'll see, too, that the data structures you choose for your program affect the algorithms available to you. Organizing your data cleverly can reduce the execution time of your procedures substantially.

Data Structures in Real Life

Why should there be different kinds of organization? It might help to look at some analogies with data structures outside of computers. First of all, think about your personal address book. It probably has specific pages reserved for each letter of the alphabet. Within a letter, the names and addresses of people starting with that letter are arranged in no particular order; you just add a new person in the first free space on the page.

Now think about the printed telephone directory for your city. In this case the names are not arranged randomly within each letter; they're in strict alphabetical order. In computer science terminology, the printed directory is a *sorted list,* while your personal directory is a *hash table.*

Obviously, if the entries in the printed directory weren't in order it would take much too long to find an address. You can get away with random ordering within each letter in your personal directory because you know a small enough number of people that it doesn't take too long to look through each one. But you probably do know enough people to make the separate page for each letter worthwhile, even though the page for Q may be practically empty. By using separate pages for each letter, with unused slots on each page reserved for expansion, you are *spending space* to *buy time.* That is, your address book is bigger than it would be if it were just one long list, but looking up a number is faster this way. This tradeoff between time and space is typical of computer programming problems also.

Why don't you keep your personal directory in strict alphabetical order, like the printed phone book? If you did that, looking up a number would be even faster. The problem is that *adding* a new number would be terribly painful; you'd have to erase all the names on the page below where the new name belongs and rewrite each of them one line below where it was.* In this case there is a tradeoff between *storage time* and *retrieval*

---

* Why doesn't the phone company have to do that whenever they get a new customer? The answer is that they maintain the directory information in two forms. The printed directory is the *external* representation, used only for looking up information; inside their computers they use an *internal* representation that allows for easier insertion of new entries.

time; you pay a small price in retrieval time to avoid a large price in storage time. This, too, is a common aspect of data structure design in computer programs.

Other kinds of real-life data structures also have computer analogues. If your desk looks like mine, with millions of little slips of paper all over the place, it is what computer scientists call a *heap.** This might be an appropriate data structure for those cases in which the program must deal with a large mass of unrelated facts. On the other hand, in a large business office there will be a *hierarchical* filing system. A file cabinet labeled "Personnel Records" might contain a drawer labeled "Inactive A-H"; that drawer would contain a file folder for each former employee whose name starts with an appropriate letter. This kind of hierarchy might be represented as a *tree* in a computer program.

Trees

We've used the idea of trees before. In Volume 1, the program to solve pitcher pouring problems was designed in terms of a tree of possible solution steps, although that tree was not represented as actual data in the program. In Volume 2, I wrote `tree.map` as an example of a higher order function operating on trees in which the leaf nodes are words and the branch nodes are phrases. In this chapter we'll work toward a general representation of trees as an abstract data type.

Here is a hierarchical grouping of some of the world's cities:

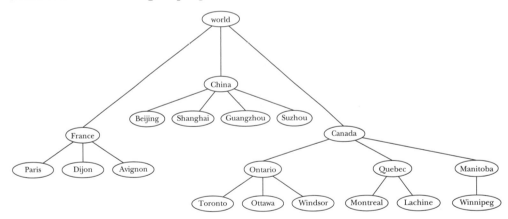

Recall that a diagram like this is called a tree because it resembles a real tree turned upside-down. Each place where a word or phrase appears in the tree is called a *node.*

---

* Unfortunately, there are two things called a "heap" in computer science. I'm thinking of the storage allocation heap, not the special tree structure used in the "heapsort" algorithm.

At the top of the diagram is the *root node* (`world`). The lines between nodes are called *branches*. The cities, which do not have branches extending below them, are called *leaf nodes*. The in-between nodes, the countries and provinces, are called *branch nodes*. (The root node is also considered a branch node since it, too, has branches below it.) This tree tells us that Toronto is in Ontario, which is in Canada, which is in the world.

A tree is a very general data structure because its shape is very flexible. For example, in the part of this tree that represents Canada I've included a level of tree structure, representing the provinces, that isn't included in the subtree that represents France. As we'll see later, some algorithms deal with restricted categories of trees. For example, a *binary* tree is a tree with at most two branches below each branch node.

So far this data structure is just a graphic representation on paper. There are many ways in which a tree can be implemented in a computer program. Let's say that I want to represent the tree of cities in a computer so that I can ask questions from this data base. That is, I'd like to write a program that will allow interactions like

```
? show locate "Montreal
[world Canada Quebec Montreal]
```

Let's pick a particular way to represent a tree in Logo. (I should warn you that later in the chapter I'm going to invent different representations, but I want to start with a simple one to meet our immediate needs. So what you're about to see is not the final version of these procedures.) Here's the way I'm going to do it: Each branch node will be represented as a Logo variable whose name is the name of the node, containing as its value a list of the names of the nodes immediately below it. For example, this tree will include a variable named `France` with the value

```
[Paris Dijon Avignon]
```

A leaf node is just a word that appears in a node list but isn't the name of a variable. For a branch node, `thing` of the node's name will provide a list of the names of its children. I can set up the tree with this procedure:

```
to worldtree
make "world [France China Canada]
make "France [Paris Dijon Avignon]
make "China [Beijing Shanghai Guangzhou Suzhou]
make "Canada [Ontario Quebec Manitoba]
make "Ontario [Toronto Ottawa Windsor]
make "Quebec [Montreal Lachine]
make "Manitoba [Winnipeg]
end
```

In principle, `locate` is a lot like `filter`, in the sense that we're looking through a data structure for something that meets a given condition. But the implementation is a bit trickier than looking through a sequential list, because each invocation gives rise to several recursive invocations (one per child), not merely one recursive invocation as usual. The program will be easier to understand if we introduce the term *forest*, which means a list of trees.

```
to locate :city
output locate1 :city "world
end

to locate1 :city :subtree
if equalp :city :subtree [output (list :city)]
if not namep :subtree [output []]
localmake "lower locate.in.forest :city (thing :subtree)
if emptyp :lower [output []]
output fput :subtree :lower
end

to locate.in.forest :city :forest
if emptyp :forest [output []]
localmake "child locate1 :city first :forest
if not emptyp :child [output :child]
output locate.in.forest :city butfirst :forest
end
```

```
? show locate "Shanghai
[world China Shanghai]
? show locate "Montreal
[world Canada Quebec Montreal]
```

Once we've set up this data base, we can write procedures to ask it other kinds of questions, too.

```
to cities :tree
if not namep :tree [output (list :tree)]
output map.se [cities ?] thing :tree
end
```

```
? show cities "France
[Paris Dijon Avignon]
? show cities "Canada
[Toronto Ottawa Windsor Montreal Lachine Winnipeg]
```

Improving the Data Representation

There's a problem with the representation I've chosen for this tree. Suppose we want to expand the data base to include the city of Quebec. This city is in the province of Quebec, so all we have to do is add the name to the appropriate list:

```
make "Quebec [Montreal Quebec Lachine]
```

If you try this, however, you'll find that `locate` and `cities` will no longer work. They'll both be trapped in infinite loops.

The problem with this program can't be fixed just by changing the program. It's really a problem in the way I decided to represent a tree. I said, "a leaf node is just a word that appears in a node list but isn't the name of a variable." But that means there's no way to allow a leaf node with the same name as a branch node. To solve the problem I have to rethink the conventions I use to represent a tree.

Being lazy, I'd like to change as little as possible in the program, so I'm going to try to find a new representation as similar as possible to the old one. Here's my idea: In my mind I associate a *level* with each node in the tree. The node `world` is at level 1, `France` and `Canada` at level 2, and so on. The names of the variables used to hold the contents of a node will be formed from the node name and the level: `world1`, `France2`, `Ontario3`, and so on. This solves the problem because the node for Quebec province will be a branch node by virtue of the variable `Quebec3`, but the node for Quebec city will be a leaf node because there will be no `Quebec4` variable.

As it turns out, though, I have to change the program quite a bit to make this work. Several procedures must be modified to take the level number as an additional input. Also, since the variable that holds the information about a place is no longer exactly named with the place's name, `cities` has some extra work to do, just to find the node whose cities we want to know. It can almost use `locate` for this purpose, but with a slight wrinkle: If we ask for the cities in Quebec, we mean Quebec province, not Quebec city. So we need a variant of `locate` that finds the node highest up in the tree with the desired place name. I gave subprocedure `locate1` an extra input, named `highest`, that's `true` if we want the highest matching tree node (when called from `cities`) or `false` if we want a matching leaf node (when called from `locate`).

```
to worldtree
make "world1 [France China Canada]
make "France2 [Paris Dijon Avignon]
make "China2 [Beijing Shanghai Guangzhou Suzhou]
make "Canada2 [Ontario Quebec Manitoba]
make "Ontario3 [Toronto Ottawa Windsor]
make "Quebec3 [Montreal Quebec Lachine]
make "Manitoba3 [Winnipeg]
end


to locate :city
output locate1 :city "world 1 "false
end


to locate1 :city :subtree :level :highest
localmake "name (word :subtree :level)
if and :highest equalp :city :subtree [output (list :city)]
if not namep :name
   [ifelse equalp :city :subtree
           [output (list :city)]
           [output []]]
localmake "lower locate.in.forest :city (thing :name) :level+1 :highest
if emptyp :lower [output []]
output fput :subtree :lower
end


to locate.in.forest :city :forest :level :highest
if emptyp :forest [output []]
localmake "child locate1 :city first :forest :level :highest
if not emptyp :child [output :child]
output locate.in.forest :city butfirst :forest :level :highest
end


to cities :tree
localmake "path locate1 :tree "world 1 "true
if emptyp :path [output []]
output cities1 :tree count :path
end


to cities1 :tree :level
localmake "name (word :tree :level)
if not namep :name [output (list :tree)]
output map.se [(cities1 ? :level+1)] thing :name
end
```

```
? show locate "Quebec
[world Canada Quebec Quebec]
? show cities "Canada
[Toronto Ottawa Windsor Montreal Quebec Lachine Winnipeg]
```

This new version solves the Quebec problem. But I'm still not satisfied. I'd like to add the United States to the data base. This is a country whose name is more than one word. How can I represent it in the tree structure? The most natural thing would be to use a list: [United States]. Unfortunately, a list can't be the name of a variable in Logo. Besides, now that I've actually written the program using this representation I see what a kludge it is!

Trees as an Abstract Data Type

My next idea for representing a tree is to abandon the use of a separate variable for each node; instead I'll put the entire tree in one big list. A node will be a list whose first is the datum at that node and whose butfirst is a list of children of the node. So the entire tree will be represented by a list like this:

```
[world [France ...] [[United States] ...] [China ...] [Canada ...]]
```

The datum at each node can be either a word or a list.

But this time I'm going to be smarter than before. I'm going to recognize that the program I'm writing should logically be separated into two parts: the part that implements the *tree* data type, and the part that uses a tree to implement the data base of cities. If I write procedures like locate and cities in terms of general-purpose tree subprocedures like leafp, a predicate that tells whether its input node is a leaf node, then I can change my mind about the implementation of trees (as I've done twice already) without changing that part of the program at all.

I'll start by implementing the abstract data type. I've decided that a tree will be represented as a list with the datum of the root node as its first and the subtrees in the butfirst. To make this work I need *selector* procedures:

```
to datum :node
output first :node
end

to children :node
output butfirst :node
end
```

and a *constructor* procedure to build a node out of its pieces:

```
to tree :datum :children
output fput :datum :children
end
```

Selectors and constructors are the main procedures needed to define any data structure, but there are usually some others that can be useful. For the tree, the main missing one is `leafp`.

```
to leafp :node
output emptyp children :node
end
```

Now I can use these tools to write the data base procedures.

```
to locate :city
output locate1 :city :world "false
end
```

```
to locate1 :city :subtree :wanttree
if and :wanttree (equalp :city datum :subtree) [output :subtree]
if leafp :subtree ~
    [ifelse equalp :city datum :subtree
            [output (list :city)]
            [output []]]
localmake "lower locate.in.forest :city (children :subtree) :wanttree
if emptyp :lower [output []]
output ifelse :wanttree [:lower] [fput (datum :subtree) :lower]
end
```

```
to locate.in.forest :city :forest :wanttree
if emptyp :forest [output []]
localmake "child locate1 :city first :forest :wanttree
if not emptyp :child [output :child]
output locate.in.forest :city butfirst :forest :wanttree
end
```

```
to cities :name
output cities1 (finddatum :name :world)
end
```

```
to cities1 :subtree
if leafp :subtree [output (list datum :subtree)]
output map.se [cities1 ?] children :subtree
end
```

```
to finddatum :datum :tree
output locate1 :name :tree "true
end
```

Once again, `cities` depends on a variant of `locate` that outputs the subtree below
a given name, instead of the usual `locate` output, which is a list of the names on the
path from `world` down to a city. But instead of having `cities` call `locate1` directly, I
decided that it would be more elegant to provide a procedure `finddatum` that takes a
datum and a tree as inputs, whose output is the subtree below that datum.

In `cities1`, the expression

```
(list datum :subtree)
```

turns out to be equivalent to just `:subtree` for the case of a leaf node. (It is only for leaf
nodes that the expression is evaluated.) By adhering to the principle of data abstraction
I'm making the program work a little harder than it really has to. The advantage, again,
is that this version of `cities` will continue working even if we change the underlying
representation of trees. The efficiency cost is quite low; changing the expression to
`:subtree` is a local optimization comparable to the common subexpression elimination
we considered early in the chapter.

I also have to revise the procedure to set up the tree. It's going to involve many
nested invocations of `tree`, like this:

```
to worldtree
make "world tree "world
                (list (tree "France
                                (list (tree "Paris [])
                                      (tree "Dijon [])
                                      (tree "Avignon []) ) )
                      (tree "China
                                (list ...
```

and so on. I can shorten this procedure somewhat by inventing an abbreviation for
making a subtree all of whose children are leaves.

```
to leaf :datum
output tree :datum []
end

to leaves :leaves
output map [leaf ?] :leaves
end
```

```
to worldtree
make "world
     tree "world
          (list (tree "France leaves [Paris Dijon Avignon])
                (tree "China leaves [Beijing Shanghai Guangzhou Suzhou])
                (tree [United States]
                     (list (tree [New York]
                                leaves [[New York] Albany Rochester
                                        Armonk] )
                           (tree "Massachusetts
                                leaves [Boston Cambridge Sudbury
                                        Maynard] )
                           (tree "California
                                leaves [[San Francisco] Berkeley
                                        [Palo Alto] Pasadena] )
                           (tree "Washington
                                leaves [Seattle Olympia] ) ) )
                (tree "Canada
                     (list (tree "Ontario
                                leaves [Toronto Ottawa Windsor] )
                           (tree "Quebec
                                leaves [Montreal Quebec Lachine] )
                           (tree "Manitoba leaves [Winnipeg]) ) ) )
end

? worldtree
? show cities [United States]
[[New York] Albany Rochester Armonk Boston Cambridge Sudbury Maynard
 [San Francisco] Berkeley [Palo Alto] Pasadena Seattle Olympia]
? show locate [Palo Alto]
[world [United States] California [Palo Alto]]
```

Tree Modification

So far, so good. But the procedure worldtree just above is very error-prone because of its high degree of nesting. In the earlier versions I could create the tree a piece at a time instead of all at once. In a practical data base system, people should be able to add new information at any time, not just ask questions about the initial information. That is, I'd like to be able to say

```
addchild :world (tree "Spain leaves [Madrid Barcelona Orense])
```

to add a subtree to the world tree. New nodes should be possible not only at the top of the tree but anywhere within it:

```
addchild (finddatum "Canada :world) (tree [Nova Scotia] leaves [Halifax])
```

Most versions of Logo do not provide tools to add a new member to an existing list. We could write a program that would make a new copy of the entire tree, adding the new node at the right place in the copy, so that `addchild` would take the form

```
make "world newcopy :world ...
```

but there are two objections to that. First, it would be quite slow, especially for a large tree. Second, it would work only if I refrain from assigning subtrees as the values of variables other than `world`. That is, I'd like to be able to say

```
? make "Canada finddatum "Canada :world
? addchild :Canada (tree [Nova Scotia] leaves [Halifax])
? show locate "Halifax
[world Canada [Nova Scotia] Halifax]
```

Even though I've added the new node to the tree `:Canada`, it should also be part of `:world` (which is where `locate` looks) because `:Canada` is a subtree of `:world`. Similarly, I'd like to be able to add a node to the Canadian subtree of `:world` and have it also be part of `:Canada`. That wouldn't be true if `addchild` makes a copy of its tree input instead of modifying the existing tree.

I'm going to solve this problem two ways. In the Doctor project in Volume 2 of this series, you learned that Berkeley Logo does include primitive procedures that allow the modification of an existing list structure. I think the most elegant solution to the `addchild` problem is the one that takes advantage of that feature. But I'll also show a solution that works in any version of Logo, to make the point that list mutation isn't absolutely necessary; we can achieve the same goals, with the same efficiency, by other means. First here's the list mutation version of `addchild`:

```
to addchild :tree :child
.setbf :tree (fput :child butfirst :tree)
end
```

```
? make "GB leaf [Great Britain]
? addchild :world :GB
? addchild :GB tree "England leaves [London Liverpool Oxford]
? addchild :GB tree "Scotland leaves [Edinburgh Glasgow]
? addchild :GB tree "Wales leaves [Abergavenny]
? show locate "Glasgow
[world [Great Britain] Scotland Glasgow]
```

Just as `tree` is a constructor for the tree data type, and `children` is a selector, `addchild` is called a *mutator* for this data type. Notice, by the way, that `:GB`, which was originally built as a leaf node, can be turned into a branch node by adding children to it; `addchild` is not limited to nodes that already have children.

The solution using `.setbf` is elegant because I didn't have to change any of the procedures I had already written; this version of `addchild` works with the same tree implementation I had already set up. But suppose we didn't have `.setbf` or didn't want to use it. (As we'll see shortly, using list mutators does open up some possible pitfalls.) We can write a mutator for the tree abstract data type even if we don't have mutators for the underlying Logo lists! The secret is to take advantage of variables, whose values can be changed—mutated—in any version of Logo.

To make this work I'm going to go back to a tree representation somewhat like the one I started with, in which each node is represented by a separate variable. But to avoid the problems I had earlier about Quebec and San Francisco, the variable name won't be the datum it contains. Instead I'll use a *generated symbol,* an arbitrary name made up by the program. (This should sound familiar. I used the same trick in the Doctor project, and there too it was an alternative to list mutation.)

This is where my use of data abstraction pays off. Look how little I have to change:

```
to tree :datum :children
localmake "node gensym
make :node fput :datum :children
output :node
end

to datum :node
output first thing :node
end

to children :node
output butfirst thing :node
end

to addchild :tree :child
make :tree lput :child thing :tree
end
```

That's it! `Leafp`, `finddatum`, `locate`, `cities`, and `worldtree` all work perfectly without modification, even though I've made a profound change in the actual representation of trees. (Try printing `:world` in each version.)

`Addchild` is only one of the possible ways in which I might want to modify a tree structure. If we were studying trees more fully, I'd create tool procedures to delete a node, to move a subtree from one location in the tree to another, to insert a new node between a parent and its children, and so on. There are also many more questions one might want to ask about a tree. How many nodes does it have? What is its maximum depth?

I've mentioned general tree manipulation tools. There are also still some unresolved issues about the particular use of trees in the city data base. For example, although the problem of Quebec city and Quebec province is under control, what if I want the data base to include Cambridge, England as well as Cambridge, Massachusetts? What should `locate` do if given `Cambridge` as input?

But instead of pursuing this example further I want to develop another example, in which trees are used for a very different purpose. In the city data base, the tree represents a *hierarchy* (Sudbury is *part of* Massachusetts); in the example below, a tree is used to represent an *ordering* of data, as in the sorting algorithms discussed earlier.

Searching Algorithms and Trees

Forget about trees for a moment and consider the general problem of *searching* through a data base for some piece of information. For example, suppose you want a program to find the city corresponding to a particular telephone area code. That is, I want to be able to say

```
? print listcity 415
San Francisco
```

The most straightforward way to do this is to have a list containing code-city pairs, like this:

```
make "codelist [[202 Washington] [206 Seattle] [212 New York]
    [213 Los Angeles] [215 Philadelphia] [303 Denver] [305 Miami]
    [313 Detroit] [314 St. Louis] [401 Providence] [404 Atlanta]
    [408 Sunnyvale] [414 Milwaukee] [415 San Francisco] [504 New Orleans]
    [608 Madison] [612 St. Paul] [613 Kingston] [614 Columbus]
    [615 Nashville] [617 Boston] [702 Las Vegas] [704 Charlotte]
    [712 Sioux City] [714 Anaheim] [716 Rochester] [717 Scranton]
    [801 Salt Lake City] [804 Newport News] [805 Ventura] [808 Honolulu]]
```

This is a list of lists. Each sublist contains one pairing of an area code with a city. We can search for a particular area code by going through the list member by member, comparing the first word with the desired area code. (By the way, in reality a single area code can contain more than one city, and vice versa, but never mind that; I'm trying to keep this simple.) In accordance with the idea of data abstraction, we'll start with procedures to extract the area code and city from a pair.

```
to areacode :pair
output first :pair
end

to city :pair
output butfirst :pair
end
```

The city is the `butfirst` rather than the `last` to accommodate cities with names of more than one word.

The iteration tool `find` does exactly what's needed, going through a list member by member until it finds one that matches some criterion:

```
to listcity :code
output city find [equalp :code areacode ?] :codelist
end
```

Time for a little analysis of algorithms. What is the time behavior of this *linear* search algorithm as the data base gets bigger? As for the case of the sorting algorithms, I'll concentrate on the number of comparisons. How many times is `equalp` invoked? The best case is if we're looking for the first code in the list, 202. In this case only one comparison is made. The worst case is if we're looking for the last code in the list, 808, or if we're looking for an area code that isn't in the list at all. This requires 31 comparisons. (That's how many code-city pairs happen to be in this particular data base.) On the average this algorithm requires a number of comparisons half way between these extremes, or 16. As we increase the size of the data base, the number of comparisons required grows proportionally; this algorithm is $O(n)$.

The area codes in `:codelist` are in ascending order. If you were looking through the list yourself, you wouldn't look at every entry one after another; you'd take advantage of the ordering by starting around the middle and moving forward or backward depending on whether the area code you found was too low or too high. That's called a *binary* search algorithm. `Listcity`, though, doesn't take advantage of the ordering in the list; the pairs could just as well be jumbled up and `listcity` would be equally happy.

Binary search works by starting with the median-value area code in the data base. If that's the one we want, we're finished; otherwise we take the higher or lower half of the remaining codes and examine the median value of that subset. One way we could implement that algorithm would be to use a binary tree to represent the code-city pairs:

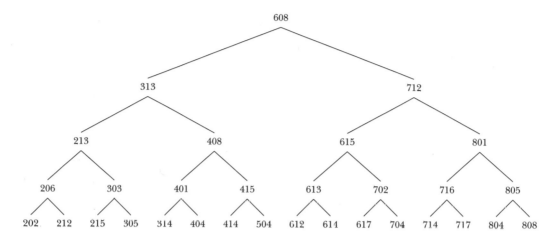

(In this picture I've just shown the area codes, but of course the actual data structure will have a code-city pair at each node.)

We could construct the tree from scratch, using **tree** and **leaves** as I did earlier, but since we already have the pairs in the correct sorted order it's easier to let the computer do it for us:

```
to balance :list
if emptyp :list [output []]
if emptyp butfirst :list [output leaf first :list]
output balance1 (int (count :list)/2) :list []
end


to balance1 :count :in :out
if equalp :count 0 ~
   [output tree (first :in) (list balance reverse :out
                                  balance butfirst :in )]
output balance1 (:count-1) (butfirst :in) (fput first :in :out)
end
```

In this program I'm using the trick of building :out using fput instead of lput and then using **reverse** to get the left branch back in ascending order, to make the construction a little faster.

Chapter 3   Algorithms and Data Structures

```
make "codetree balance :codelist
```

will generate the tree.

Now we're ready to write `treecity`, the tree-based search program analogous to `listcity` for the linear list.

```
to treecity :code
output city treecity1 :code :codetree
end

to treecity1 :code :tree
if emptyp :tree [output [000 no city]]
localmake "datum datum :tree
if :code = areacode :datum [output :datum]
if :code < areacode :datum [output treecity1 :code lowbranch :tree]
output treecity1 :code highbranch :tree
end

to lowbranch :tree
if leafp :tree [output []]
output first children :tree
end

to highbranch :tree
if leafp :tree [output []]
output last children :tree
end
```

? print treecity 415
San Francisco

Treecity gives the same output as `listcity`, but it's faster. At worst it makes two comparisons (for equal and less than) at each level of the tree. This tree is five levels deep, so if the input area code is in the tree at all we'll make at most 9 comparisons, compared to 31 for `listcity`. The average number is less. (How much less?) The difference is even more striking for larger data bases; if the number of pairs is 1000, the worst-case times are 1000 for `listcity` and 19 for `treecity`.

In general the depth of the tree is the number of times you can divide the number of pairs by two. This is like the situation we met in analyzing the partition sort algorithm; the depth of the tree is the log base two of the number of pairs. This is an $O(\log n)$ algorithm.

The procedures `lowbranch` and `highbranch` are data abstraction at work. I could have used `first children :tree` directly in `treecity1`, but this way I can change my mind about the representation of the tree if necessary. In fact, in a practical program I would want to use a representation that allows a node to have a right child (a `highbranch`) without having a left child. Also, `lowbranch` and `highbranch` are written robustly; they give an output, instead of causing an error, if applied to a leaf node. (That happens if you ask for the city of an area code that's not in the data base.) I haven't consistently been writing robust programs in this chapter, but I thought I'd give an example here.

The efficiency of the tree searching procedure depends on the fact that the tree is *balanced*. In other words, the left branch of each node is the same size as its right branch. I cheated slightly by starting with 31 area codes, a number that allows for a perfectly balanced tree. Suppose I had started with 35 area codes. How should I have built the tree? What would happen to the efficiency of the program? What is the maximum possible number of trials necessary to find a node in that tree? What other numbers of nodes allow for perfect balance?

There are two important ideas to take away from this example. The first is that the choice of data representation can have a substantial effect on the efficiency of a program. The second, as I mentioned at the beginning of this section, is that we have used the same kind of data structure, a tree, for two very different purposes: first to represent a *hierarchy* (Sudbury is *part of* Massachusetts) and then to represent an *ordering* (313 is *before* 608).

Logo's Underlying Data Structures

An abstract data type, such as the tree type we've been discussing, must be implemented using some lower-level means for data aggregation, that is, for grouping separate things into a combined whole. In Berkeley Logo, there are two main built-in means for aggregation: lists and arrays. (Every dialect of Logo has lists, but not all have arrays.) Words can be thought of as a third data aggregate, in which the grouped elements are letters, digits, and punctuation characters, but we don't ordinarily use words as the basis for abstract data types.

Logo was designed to be used primarily by people whose main interest is in something other than computer programming, and so a design goal was to keep to a minimum the extent to which the Logo programmer must know about how Logo itself works internally. Even in these books, which *are* focused on computing itself, we've gotten this far without looking very deeply into how Logo's data structures actually work. But for the purposes of this chapter it will be useful to take that step.

Essentially all computers today are divided into a *processor* and a *memory*. (The exceptions are experimental "parallel processing" machines in which many small sub-processors and sub-memories are interconnected, sometimes combining both capabilities within a single intergrated circuit.) Roughly speaking, the processor contains the circuitry that implements hardware primitive procedures such as arithmetic operations. (Not every Logo primitive is a hardware primitive.) The memory holds the information used in carrying out a program, including the program itself and whatever data it uses. The memory is divided into millions of small pieces, each of which can hold a single value (a number, a letter, and so on).* Each small piece has an *address,* which is a number used to select a particular piece; the metaphor is the street address of each house on a long street. The hardware primitive procedures include a `load` operation that takes a memory address as its input and finds the value in the specified piece of memory, and a `store` command that takes an address and a value as inputs and puts the given value into the chosen piece of memory.

With this background we can understand how lists and arrays differ. To be specific, suppose that we have a collection of five numbers to store in memory. If we use an array, that means that Logo finds five *consecutive* pieces of memory to hold the five values, like this:

If instead we use a list, Logo finds the memory for each of the five values as that value is computed. The five memory slots might not be consecutive, so each memory slot must contain not only the desired value but also a *pointer* to the next slot. That is, each slot must contain an additional number, the address of the next slot. (What I'm calling a "slot" must therefore be big enough to hold two numbers, and in fact Logo uses what we call a *pair* for each, essentially an array of length two.) Since we don't care about the actual numeric values of the addresses, but only about the pairs to which they point, we generally use arrows to represent pointers pictorially:

---

* I'm being vague about what a "value" is, and in fact most computer memories can be divided into pieces of different sizes. In most current computers, a *byte* is a piece that can hold any of 256 different values, while a *word* is a piece that can hold any of about four billion different values. But these details aren't important for my present purposes, and I'm going to ignore them. I'll talk as if memories were simply word-addressable.

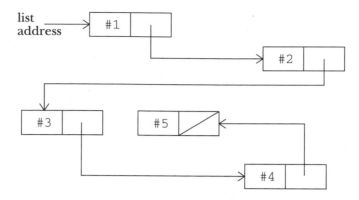

The last pair of the list has a *null pointer,* a special value to indicate that there is no next pair following it, indicated by the diagonal line.

Why do we bother to provide two aggregation mechanisms? Why don't language designers just pick the best one? Clearly the answer will be that each is "the best" for different purposes. In the following paragraphs I'll compare several characteristics of lists and arrays.

One advantage of arrays that should be obvious from these pictures is that a list uses twice as much memory to hold the same number of values. But this is not generally an important difference for modern computers; unless your problem is really enormous, you don't have to worry about running out of memory.

The most important advantage of arrays is that they are *random access.* This means that each member of an array can be found just as quickly as any other member, regardless of its position within the array. If the program knows the address at which the array begins, and it wants to find the nth member of the array, only two operations are needed: First add n to the array's address, then `load` the value from the resulting address. This takes a constant (and very short) amount of time, $O(1)$. By contrast, in a list there is no simple arithmetic relationship between the address of the list's first member and the address of its nth member. To find the nth member, the program must `load` the pointer from the first pair, then use that address to `load` the pointer from the second pair, and so on, n times. The number of operations needed is $O(n)$.

On the other hand, the most important advantage of lists is *dynamic allocation.* This means that the programmer does not have to decide ahead of time on how big the data aggregate will become. (We saw an example recently when we wanted to add a child to a node of an existing tree.) Consider the five-member aggregates shown earlier, and suppose we want to add a sixth member. If we've used a list, we can say, for example,

```
make "newlist fput "A :oldlist
```

and all Logo has to do is find one new pair:

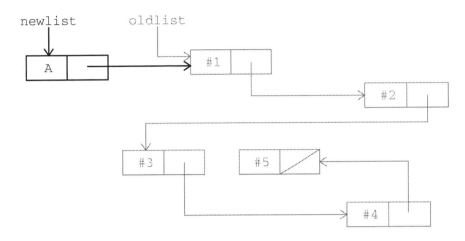

By contrast, once an array has been created we can't expand it, because the new address would have to be adjacent to the old addresses, and that piece of memory might already be used for something else. To make an array bigger, you have to allocate a complete new array and copy the old values into it.

Remember that arrays sacrifice efficient expansion in order to get efficient random access. From the standpoint of program speed, one is not absolutely better than the other; it depends on the nature of the problem you're trying to solve. That's why it's best if a language offers both structures, as Berkeley Logo does. For the very common case of `foreach`-like iteration through an aggregate, neither random access nor dynamic allocation is really necessary. For a data base that can grow during the running of a program, the flexibility of dynamic allocation is valuable. For many sorting algorithms, on the other hand, it's important to be able to jump around in the aggregate and so random access is useful. (A programmer using arrays can partially overcome the lack of dynamic allocation by preallocating a too-large array and leaving some of it empty at first. But if the order of members in the array matters, it may turn out that the "holes" in the array aren't where they're needed, and so the program still has to copy blocks of members to make room. Also, such programs have occasional embarrassing failures because what the programmer thought was an extravagantly large array turns out not quite large enough for some special use of the program, or because a malicious user deliberately "overruns" the length of the array in order to evade a program restriction.)

The solitaire program in Volume 2 of this series illustrates the different advantages of lists and arrays. As in any card game, a solitaire player distributes the cards into several small groups, each of which varies in size as the play continues. For example, a typical step is to deal a card from the *hand* onto the *pile*, each of which is represented as a list:

```
make "pile fput (first :hand) :pile
make "hand butfirst :hand
```

(The actual solitaire program uses somewhat different instructions to accomplish the same effect, with a `deal` procedure that outputs the next available card after removing it from the hand.)

On the other hand (no pun intended), *shuffling* the deck is easier when an array is used to hold the card values, because the shuffling algorithm requires random jumping around in the deck, but does not change the total number of cards, so that random access is more important than dynamic allocation. Therefore, the program starts each round of play with the deck in the form of an array of 52 cards. It shuffles the deck in array form, and then copies the members of the array into a list, which is used for the rest of that round. The advantage of an array for shuffling, and the advantage of a list for dealing cards, together outweigh the time spent copying the array into the list.

An important consequence of dynamic allocation is that lists are *sharable* data structures. In the example above, `:oldlist` contains five pairs and `:newlist` contains six, but the total number of pairs used is six, not 11, because most of the same pairs are part of both lists. That's why the `fput` operation takes $O(1)$ time, unaffected by the length of the list, as do `first` and `butfirst`. (Now that you know how lists are constructed using pairs and pointers, you should be able to understand something I've mentioned earlier without explanation: `Lput`, `last`, and `butlast` require $O(n)$ time. It's much faster to operate near the beginning of a list than near the end.) Arrays are not sharable; each array occupies its own block of consecutive memory addresses.

When a data structure is both sharable and mutable, it's possible to get into some very mysterious, hard-to-detect bugs. Suppose we do this:

```
? make "one [Ice cream is delicious.]
? make "two fput "Spinach butfirst butfirst :one
```

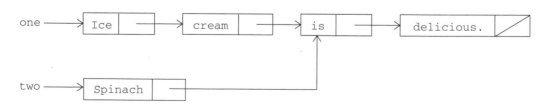

Chapter 3   Algorithms and Data Structures

Then suppose you decide you don't like spinach. You might say

```
? .setfirst butfirst butfirst :two "disgusting.
? print :two
Spinach is disgusting.
```

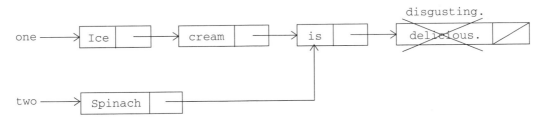

But you haven't taken into account that :one and :two share memory, so this instruction has an unintended result:

```
? print :one
Ice cream is disgusting.
```

This is definitely a bug!

It's the combination of mutation and sharing that causes trouble. Arrays are mutable but not sharable; the result of using setitem to change a member of an array is easily predictable. The trouble with list mutation is that you may change other lists besides the one you think you're changing. That's why Berkeley Logo's .setfirst and .setbf primitives have names starting with periods, the Logo convention for "experts only!" It's also why many other Logo dialects don't allow list mutation at all.*

In order to explain to you about how something like this might happen, I've had to tell you more about Logo's storage allocation techniques than is ordinarily taught. One of the design goals of Logo was that the programmer shouldn't have to think in terms of boxes and arrows as we're doing now. But if you mutate sharable lists, you'd better understand the boxes and arrows. It's not entirely obvious, you see, when two lists *do* share storage. Suppose the example had been backwards:

---

* Also, this helps to explain the importance of property lists in Logo. Property lists are a safe form of mutable list, because they are not sharable; that's why the plist primitive outputs a newly-allocated *copy* of the property list.

```
? make "one [Delicious, that's ice cream.]
? make "two lput "spinach. butlast butlast :one
? print :two
Delicious, that's spinach.
? .setfirst :two "Disgusting,
? print :two
Disgusting, that's spinach.
? print :one
Delicious, that's ice cream.
```

In this case the other list is *not* mysteriously modified because when lput is used, rather than fput as in the previous example, the two lists do *not* share memory. That's a consequence of the front-to-back direction of the arrows connecting the boxes; it's possible to have two arrows pointing *into* a box, but only one arrow can *leave* a box. You can't do this:

The combination of mutation and sharing, although tricky, is not all bad. The same mutual dependence that made a mess of :one and :two in the example above was desirable and helpful in the case of :world and :Canada earlier. That's why Lisp has always included mutable lists, and why versions of Logo intended for more expert users have also chosen to allow list mutation.

Don't think that without mutable lists you are completely safe from mutual dependence. Any language in which it's possible to give a datum a *name* allows the programmer to set up the equivalent of sharable data, just as I did in the final version of the tree of cities. As far as the Logo interpreter is concerned, the value of the variable world is some generated symbol like G47. That value is immune to changes in other data structures. But if we think of :world as containing, effectively, the entire tree whose root node is called G47, then changes to other variables do, in effect, change the value of world. What is true is that without mutable lists you can't easily set up a mutual dependence *by accident;* you have to intend it.

By the way, by drawing the box and pointer diagrams with the actual data inside the boxes, I may have given you the impression that each member of a list or array must be a single number or letter, so that the value will fit in one memory address. Actually, each member can be a pointer to anything. For example, here's a picture of an array that includes lists,

{[A B C] D [E F]}

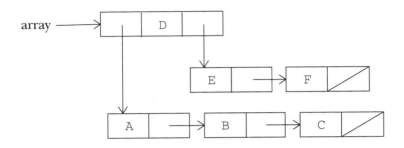

Program Listing

```
;;; Algorithms and Data Structures

;; Local optimization of quadratic formula

to quadratic :a :b :c
localmake "root sqrt (:b * :b-4 * :a * :c)
localmake "x1 (-:b+:root)/(2 * :a)
localmake "x2 (-:b-:root)/(2 * :a)
print (sentence [The solutions are] :x1 "and :x2)
end


;; Memoization of T function

to t :n :k
localmake "result gprop :n :k
if not emptyp :result [output :result]
make "result realt :n :k
pprop :n :k :result
output :result
end

to realt :n :k
if equalp :k 0 [output 1]
if equalp :n 0 [output 0]
output (t :n :k-1) + (t :n-1 :k)
end
```

```
;; Speedup of Simplex function

to simplex :buttons
output 2 * first (cascade :buttons
                          [fput (sumprods butfirst ?2 ?1) ?1] [1]
                          [fput 1 nextrow ?2] [1 1])
end

to sumprods :a :b
output reduce "sum (map "product :a :b)
end

to nextrow :combs
if emptyp butfirst :combs [output :combs]
output fput (sum first :combs first butfirst :combs) ~
            nextrow butfirst :combs
end

;; Sorting -- selection sort

to ssort :list
if emptyp :list [output []]
output ssort1 (first :list) (butfirst :list) []
end

to ssort1 :min :in :out
if emptyp :in [output fput :min ssort :out]
if lessthanp :min (first :in) ~
   [output ssort1 :min (butfirst :in) (fput first :in :out)]
output ssort1 (first :in) (butfirst :in) (fput :min :out)
end

;; Sorting -- partition sort

to psort :list
if emptyp :list [output []]
if emptyp butfirst :list [output :list]
localmake "split ((first :list) + (last :list)) / 2
if lessthanp first :list :split ~
   [output psort1 :split (butfirst :list) (list first :list) []]
output psort1 :split (butlast :list) (list last :list) []
end
```

```
to psort1 :split :in :low :high
if emptyp :in [output sentence (psort :low) (psort :high)]
if lessthanp first :in :split ~
   [output psort1 :split (butfirst :in) (fput first :in :low) :high]
output psort1 :split (butfirst :in) :low (fput first :in :high)
end


;; Sorting -- count comparisons

to lessthanp :a :b
if not namep "comparisons [make "comparisons 0]
make "comparisons :comparisons+1
output :a < :b
end

to howmany
print :comparisons
ern "comparisons
end

;; Abstract Data Type for Trees: Constructor

to tree :datum :children
output fput :datum :children
end

;; Tree ADT: Selectors

to datum :node
output first :node
end

to children :node
output butfirst :node
end

;; Tree ADT: Mutator

to addchild :tree :child
.setbf :tree (fput :child butfirst :tree)
end
```

```
;; Tree ADT: other procedures

to leaf :datum
output tree :datum []
end

to leaves :leaves
output map [leaf ?] :leaves
end

to leafp :node
output emptyp children :node
end

;; The World tree

to worldtree
make "world ~
    tree "world ~
        (list (tree "France leaves [Paris Dijon Avignon])
              (tree "China leaves [Beijing Shanghai Guangzhou Suzhou])
              (tree [United States]
                    (list (tree [New York]
                                leaves [[New York] Albany Rochester
                                        Armonk] )
                          (tree "Massachusetts
                                leaves [Boston Cambridge Sudbury
                                        Maynard] )
                          (tree "California
                                leaves [[San Francisco] Berkeley
                                        [Palo Alto] Pasadena] )
                          (tree "Washington
                                leaves [Seattle Olympia] ) ) )
              (tree "Canada
                    (list (tree "Ontario
                                leaves [Toronto Ottawa Windsor] )
                          (tree "Quebec
                                leaves [Montreal Quebec Lachine] )
                          (tree "Manitoba leaves [Winnipeg]) ) ) )
end

to locate :city
output locate1 :city :world "false
end
```

```
to locate1 :city :subtree :wanttree
if and :wanttree (equalp :city datum :subtree) [output :subtree]
if leafp :subtree ~
   [ifelse equalp :city datum :subtree
           [output (list :city)]
           [output []]]
localmake "lower locate.in.forest :city (children :subtree) :wanttree
if emptyp :lower [output []]
output ifelse :wanttree [:lower] [fput (datum :subtree) :lower]
end

to locate.in.forest :city :forest :wanttree
if emptyp :forest [output []]
localmake "child locate1 :city first :forest :wanttree
if not emptyp :child [output :child]
output locate.in.forest :city butfirst :forest :wanttree
end

to cities :name
output cities1 (finddatum :name :world)
end

to cities1 :subtree
if leafp :subtree [output (list datum :subtree)]
output map.se [cities1 ?] children :subtree
end

to finddatum :datum :tree
output locate1 :name :tree "true
end

;; Area code/city pairs ADT

to areacode :pair
output first :pair
end

to city :pair
output butfirst :pair
end
```

```
;; Area code linear search

make "codelist [[202 Washington] [206 Seattle] [212 New York]
                [213 Los Angeles] [215 Philadelphia] [303 Denver]
                [305 Miami] [313 Detroit] [314 St. Louis]
                [401 Providence] [404 Atlanta] [408 Sunnyvale]
                [414 Milwaukee] [415 San Francisco] [504 New Orleans]
                [608 Madison] [612 St. Paul] [613 Kingston]
                [614 Columbus] [615 Nashville] [617 Boston]
                [702 Las Vegas] [704 Charlotte]
                [712 Sioux City] [714 Anaheim] [716 Rochester]
                [717 Scranton] [801 Salt Lake City] [804 Newport News]
                [805 Ventura] [808 Honolulu]]

to listcity :code
output city find [equalp :code areacode ?] :codelist
end


;; Area code binary tree search

to balance :list
if emptyp :list [output []]
if emptyp butfirst :list [output leaf first :list]
output balance1 (int (count :list)/2) :list []
end


to balance1 :count :in :out
if equalp :count 0 ~
   [output tree (first :in) (list balance reverse :out
                                  balance butfirst :in)]
output balance1 (:count-1) (butfirst :in) (fput first :in :out)
end


to treecity :code
output city treecity1 :code :codetree
end


to treecity1 :code :tree
if emptyp :tree [output [0 no city]]
localmake "datum datum :tree
if :code = areacode :datum [output :datum]
if :code < areacode :datum [output treecity1 :code lowbranch :tree]
output treecity1 :code highbranch :tree
end
```

```
to lowbranch :tree
if leafp :tree [output []]
output first children :tree
end

to highbranch :tree
if leafp :tree [output []]
output last children :tree
end
```

4   Programming Language Design

Program file for this chapter: `pascal`

This chapter and the next are about two related things: why different programming languages are different and how a programming language is implemented. To make the discussion concrete, I've chosen a specific language as an example: Pascal. That choice seems appropriate partly because Pascal is very different from Logo and partly because it is widely used as a vehicle for teaching introductory computer science, the same task I'm attempting in this book using Logo.*

For the purposes of this book I've written a program that translates a *small subset* of Pascal into a simulated machine language. You can get a real Pascal compiler for your computer that accepts the full language, and that's what you should do if you want to learn how to program in Pascal. I had two reasons for writing this subset compiler. One is that some readers may not otherwise have access to a Pascal compiler, and mine, despite its limitations, will enable you to explore the parts of the language I'm going to be talking about. The other is that the next chapter is about how a compiler works, and this compiler is accessible to examination because it's written in Logo.

When you're comparing two programming languages an obvious question to ask is "which is better?" Please don't use my partial Pascal compiler as the basis for an answer to that question; it wouldn't be fair. You already know my opinion, but my purpose in this chapter is not to convince you of it. Instead I want you to understand *why* each

---

* The recent trend in computer science education has been a shift from Pascal to C or C++. I haven't followed that trend in this book because from my perspective C illuminates no new issues, it has a more complicated syntax, and it leaves out one interesting Pascal feature: nested procedure definitions (block structure). C++ does introduce the issue of object-oriented programming, but, I think, not in a way that clarifies the issues; if you want to understand OOP you'd do better to learn Object Logo.

language is designed the way it is. For each of the language differences we'll examine, there are good reasons for either choice; the reasons that influence a language designer will depend on the overall goals he or she has for this language.

Programming paradigms

Perhaps the most important aspect of the design of a programming language is the *programming paradigm* that it encourages. A paradigm (it's pronounced "para" as in "parakeet" followed by "dime" as in ten cents) is an approach to organizing a complex program: How do you combine the primitives of a language to accomplish harder tasks? It's an aspect of programming style, but when people say "style" they're usually thinking of smaller details, such as the use of comments in procedure definitions or choosing sensible variable names. Perhaps an example of different paradigms will help.

Here's how the factorial function is usually computed in Logo, using a recursive operation:

```
to fact :n
if :n=0 [output 1]
output :n * fact :n-1
end
```

The goal is to multiply several numbers together, the integers from 1 to :n. We do this by carrying out one multiplication in each recursive invocation. This procedure is written in the *functional programming* paradigm; the main tool for building up complexity is composition of functions. In this example, the result of the recursive `fact` invocation is composed with the primitive * (multiplication) function.

Now consider this alternate approach:

```
to fact.seq :n
localmake "product 1
for [i 1 :n] [make "product (:product * :i)]
output :product
end
```

This is an example of the *sequential programming* paradigm, so called because the `for` instruction carries out a sequence of steps:

• Multiply the accumulated product by 1.
• Multiply the product by 2.
• Multiply it by 3.

... and so on. Instead of a composition of functions, we have a partial result stored in a box, the variable `product`. At each step, the old value is replaced with an updated value.

Although `fact.seq` can be written in Logo, it's not the most natural Logo style. Most versions of Logo don't even provide `for` as a primitive command, although (as we saw in Volume 2) it can be written in Logo.* As we've seen, Logo encourages the functional programming paradigm, in which complicated computations are achieved by means of function composition and recursion. Logo encourages functional programming partly through its emphasis on recursion rather than on iterative control structures, and partly because lists are used as the main data aggregation mechanism. As we saw in Chapter 3, lists encourage an aggregate to be built up one member at a time (as recursive functions do), and discourage mutation (which is crucial to the sequential approach).

In Pascal, the opposite is true. It's possible to write a recursive factorial function in Pascal:

```
function fact(n:integer): integer;
  begin
  if n=0 then
    fact := 1
  else
    fact := n * fact(n-1)
  end;
```

but a habitual Pascal programmer would be much more likely to write this function in sequential style:

```
function fact(n:integer): integer;
  var product, i: integer;

  begin
    product := 1;
    for i := 1 to n do
      product := product * i;
    fact := product
  end;
```

(Don't worry, I know the details of the notation are a mystery to you, but you should still be able to see the relationship between each Pascal version and the corresponding Logo version. The only crucial point about notation right now is that `:=` is the Pascal assignment operator, like `make` in Logo. We'll go into the details of Pascal syntax later.)

---

* Even in Berkeley Logo, `for` is a library procedure rather than a true primitive.

Here's a more complicated example, showing how data aggregates are used in the two paradigms. In Chapter 2 we explored the Simplex lock problem by computing the function

$$f(n) = \begin{cases} \sum_{i=0}^{n-1} \binom{n}{i} \cdot f(i), & \text{if } n > 0; \\ 1, & \text{if } n = 0. \end{cases}$$

using these procedures:

```
to simplex :buttons
output 2 * f :buttons
end

to f :n
if equalp :n 0 [output 1]
output cascade :n [? + ((choose :n (#-1)) * f (#-1))] 0
end
```

Here, the mathematical definition of f in terms of itself is reflected in the recursive nature of the operation f. In Chapter 3, we improved the efficiency of the procedure by remembering smaller values of f to avoid recomputing them; similarly, instead of computing the choose function separately each time, we used old values to compute new ones:

```
to simplex :buttons
output 2 * first (cascade :buttons
                           [fput (sumprods butfirst ?2 ?1) ?1] [1]
                           [fput 1 nextrow ?2] [1 1])
end

to sumprods :a :b
output reduce "sum (map "product :a :b)
end

to nextrow :combs
if emptyp butfirst :combs [output :combs]
output fput (sum first :combs first butfirst :combs) ~
            nextrow butfirst :combs
end
```

The recursive nature of f is less obvious in the second implementation, but the overall technique is still composition of functions. (Recall that the job of `cascade` is to invoke a function repeatedly, in the pattern $f(f(f(\cdots f(x))))$. In this case, `cascade` is computing two functions in parallel; one is a list of values of the Simplex function f and the other is a row of Pascal's triangle.) The availability of higher order functions (in this program I've used `cascade`, `map`, and `reduce`) is another way in which Logo encourages the functional paradigm.

In sequential style, the composition of functions is replaced by a sequence of steps in which values are stored in boxes (members of arrays) and repeatedly replaced with different values:

```
to simplex.seq :buttons
localmake "f (array :buttons+1 0)
localmake "combs (array :buttons+1 0)
local [left right]
setitem 0 :f 1
setitem 0 :combs 1
for [i 1 :buttons] [
  setitem :i :f 0
  make "right 0
  for [j 0 :i-1] [
    make "left :right
    make "right item :j :combs
    setitem :j :combs :left+:right
    setitem :i :f (item :i :f) + (item :j :f)*(item :j :combs)
  ]
  setitem :i :combs 1
]
output 2 * item :buttons :f
end
```

It may take some effort to convince yourself that this procedure really computes the same results as the other versions! Within the procedure, the array `f` contains the values $f(0), f(1), \ldots$ as they are computed one by one; the array `combs` contains one row (at a time) of Pascal's triangle.

The procedure first puts $f(0)$ into the zeroth position of the `f` array and the first row of Pascal's triangle (containing just one 1) in the `combs` array. Then comes a `for` loop that computes $f(1)$, then $f(2)$, and so on, until the desired value is reached. An inner `for` loop fills the same purpose as the `sumprods` function in the previous version of `simplex`: It computes the sum of several terms, not by function composition but by adding each term into the sum separately. The instruction

```
setitem :i :f (item :i :f) + (item :j :f)*(item :j :combs)
```

adds one additional term to the sum each time it's carried out.

The sequential Simplex calculation looks bizarre in Logo, but it's much more natural in Pascal:

```
function simplex(buttons:integer): integer;
var left, right, i, j: integer;
    f, combs: array [0..30] of integer;

  begin
  f[0] := 1;
  combs[0] := 1;
  for i := 1 to buttons do
    begin
    f[i] := 0;
    right := 0;
    for j := 0 to i-1 do
      begin
        left := right;
        right := combs[j];
        combs[j] := left+right;
        f[i] := f[i] + (f[j] * combs[j])
      end;
      combs[i] := 1
    end;
    simplex := 2 * f[buttons]
  end;
```

Pascal is well suited to this style of programming for several reasons. One is that the `f[i]` notation for a member of an array is more compact and more readable than Logo's use of procedure invocations (calling `item` to examine an array member and `setitem` to modify its value). Another, already mentioned, is that `for` is built into Pascal. Perhaps most important is Pascal's *block structure:* the keywords `begin` and `end` can be used to group what would otherwise be separate instructions into one larger instruction. In Logo, the instructions that are repeated in a `for` loop must be part of a list, one of the inputs to the `for` procedure; in principle, the entire `for` invocation is one Logo instruction line.

Both Logo and Pascal are compromises between the functional paradigm and the sequential paradigm. (In Logo, turtle graphics programs are most often done sequentially, whereas the manipulation of words and sentences is generally done functionally.) But Logo is much more of a functional language than Pascal, partly because it supports list processing (you can create lists in Pascal, but it's painful), and even more importantly because in Logo it's easy to invent higher order functions such as `map` and `cascade`. Pascal programmers can't readily invent their own control structures because there's nothing like `run` or `apply` in Pascal, and the built-in control structures are all sequential ones. (In addition to `for`, Pascal has equivalents to the `while` and `do.until` commands in the Berkeley Logo library.) As another example, Logo's `ifelse` primitive can be used either as a command or as an operation, but the Pascal equivalent works only as a command.

Not all programming languages compromise between paradigms. It's rare these days to see a purely sequential language, but it used to be common; both the original Fortran language and the early microcomputer versions of BASIC lacked the ability to handle recursive procedures. Purely functional languages are not widely used in industry, but are of interest to many computer science researchers; the best known example is called ML. In a purely functional language, there is no assignment operator (like `make` in Logo) and no mutators (like `setitem` or `.setfirst`).

There are other programming paradigms besides sequential and functional, although those are the oldest. The sequential paradigm came first because the actual digital computer hardware works sequentially; Fortran, which was the first higher level programming language, was initially viewed as merely an abbreviation for the computer's hardware instruction sequences.* The functional paradigm was introduced with Lisp, the second-oldest programming language still in use. Although Lisp is not a pure functional language (it does have assignment and mutation), its design is firmly based on the idea of functions as the way to express a computation.

Another paradigm that's very popular today is *object-oriented programming*. In this paradigm, we imagine that instead of having a single computer carrying out a single program, the computational world includes many independent "objects," each of which can carry out programs on its own. Each object includes *methods,* which are like local procedures, and *variables,* just like the variables we've used all along except that each belongs to a particular object. If one object wants to know the value of another object's variable, the first object must send a *message* to the second. A message is a request to carry out a method, so the messages that each object accepts depends on the methods that it knows.

---

* Today, we think of programming languages primarily as ways to express problems, rather than as ways to model how computer hardware works. This shift in attitude has allowed the development of non-sequential paradigms. We design languages that are well matched to the problems we want to solve, rather than well matched to the hardware we're using.

Logo has had a sort of glimmer of the object paradigm for many years, because many dialects of Logo include multiple turtles. To move a turtle, you send it a message, using a notation something like

```
ask 7 [forward 100]
```

to send a message to turtle number 7. But this notation, even though it conveys some of the flavor of object-oriented programming, is not truly representative of the paradigm. In a real object system, it would be possible for specific turtles to have their own, specialized `forward` methods. Turtle 7, for example, might be a special "dotted turtle" that draws dotted lines instead of solid lines when it moves forward. One Logo dialect, called Object Logo, does provide a genuine object capability.

Object-oriented programming fits naturally with the sort of problem in which the computer is modeling or simulating a bunch of real-world objects; in fact, the paradigm was invented for *simulation* programs, used to try to answer questions such as "Will it eliminate the traffic jams if we add another lane to this highway, or should we spend the money on more frequent bus service instead?" The objects in the simulation program are people, cars, buses, and lanes. Another example of a problem that lends itself to the object paradigm is a window system, such as the one in Mac OS or in Microsoft Windows. Each window is an object; when a window is displayed so as to hide part of another window, the new window must send a message to the hidden one telling it not to display the hidden region.

Some people argue that object-oriented programming should be used for *every* programming problem, not because the independent object metaphor is always appropriate but because using objects helps with *information hiding;* if every variable belongs to a specific object, the program is less likely to have the kind of bug in which one part of a program messes up a data structure that's used in another part. This can be particularly important, they say, in a large programming problem in which several programmers work on different pieces of the program. When the different programmers' procedures are put together, conflicts can arise, but the object paradigm helps isolate each programmer's work from the others. Although this argument has some merit, I'm cautious about any claim that one particular paradigm is best for all problems. I think programmers should be familiar with all of the major paradigms and be able to pick one according to the needs of each task.

Another important programming paradigm is called *logic programming* or *declarative programming.* In this approach, the programmer doesn't provide an algorithm at all, but instead lists known facts about the problem and poses questions. It's up to the language implementation to search out all the possible solutions to a question. We saw a very simplified version of this paradigm in the discussion of logic problems in Chapter 2. Logic programming is especially well suited to *database* problems, in which we pose questions such as "Who are all the employees of this company who work in the data processing division and have a salary above $40,000?" But, like all the paradigms I've mentioned, logic programming is *universal;* any problem that can be solved by a computer at all can be expressed as a logic program. Logic programming is quite popular in Japan and in Europe, but not so much in the United States, perhaps just because it wasn't invented here.

Interactive and Non-interactive Languages

You use Logo by interacting with the language processor. You issue an instruction, Logo does what you've told it and perhaps prints a result, and then you issue another instruction. You can preserve a sequence of instructions by defining a procedure, in which case that procedure can be invoked in later instructions. But you don't have to define procedures; young children generally start using Logo by issuing primitive turtle motion commands one at a time. Defining procedures can be thought of as extending the repertoire of things Logo knows how to do for future interaction.

By contrast, you write a Pascal program as a complete entity, "feed" the program to the Pascal language processor all at once, and then wait for the results. Often, when you type your program into the computer you aren't dealing with the Pascal processor at all; you use another program, a text editor, to let you enter your Pascal program into the computer. *Then* you start up Pascal itself. (Most microcomputer versions of Pascal include a simple text editor for program entry, just as Logo includes a procedure editor.) Typically you store your Pascal program as a file on a disk and you give the file name as input to the Pascal language processor.

Keep in mind that it's the process of writing and entering a program that's non-interactive in Pascal. It's perfectly possible to write a Pascal program that interacts with the user once it's running, alternating **read** and **write** statements. (However, user input is one of the things I've left out of my Pascal subset, as you'll see shortly.)

If you want to write your own Pascal programs for use with my compiler, you'll need a way to create a disk file containing your new program, using either Logo's procedure editor or some separate editing program. The sample Pascal programs in this chapter are included along with the Logo program files that accompany this book.

Our first example of a complete Pascal program is a version of the Tower of Hanoi puzzle. I described this problem in the first volume of this series. The Logo solution consists of two procedures:

```
to hanoi :number :from :to :other
if equalp :number 0 [stop]
hanoi :number-1 :from :other :to
movedisk :number :from :to
hanoi :number-1 :other :to :from
end

to movedisk :number :from :to
print (sentence [Move disk] :number "from :from "to :to)
end
```

To use these procedures you issue an instruction like

```
? hanoi 5 "a "b "c
Move disk 1 from a to b
Move disk 2 from a to c
Move disk 1 from b to c
Move disk 3 from a to b
Move disk 1 from a to c
... and so on.
```

Here is the corresponding Pascal program. This program is in the file `tower`. (As you can see, Pascal programs begin with a *program name;* in all of the examples in this chapter the file name is the same as the program name, although that isn't a requirement of Pascal.) Never mind the program details for the moment; right now the point is to make sure you know how to get the Pascal compiler to translate it into Logo.

```
program tower;
 {This program solves the 5-disk tower of hanoi problem.}

procedure hanoi(number:integer;from,onto,other:char);
 {Recursive procedure that solves a subproblem of the original problem,
 moving some number of disks, not necessarily 5.  To move n disks, it
 must get the topmost n-1 out of the way, move the nth to the target
 stack, then move the n-1 to the target stack.}

  procedure movedisk(number:integer;from,onto:char);
   {This procedure moves one single disk.  It assumes that the move is
   legal, i.e., the disk is at the top of its stack and the target stack
   has no smaller disks already.  Procedure hanoi is responsible for
   making sure that's all true.}

  begin {movedisk}
    writeln('Move disk ',number:1,' from ',from,' to ',onto)
  end; {movedisk}
```

```
begin {hanoi}
  if number <> 0 then
    begin
      hanoi(number-1,from,other,onto);
      movedisk(number,from,onto);
      hanoi(number-1,other,onto,from)
    end
end; {hanoi}

begin {main program}
  hanoi(5,'a','b','c')
end.
```

Once you have a Pascal program in a disk file, you compile it using the `compile` command with the file name as input:

? compile "tower

The compiler types out the program as it compiles it, partly to keep you from falling asleep while it's working but also so that if the compiler detects an error in the program you'll see where the error was found.

When the compiler has finished processing the *source file* (the file containing the Pascal program) it stops and you see a Logo prompt. At this point the program has been translated into a simulated machine language. To run the program, say

```
? prun "tower
Move disk 1 from a to b
Move disk 2 from a to c
Move disk 1 from b to c
Move disk 3 from a to b
Move disk 1 from a to c
```
... and so on.

The input to the `prun` (Pascal run) command is the program name—the word that comes after `program` at the beginning of the source file.

The difference between an interactive and a non-interactive language is not just an arbitrary choice of "user interface" style. This choice reflects a deeper distinction between two different ways of thinking about what a computer program is. In Logo there is really no such thing as a "program." Each procedure is an entity on its own. You may think of one particular procedure as the top-level one, but Logo doesn't know that; you could invoke any procedure directly by using an interactive instruction naming that procedure. Logo does have the idea of a *workspace*, a collection of procedures stored together in a file because they are related. But a workspace need not be a tree-structured hierarchy with one top-level procedure and the others as subprocedures. It can be a collection of utility procedures with no top-level umbrella, like the Berkeley Logo library. It can be a group of projects that are conceptually related but with several independent top-level procedures, like the two memoization examples, the two sorting algorithms, the tree data base, and other projects in the `algs` workspace of Chapter 3.

By contrast, a Pascal program is considered a single entity. It always begins with the word `program` and ends with a period, by analogy with an English sentence. (The subprocedures and the individual statements within the program are separated with semicolons because they are analogous to English clauses.*) It makes no sense to give the Pascal compiler a source file containing just procedures without a main program.

Why did Logo's designers choose an interactive program development approach, while Pascal's designers chose a whole-program paradigm? Like all worthwhile questions, this one has more than one answer. And like many questions in language design, this one has two broad *kinds* of answer: the answers based on the implementation strategy for the language and the ones based on underlying programming goals.

The most obvious answer is that Pascal is a *compiled* language and Logo is an *interpreted* one. That is, most Pascal language processors are *compilers:* programs that translate a program from one language into another, like translating a book from English into Chinese. Most compilers translate from a source language like Pascal into the native *machine language* of whatever computer you're using. (My Pascal compiler translates into a *simulated* machine language that's actually processed by Logo procedures.) By contrast, most Logo versions are *interpreters:* programs that directly carry out the instructions in your source program, without translating it to a different ("object") language.**

To understand why interpreters tend to go with interactive languages, while compilers usually imply "batch mode" program development, think about the "little person" metaphor that's often used in teaching Logo. If you think of the computer as being full of little people who know how to carry out the various procedures you've written, the one who's really in charge is not the one who carries out your top-level procedure, but

---

* I say "English" because I am writing for an English-speaking audience, but in fact Pascal was designed by a largely European committee including native speakers of several languages; principal designer Niklaus Wirth is Swiss. Their languages all have periods and semicolons, though.

** This is another case in which the same word has two unrelated technical meanings. The use of "object" in describing the result of a compilation (object program, object language) has nothing to do with object-oriented programming.

rather the one representing the Logo interpreter itself. If the procedure specialists are like circus performers, the Logo interpreter is the ringmaster. The circus metaphor is actually a pretty good one, because on the one hand each performer is an autonomous person, but at the same time the performers have to cooperate in order to put on a show. The relevance of the metaphor to this discussion is that in a compiled language there is no "ringmaster." The compiler is more closely analogous to a bird that hatches an egg (your program) and then pushes the new bird out of the nest to fend for itself. In a compiled language there is no provision for an interactive interface to which you can give commands that control the running of your program, unless your program itself includes such an interface.

Saying the same thing in a different way, the Logo interpreter is part of the environment in which any Logo program operates. (That's why Logo can provide a facility like the `run` command to allow your program to construct new Logo instructions as it progresses.) But a Pascal compiler does its job, translating your program into another form, and then disappears. Whatever mechanisms are available to control your program have to be built into the program. For example, my Pascal version of the Tower of Hanoi program includes the top-level instruction that starts up the solution for five disks. In the Logo version, that instruction isn't considered part of the program; instead, you direct Logo interactively to invoke the `hanoi` procedure.

The distinction between compiled and interpreted languages is not as absolute as it once was. There are versions of Logo in which each procedure is compiled as you define it, but it's still possible to give instructions interactively. (Some such versions include both a compiler and an interpreter; in others, the "interpreter" just arranges to compile each instruction you type as if it were a one-line program.) And many current Pascal compilers don't compile into the machine language of the host computer, but rather into an *intermediate* language called "P-code" that is then interpreted by another program, a P-code interpreter. P-code is called an intermediate language because the level of detail in a P-code program is in between that of a language you'd want to use and that of the underlying machine language. Its primitives are simple and quick, not complex control structures like `if` or `for`. The advantage of a Pascal language processor based on P-code is that the compiler is *portable*—it can work on any computer. All that's needed to start using Pascal on a new computer is a P-code interpreter, which is a relatively easy programming project.

So far I've been explaining a language design decision (interactive or non-interactive development) in terms of an implementation constraint (interpreted or compiled). But it's possible to look beyond that explanation to ask *why* someone would choose to design a compiler rather than an interpreter or vice versa.

The main advantage of a compiler is that the finished object program runs fast, since it is directly executed in the native language of the host computer. (An interpreter, too, ultimately carries out the program in the computer's native language. But the interpreter must decide which native language instructions to execute for a given source language instruction each time that instruction is evaluated. In a compiled language that translation process happens only once, producing an object program that requires no further translation while it's running.) The tradeoff is that the compilation process itself is slow. If you're writing a program that will be used every day forever, the compiled language has the advantage because the development process only happens once and then the program need not be recompiled. On the other hand, during program development the compiled language may be at a disadvantage, because any little change in one instruction requires that the entire program be recompiled. (For some languages there are *incremental* compilers that can keep track of what part of the program you've changed and only recompile that part.)

A compiled language like Pascal (or Fortran or C), then, makes sense in a business setting where a program is written for practical use, generally using well-understood algorithms so that the development process should be straightforward. An interpreted language like Logo (or Lisp or BASIC) makes more sense in a research facility where new algorithms are being explored and the development process may be quite lengthy, but the program may never be used in routine production. (In fact nobody uses BASIC for research purposes, because of other weaknesses, but its interactive nature is a plus.) Another environment in which interaction is important is education; a computer science student writes programs that may *never* actually be run except for testing. The program is of interest only as long as it doesn't work yet. For such programs the speed advantage of a compiled program is irrelevant.

There are also reasons that have nothing to do with implementation issues. I've spoken earlier of two conflicting views of computer science, which I've called the software engineering view and the artificial intelligence view. In the former, the program development process is seen as beginning with a clear, well-defined idea of what the program should do. This idea is written down as a *program specification* that forms the basis for the actual programming. From that starting point, the program is developed top-down; first the main program is written in terms of subprocedures that are planned but not written yet; then the lower-level procedures are written to fill in the details. No procedure is written until it's clear how that procedure fits into a specific overall program. Since Pascal's developers are part of the software engineering camp, it's not surprising that a Pascal program takes the form of an integrated whole in which each procedure must be *inside* a larger one, rather than a collection of more autonomous procedures. By contrast, Logo is a product of the artificial intelligence camp, for whom program development is a more complicated process involving bottom-up as well as top-down design. AI researchers recognize that they may begin a project with only a vague idea of what the finished program will do or how it will be organized. It's appropriate, then, to start by writing program fragments that deal with whatever subtasks you *do* understand, then see how those pieces can fit together to complete the overall project. Development isn't a straight line from the abstract specification to the concrete subprocedures; it's a zigzag path in which the programmer gets an idea, tries it out, then uses the results as the basis for more thinking about ideas.

Traditionally, an interpreter has been the primary tool to facilitate interactive program development. Recently, though, software developers have brought a more interactive flavor to compiled languages by inventing the idea of an *integrated development environment* (IDE), in which a compiler is one piece of a package that also includes a language-specific editor (one that knows about the syntax of the language and automatically provides, for example, the keyword `do` that must follow a `for` in Pascal), online documentation, and a *debugger,* which is a program that permits you to follow the execution of your program one step at a time, like the `step` command in Berkeley Logo. The idea is to have your cake and eat it too: You use the IDE tools during program development, but once your program is debugged, you're left with a fast compiled version that can be run without the IDE.

Block Structure

So far we've been looking at how each language thinks about a program as a whole. We turn now to the arrangement of pieces within a program or a procedure.

A Logo procedure starts with a *title line,* followed by the instructions in the procedure *body* and then the `end` line. The purpose of the title line is to give names to the procedure itself and to its inputs.

The structure of a Pascal program is similar in some ways, but with some complications. The program starts with a *header* line, very much analogous to the title line in Logo. The word `tower` in the header line of our sample program is the name of the program. Skipping over the middle part of the program for the moment, the part between `begin` and `end` in the last few lines is the *statement part* of the program, just as in Logo. The word `end` in the Pascal program is not exactly analogous to the `end` line in a Logo procedure; it's a kind of closing bracket, matching the `begin` before it. The period right after the final `end` is what corresponds to the Logo `end` line.

What makes Pascal's structure different from Logo's is the part I've skipped over, the declaration of procedures. In Logo, every procedure is a separate entity. In Pascal, the declaration of the procedure `hanoi`, for example, is *part of* the program `tower`. This particular program uses no global variables, but if it did, those variables would also have to be declared within the program. If the program used global variables `a`, `b`, `i`, and `j` then it might begin

```
program tower;
var a,b:real;
    i,j:integer;
procedure hanoi(number:integer;from,onto,other:char);
```

In summary, a Pascal program consists of

1. the header line
2. the declaration part (variables and procedures)
3. the statement part
4. the final punctuation (period)

But notice that the procedure `hanoi`, declared inside `tower`, has the *same* structure as the entire program. It begins with a header line; its declaration part includes the declaration of procedure `movedisk`; it has a statement part between `begin` and `end`; its final punctuation is a semicolon instead of a period.

What does it *mean* for one procedure to be declared inside another? You already know what a *local variable* means; if a variable `v` belongs to a procedure `p` then that variable exists only while the procedure is running; at another point in the program there might be a different variable with the same name. In Pascal, the same is true for local procedures. In our example program, the procedure `movedisk` exists only while procedure `hanoi` is running. It would be an error to try to invoke `movedisk` directly from the main program.

The header line for a procedure can include names for its inputs, just as the title line of a Logo procedure names its inputs. A useful bit of terminology is that the variable names in the procedure header are called *formal parameters* to distinguish them from the expressions that provide particular input values when the procedure is actually invoked; the latter are called *actual arguments*. The words "parameter" and "argument" are both used for what we call an "input" in Logo.*

---

* I'm misleading you a little bit by calling it a "header line." Like any part of a Pascal program, the header can extend over more than one line, or can be on the same line with other things. The end of the header is marked with a semicolon. In Pascal a line break is just like a space between words. However, there are conventions for properly formatting a Pascal program. Even though

The sequence of header, declarations, statements, and punctuation is called a *block*. Pascal is called a *block structured* language because of the way blocks can include smaller blocks. Another aspect of block structure is Pascal's use of *compound statements*. A sequence of the form

```
begin statement ; statement ; statement end
```

is called a compound statement. An example from the `tower` program is

```
begin
  hanoi(number-1,from,other,onto);
  movedisk(number,from,onto);
  hanoi(number-1,other,onto,from)
end
```

(Notice that semicolons go *between* statements within this sequence; none is needed after the last statement of the group. This syntactic rule is based on the analogy between Pascal statements and English clauses that I mentioned earlier.) For example, Pascal includes a conditional statement whose form is

```
if condition then statement
```

The "statement" part can be a single *simple* statement, like a procedure call, or it can be a compound statement delimited by `begin` and `end`. Because the general term "block structured language" refers to any syntactic grouping of smaller units into a larger one, including compound statements, you may hear the word "block" used to refer to a compound statement even though that's not the official Pascal meaning.

Statement Types

In Logo we don't talk about different kinds of statements like compound, simple, and so on. *Every* Logo instruction (well, all but `to`) is a procedure invocation. `If`, for example, is a procedure whose first input is `true` or `false` and whose second input is a list containing instructions to be carried out if the first input is `true`. In Pascal there are several different kinds of statements, each with its own syntax.

---

the Pascal compiler doesn't care about spacing and line breaks, people always do it as I've shown you here, with subordinate parts of the program indented and each statement on a separate line.

You know about compound statements. You've seen one example of if, which is one of several *structured* statements in Pascal. Other examples include

```
while condition do statement;
repeat statements until condition

while x < 0 do
  begin
    increase(x);
    writeln(x)
  end;

repeat
  increase(x);
  writeln(x)
until x >= 0;
```

These are like the `while` and `do.until` tools in Berkeley Logo. `While`, like if, requires a single statement (which can be a compound statement between `begin` and `end`) after the `do`. However, the words `repeat` and `until` implicitly delimit a compound statement, so you can put more than one statement between them without using `begin` and `end`. Another example is `for`, which you'll see in use in a moment. Continuing the analogy with English grammar, a compound statement is like a compound sentence with several independent (or coordinate) clauses; a structured statement is like a complex sentence, with a dependent (or subordinate) clause. (If you always hated grammar, you can just ignore this analogy.)

There are basically only two kinds of simple statement: the procedure call, which you've already seen, and the *assignment* statement used to give a variable a new value. This latter is Pascal's version of `make` in Logo; it takes the form

```
variable := expression

slope := ychange/xchange
```

As I've already mentioned, the variable must have been declared either in a procedure heading or in a `var` declaration. (Assignment is represented with the two-character symbol `:=` because `=` by itself means `equalp` rather than `make`.)

I say there are "basically" only two kinds because each of these has some special cases that look similar but follow different rules. For example, printing to the computer screen is done by what looks like an invocation of `write` (analogous to `type` in Logo) or `writeln` ("write line," analogous to `print`). But these are not ordinary procedures.

Not only do they take a variable number of arguments, but the arguments can take a special form not ordinarily allowed. In the `movedisk` procedure in the `tower` program, one of the arguments to `writeln` is

```
number:1
```

The ":1" here means "using one print position unless more are needed to fit the number." Pascal print formatting is designed to emphasize the printing of numbers in columns, so the default is to print each number with a fairly large number of characters, with spaces at the left if the number doesn't have enough digits. The exact number of characters depends on the type of number and the dialect of Pascal, but 10 is a typical number for integers. So

```
writeln(1,2,3,4);
writeln(1000,2000,3000,4000);
```

will give a result looking something like this:

```
         1         2         3         4
      1000      2000      3000      4000
```

In `movedisk` I had to say ":1" to avoid all that extra space.

What are the pros and cons of using a variety of syntax rules for different kinds of statements? One reason for the Pascal approach is that differences in meaning can be implicit in the definitions of different statement types instead of having to be made explicit in a program. Don't worry; you're not expected to understand what that sentence meant, but you will as soon as you see an example. In Logo we say

```
if :x < 10 [increment "x]
while [:x < 10] [increment "x]
```

Why is the predicate expression `:x < 10` in a quoted list in the case of `while` but not for `if`? `If` wants the expression to be evaluated once, *before* `if` is invoked. The actual input to `if` is not that expression but the value of the expression, either `true` or `false`. `While`, on the other hand, wants to evaluate that expression repeatedly. If Logo evaluated the expression ahead of time and gave `while` an input of `true` or `false` it wouldn't be able to know when to stop repeating.

The fact that `if` wants the condition evaluated once but `while` wants to evaluate it repeatedly has nothing to do with the syntax of Logo; the same is true in Pascal. But in Pascal you say

```
if x<10 then increment(x);
while x<10 do increment(x);
```

In Logo the fact that `if`'s condition is evaluated in advance but `while`'s isn't is made explicit by the use of square brackets. In Pascal it's just part of the *semantic* definitions of the `if` and `while` statements. (*Syntax* is the form in which something is represented; *semantics* is the meaning of that something.)

One more example: Beginning students of Logo often have trouble understanding why you say

```
make "new :old
```

to assign the value of one variable to another variable. Why is the first quoted and the second dotted? Of course you understand that it's because the first input to `make` is the *name* of the variable you want to set, while the second is the *value* that you want to give it. But in Pascal this distinction is implicit in the semantic definition of the assignment statement; you just say

```
new := old
```

Since beginning Logo students have trouble with quotes and dots in `make`, you might think that the Pascal approach is better. But beginning Pascal students have a trouble of their own; they tend to get thrown by statements like

```
x := x+1
```

This doesn't look quite as bad as the BASIC or Fortran version in which the symbol for assignment is just an equal sign, but it's still easy to get confused because the symbol "`x`" means two very different things in its two appearances here. In the Logo version

```
make "x :x+1
```

the explicit difference in appearance between `"x` and `:x` works to our advantage.

Which way do you find it easier to learn something: Do you want to start with a simple, perhaps partly inaccurate understanding and learn about the difficult special cases later, or do you prefer to be told the whole truth from the beginning? I've posed the question in a way that shows my own preference, I'm afraid, but there are many people with the opposite view.

The issue about whether or not to make the semantics of some action implicit in the syntax of the language is the most profound reason for the difference between Logo's single instruction syntax and Pascal's collection of statement types, but there are other implications as well. One virtue of the Pascal compound statement is that it makes for short, manageable instruction lines. You've seen Logo procedures in these books in which one "line" goes on for three or four printed lines on the page, e.g., when the instruction list input to `if` contains several instructions. It's a particularly painful problem in the versions of Logo that don't allow continuation lines.

On the other hand, Logo's syntactic uniformity contributes to its *extensibility*. In the example above, `if` is a Logo primitive, whereas `while` is a library procedure written in Logo. But the difference isn't obvious; the two are used in syntactically similar ways. You can't write control structures like `while` in Pascal because there's nothing analogous to `run` to allow a list of instructions to be an input to a procedure, but even if you could, it would have to take the form

```
while(condition,statement)
```

because that's what a procedure call looks like. But it's not what a built-in Pascal control structure looks like.

Shuffling a Deck Using Arrays

It's time for another sample Pascal program. Program `cards` is a Pascal version of the problem of shuffling a deck of cards that we discussed in Chapter 3. It includes local variables, assignment statements, and the `for` structured statement. It also will lead us into some additional language design issues.

```
program cards;
  {Shuffle a deck of cards}

var ranks:array [0..51] of integer;
    suits:array [0..51] of char;
    i:integer;

procedure showdeck;
  {Print the deck arrays}

  begin {showdeck}
    for i := 0 to 51 do
      begin
        if i mod 13 = 0 then writeln;
        write(ranks[i]:3,suits[i]);
      end;
    writeln;
    writeln
  end; {showdeck}
```

```
   procedure deck;
     {Create the deck in order}

      var i,j:integer;
          suitnames:packed array [0..3] of char;

      begin {deck}
        suitnames := 'HSDC';
        for i := 0 to 12 do
          for j := 0 to 3 do
            begin
              ranks[13*j+i] := i+1;
              suits[13*j+i] := suitnames[j]
            end;
        writeln('The initial deck:');
        showdeck
      end; {deck}

   procedure shuffle;
    {Shuffle the deck randomly}

      var rank,i,j:integer;
          suit:char;

      begin {shuffle}
        for i := 51 downto 1 do {For each card in the deck}
          begin
            j := random(i+1); {Pick a random card before it}
            rank := ranks[i]; {Interchange ranks}
            ranks[i] := ranks[j];
            ranks[j] := rank;
            suit := suits[i]; {Interchange suits}
            suits[i] := suits[j];
            suits[j] := suit
          end;
        writeln('The shuffled deck:');
        showdeck
      end; {shuffle}

   begin {main program}
     deck;
     shuffle
   end.
```

Experienced Pascal programmers will notice that this program isn't written in the most elegant possible Pascal style. This is partly because of issues in Pascal that I don't want to talk about (records) and partly because of issues that I *do* want to talk about in the next section (scope).

Here's what happens when you run the program:

```
? prun "cards
The initial deck:

   1H   2H   3H   4H   5H   6H   7H   8H   9H  10H  11H  12H  13H
   1S   2S   3S   4S   5S   6S   7S   8S   9S  10S  11S  12S  13S
   1D   2D   3D   4D   5D   6D   7D   8D   9D  10D  11D  12D  13D
   1C   2C   3C   4C   5C   6C   7C   8C   9C  10C  11C  12C  13C

The shuffled deck:

   2D  11D   6S   9D   6C  10H   8D  11C   3D   4C   5H   4S   1D
   5C   5D   6D   9S   4D   8C  13S  13D  10C   9H  10D   5S  12D
  13H   9C   3C   1S  10S   4H  12S  11S  12H  11H   2H   3H   1H
  13C   8H   7C   2C   1C   7S   6H   2S   7D   8S  12C   3S   7H
```

The Pascal `for` is somewhat like the Berkeley Logo `for` in its semantics, although of course the syntax is quite different. The step value must be either 1 (indicated by the keyword `to`) or −1 (`downto`). By the way, if you've been wondering why I changed one of the variable names in the Tower of Hanoi program from `to` in the Logo version to `onto` in the Pascal version, it's because `to` is a *reserved word* in Pascal and can't be used as the name of anything.

The Pascal standard does not include a `random` function. Most practical versions of Pascal do provide a random number generator of some sort; since there's no standard, I've chosen to implement the kind that's most useful for the kind of programming I'm interested in, namely the Logo `random` that takes an integer argument and returns an integer between zero and one less than the argument.

Lexical Scope

Program `cards` has three procedures: `showdeck`, `deck`, and `shuffle`. Each of these is declared directly in the top-level program. However, `showdeck` is not *invoked* directly at top level; it's used by the other two procedures. (This is one of the questionable bits of programming style I've put in for the sake of the following discussion; ordinarily I think I'd have put the statements that invoke `showdeck` in the main program block.)

If you read the program carefully you'll see that `showdeck` uses a variable `i` but does *not* declare that variable.* (When a variable is used but not declared within a certain procedure, that use of the variable is called a *free reference*. A use of a variable that *is* declared in the same block is called a *bound* reference.) There are three variables named `i` in the program: one in the outer block, one in `deck`, and one in `shuffle`. When, for example, the main program calls `deck` and `deck` calls `showdeck`, which variable `i` does `showdeck` use?

In Logo the answer would be that `showdeck` uses the `i` belonging to `deck`, the procedure that invoked it. That's because Logo follows the rules of *dynamic scope:* A free reference to a variable is directed to the variables of the procedure that invoked the current one, then if necessary to the variables of the procedure that invoked that one, and so on up to the global variables. (Dynamic scope is discussed more fully in the first volume of this series.)

In Pascal, `showdeck` uses the `i` belonging to the main program. That's because a free reference to a variable is directed to *the block within which the current procedure was declared,* then to the block surrounding that one, and so on up to the outermost program block. This rule is called *lexical* scope. The set of blocks surrounding a given block, smaller to larger, is its *lexical environment.* The lexical environment of `showdeck` is

```
{showdeck, cards}
```

The lexical environment of `movedisk` in the `tower` program is

```
{movedisk, hanoi, tower}
```

The set of procedure invocations leading to a given procedure is its *dynamic environment.* A procedure's dynamic environment isn't always the same; for example, the dynamic environment of `showdeck` is sometimes

```
{showdeck, deck, cards}
```

---

* Actually, the Pascal language requires that the variable used in a `for` statement *must* be declared in the same procedure in which the `for` appears; program `cards` is not legal Pascal for that reason. What's the purpose of that restriction? Suppose that this procedure was invoked from within another `for` loop in another procedure, and both use the same variable; then both procedures would be trying to assign conflicting values to that variable. Berkeley Logo's `for` automatically makes its variable local to the `for` procedure itself, for the same reason. But my Pascal compiler lets us get away with breaking this rule, and I've done it deliberately to make a point.

and sometimes

```
{showdeck, shuffle, cards}
```

The word "lexical" is the adjective form of *lexicon,* which means "dictionary." It's used in this computer science context because the lexical context of a procedure has to do with where it's defined, just as words are defined in a dictionary. The word "dynamic" means *in motion;* it's used because the dynamic context of a procedure keeps changing as the program runs.

What are the reasons behind the choice of lexical or dynamic scope? This is another choice that was originally made for implementation reasons. It turns out to be easy for an interpreter to use dynamic scope, but for a compiler it's much easier to use lexical scope. That's because the interpreter makes the decision about which variable to use while the program is running and the dynamic environment is known, but the compiler has to translate the program *before* it is run. At "compile time" there isn't one fixed dynamic environment, but there is a single, already-known lexical environment. Originally, interpreted languages like Logo, Lisp, and APL all used dynamic scope, while compiled ones like Fortran and Pascal used lexical scope. (There was even a period of time when Lisp systems offered both an interpreter and a compiler, and the behavior of the same program was different depending on whether you compiled it or interpreted it because of different scope rules.)

More recent dialects of Lisp, such as Common Lisp and Scheme, have been designed to use lexical scope even when interpreted. Their designers think lexical scope is better for reasons that don't depend on the implementation technique. One reason is that dynamic scope allows for programming errors that don't arise when lexical scope is used. In Logo, suppose you write a procedure that makes a free reference to some variable v. What you intended, let's say, was to use a global variable by that name. But you've forgotten that your procedure is sometimes invoked by another procedure that you wrote two weeks ago that happens to have an input named v. It can be very hard to figure out why your procedure is suddenly getting the wrong variable. With lexical scope, it's much easier to keep track of the context in which your procedure is defined, to make sure there are no local variables v in the lexical environment.

It's possible to argue in favor of dynamic scope also. One argument is that in a lexically scoped language certain kinds of tool procedures can't be written at all: the ones like `while` or `for` that take an instruction list as input and `run` the list repeatedly. Suppose you write a procedure in Logo that contains an instruction like

```
while [:degrees < 0] [make "degrees :degrees+360]
```

What variable `degrees` do you want this instruction to use? Presumably you mean the same variable `degrees` that is used by other instructions in the same procedure. But if Logo used lexical scope, then `while` wouldn't have access to the local variables of your procedure. (It's possible to design other features into a lexically scoped language to get around this limitation, but the necessary techniques are more complicated than the straightforward way you can write `while` in Logo.)

Another argument for dynamic scope, with particular relevance to Logo, is that dynamic scope fits better with the expectations of an unsophisticated programmer who hasn't thought about scope at all. One of the design goals of Logo is to be easy for such beginners. Until now we've been talking about scope in terms of naming conflicts: what happens if two variables have the same name. But suppose you write a program with a bunch of procedures, with a bunch of *distinct* variable names used as inputs. It makes life very simple if all those variables are available whenever you want them, so you don't have to think in such detail about how to get a certain piece of information down the procedure invocation chain to a subprocedure. If some variables are accessible to subprocedures but others aren't, that's one more mystery to make programming seem difficult. In particular, dynamic scope can simplify the debugging of a Logo program. If you arrange for your program to `pause` at the moment when an error happens, then you can enter Logo instructions, with all of the local variables of *all* pending procedure invocations available, to help you figure out the reason for the error. Debuggers for lexically scoped languages require a more complicated debugging mechanism in which the programmer must explicitly shift focus from one procedure to another.

In the situations we've seen, lexical scope always acts as a *restriction* on the availability of variables to subprocedures. That is, a procedure's lexical environment is always a subset of its dynamic environment. (Suppose procedure `a` includes the definition of procedure `b`, which in turn includes the definition of `c`. So the lexical environment of `c` is `{c,b,a}`. You might imagine that `c`'s dynamic environment could be `{c,a}` if procedure `a` invoked `c` directly, but in fact that's illegal. Just as `a` can't use `b`'s local variables, it can't use `b`'s local procedures either. The reason the dynamic environment can be different from the lexical one at all is that two procedures can be part of the same block, like `showdeck` and `deck` in the `cards` program.) In Lisp, it's possible for a procedure to return *another procedure* as its output—not just the name of the procedure or the text of the procedure, as we could do in Logo, but the procedure itself, lexical environment and all. When such a procedure is later invoked from some other part of the program, the procedure's lexical environment may not be a subset of its dynamic environment, and so lexical scope gives it access to variables that it couldn't use under dynamic scope rules. That's a powerful argument in favor of lexical scope for Lisp, but it doesn't apply to Pascal.

One special scope rule in Pascal applies to procedures declared in the same block: The one declared later can invoke the one declared earlier, but not the other way around. In the `cards` program, `deck` can call `showdeck` but `showdeck` can't call `deck`. There is no deep reason for this restriction; it's entirely for the benefit of the compiler. One of the design goals of Pascal was that it should be easy to write a compiler that goes through the source program once, from beginning to end, without having to back up and read part of the program twice. In particular, when the compiler sees a procedure invocation, it must already know what inputs that procedure requires; therefore, it must have already read the header of the subprocedure. Usually you can get around this restriction by rearranging the procedures in your program, but for the times when that doesn't work Pascal provides a kludge that lets you put the header in one place in the source file and defer the rest of the procedure until later.

Typed Variables

Berkeley Logo has three data types: *word, list,* and *array.* (Numbers are just words that happen to be full of digits.) But a *variable* in Logo does not have a type associated with it; any datum can be the value of any variable.

Pascal has lots of types, and every variable belongs to exactly one of them. In the sample programs so far we've used five types: *char, integer, array of char, array of integer,* and *packed array of char.* When a variable is declared, the declaration says what type it is.

The selection of data types is the area in which my Pascal compiler is most lacking; I've implemented only a few of the possible types. I'll describe the ones available in my compiler in detail and give hints about the others.

The fundamental types out of which all others are built are the *scalar* types that represent a single value, as opposed to an aggregate like an array or a list. Pascal has four:

> `integer` a positive or negative whole number (e.g., `23`)
> `real` a number including decimal fraction part (e.g., `-5.0`)
> `char` a single character (e.g., `'Q'`)
> `Boolean` `true` or `false`

Pascal also has several kinds of aggregate types. The only one that I've implemented is the array, which is a fixed number of uniform elements. By "uniform" I mean that all members of the array must be of the same type. Full Pascal allows the members to be of any type, including an aggregate type, as long as they're all the same, so you could say

```
var a : array [1..10] of array [1..4] of integer;
```

to get an array of arrays. But in my subset Pascal the members of an array must be scalars. This restriction is not too severe because Pascal arrays can have *multiple indices;* instead of the above you can use the equivalent

```
var a : array [1..10, 1..4] of integer;
```

This declaration creates a two-dimensional array whose members have names like `a[3,2]`.

The notation `1..10` is called a *range;* it indicates the extent of the array. Berkeley Logo arrays ordinarily start with index one, so a Logo instruction like

```
make "ten array 10
```

is equivalent to the Pascal declaration

```
var ten:array [1..10] of something
```

except that the Logo array need not have uniform members.* (Also, a subtle difference is that the Logo array is an independent datum that can be the value of a variable just as a number can be the value of a variable. The Pascal array *is* the variable; you can change the contents of individual members of the array but it's meaningless to speak of changing the value of that variable to be something other than that array.)

In Pascal an index range doesn't have to be numbers; you can use any scalar type except real:

```
var frequency : array ['a'..'z'] of integer;
```

might be used in a program that counts the frequency of use of letters, such as a cryptography program. The members of this array would be used by referring to things like `frequency['w']`. (In Pascal documentation there is a word for "scalar type other than real": It's called an *ordinal* type.)

A *packed array* is one that's represented in the computer in a way that takes up as little memory as possible. Ordinary arrays are stored so as to make it as fast as possible to examine or change an individual element. The distinction may or may not be important for a given type on a given computer. For example, most current home computers have their memory organized in *bytes* that are just the right size for a single character. On such

---

* The Berkeley Logo `array` primitive can take an optional second input to specify a different starting index.

a computer, an array of char and a packed array of char will probably be represented identically. But one of my favorite larger computers, the Digital Equipment Corporation PDP-10, had its memory organized in *words* of 36 bits, enough for five 7-bit characters with one bit left over. A packed array of char, on the PDP-10, would be represented with five characters per word; an ordinary array of char might store only one character per word, wasting some space in order to simplify the task of finding the *n*th character of the array.

My compiler, which is meant to be simple rather than efficient, ignores the **packed** declaration. The reason I used it in the **cards** program is to illustrate a rule of Pascal: The statement

```
suitnames := 'HSDC'
```

assigns a *constant string* to the array variable **suitnames**, and such assignments are allowed only to packed arrays of char. Also, the size of the array must equal the length of the string. If **suitnames** were an array of length 10, for example, I'd have had to say

```
suitnames := 'HSDC      '
```

filling up the unused part of the array explicitly with spaces.

In an assignment statement, the type of the variable on the left must be the same as the type of the expression on the right. An assignment can copy one array into another if it involves two variables of exactly the same type:

```
var a,b:array [3..17] of real;

a := b
```

but except for the case of packed arrays of char mentioned above there is no way to represent a constant array in a Pascal program. If you want an array of all the prime numbers less than 10 you have to initialize it one member at a time:

```
var primes : array [1..4] of integer;

primes[1] := 2;
primes[2] := 3;
primes[3] := 5;
primes[4] := 7
```

In scalar assignments, a slight relaxation of the rules is allowed in that you may assign an integer value to a real variable. The value is converted to a real number (e.g., 17 to 17.0). The opposite is *not* allowed, but there are two built-in functions trunc (for "truncate") and round that can be used to convert a real value to an integer. Trunc cuts off the fraction part, so trunc(4.99) is 4. Round rounds to the nearest integer.

Pascal provides the usual infix arithmetic operations +, −, *, and /, following the usual precedence rules, just as in Logo. The result of any of these is integer if both operands are integer, otherwise real, except that the result of / (division) is always real. There are integer division operations div (integer quotient) and mod (integer remainder); both operands to these must also be integers. The relational operators = (like equalp in Logo), < (less than), > (greater than), <= (less than or equal to), >= (greater than or equal to), and <> (not equal to) take two real or integer operands and yield a Boolean result. There are also Boolean operators and, or, and not, just like the Logo ones except that they use infix syntax:

```
(x < 0) and (y <= 28)
```

Additional Types in Standard Pascal

Standard Pascal, but not my version, includes other aggregate types besides the array. One such type is the *record;* a record is a non-uniform aggregate, but the "shape" of the aggregate must be declared in advance. For example, you can declare a record containing three integers and an array of 10 characters. In the **cards** program, instead of two separate arrays for ranks and suits I could have said

```
var carddeck: array [0..51] of record
                                  rank:integer;
                                  suit:char
                               end;
```

Then to refer to the rank of card number 4 I'd say

```
carddeck[4].rank
```

and that would be an integer. A *pointer* is a variable whose value is the memory address of a record; pointer variables can be used to implement dynamic data structures like Logo lists by building explicitly the collections of boxes and arrows illustrated in some of the pictures in Chapter 3. But it's hard to build anything in Pascal that's *quite* like Logo lists, even using pointers, because what's in each box has to belong to some particular predeclared type.

Real Pascal also includes user-defined types. There is a `type` declaration that goes before the `var` declaration in a block:

```
type string = packed array [1..10] of char;
```

Variable declarations can then use `string` as the type of the variable being declared. In fact, standard Pascal *requires* the use of named types in certain situations. For example, in a procedure header the formal parameters must be given a named type (either a built-in scalar type like `integer` or a defined type like `string`); since I haven't implemented `type` my compiler allows

```
procedure paul(words:packed array [1..10] of char);
```

although standard Pascal doesn't allow such a header.

You can also define *subrange* types:

```
type dieface = 1..6;
```

This type is really an integer, but it's constrained to have only values in the given range. This particular one might be used for a variable whose value is to represent the result of rolling a six-sided die. Finally, there are *enumerated* types:

```
type Beatle = (John, Paul, George, Ringo);
```

This type is used for a variable that represents one of a small number of possible things. In reality it's also a kind of integer; the word `John` represents 0, `Paul` is 1, and so on. In fact, it's only during the compilation of the program that Pascal remembers the names of the possible values; you can't read or print these variables during the running of the program.

Critique of Typed Variables

Why would anyone want to use a subrange or other restricted type? If the program works using a variable of type `dieface`, it would work just as well if the variable were of type `integer`. The only difference is that using a subrange type is slower because the program has to check (at run time) to make sure that any value you try to assign to that variable is in the approved range.

According to Pascal enthusiasts, the virtue of restricted types, like the virtue of typed variables in the first place, is that their use helps catch program bugs. For example, in the `cards` program, procedure `shuffle` has variables i and j that are used to index the arrays `ranks` and `suits`. How do we know there isn't an error in the program so that one of those variables is given a value that isn't a valid index for those arrays? Such an error would be caught when we *use* the index variable to try to refer to an array element that doesn't exist, but it's easier to debug the program if we get the error message at the moment when the variable is assigned the incorrect value. So I should have declared

```
var i,j : 0..51;
```

instead of using `integer`. (Of course one reason I didn't use a subrange type is that I didn't implement them in my compiler!)

The trouble is that strict typing of variables is an unnecessary pain in the neck.* Take this business of array index bounds. Here is a possible piece of Pascal program:

```
i := 0;
while i <= 51 do
   begin
     writeln(ranks[i]:3,suits[i]);
     i := i+1
   end
```

There's nothing wrong with this. It will print the value of each member of the two arrays, starting from index 0 and continuing through 51. However, at the end of the `while` statement, the variable i has the value 52. This is *not* an error; the program does *not* try to refer to member 52 of the arrays. But if we declared i as a subrange type the way we "should," the program will give an error message and die. This particular example could be rewritten using `for` instead of `while` to avoid the problem, but it turns out that there are many algorithms that jump around in an array in which the index variable sometimes takes on a value just outside the bounds of the array. Some sort algorithms, for example, are like that.

---

* I know I said I wasn't going to try to convince you which language is better, but on this particular point I really think the Pascal people don't have a leg to stand on.

Typed variables work against program robustness. (A *robust* program is one that keeps calm in the face of bad data or other user error, rather than dying abruptly.) For example, suppose we want to find the sum of a bunch of numbers. Some human being is going to type these numbers into the computer, one at a time. We don't know in advance how many there are, so we let the person type done when done. Since the typist is only human, rather than a computer, we want to make sure the program doesn't blow up if he accidentally types something other than a number or done. Here's one way to do it in Logo:

```
to addnumbers
print [Enter the numbers, one per line.]
print [Type the word 'done' when done.]
print se [The sum is] addnumbers1 0
end

to addnumbers1 :sum
localmake "next readnumber
if emptyp :next [output :sum]
output addnumbers1 :sum+:next
end

to readnumber
localmake "input readlist
if emptyp :input [output readnumber]
if equalp :input [done] [output []]
if numberp first :input [output first :input]
print [Please type numbers only.]
output readnumber
end
```

If the user makes a typing mistake, the program says so, ignores the bad input, and keeps going. Now, how shall we write this in Pascal? Into what type of variable should we read each number from the keyboard? If we pick integer, then any entry of a non-number will incite Pascal to print an error message and terminate the program. Instead we can read the keyboard entry into an array of char, one character at a time. Then anything the user types is okay, but we can't do arithmetic on the result—we can't add it into the accumulated sum. We can read it as chars and then write a procedure that knows how to look at a string of digits and compute the number that those digits represent. But this is not the sort of thing that we should need to do ourselves in a high-level programming language.

Why should a programmer have to decide in advance whether or not the numbers that a program will manipulate are integers? In Logo I can write a general numeric procedure like this one:

```
to square :x
output :x * :x
end
```

but in Pascal I need one for each kind of number:

```
function RealSquare(x:real): real;
begin
  RealSquare := x * x
end;

function IntSquare (x:integer): integer;
begin
  IntSquare := x * x
end;
```

Why pick on the distinction between integer and non-integer values? Why not positive and negative values, or odd and even values? The historical answer is that computer hardware uses two different representations for integer and real numbers, but so what? That doesn't mean the distinction is relevant to the particular program I'm writing.

The language ML, which I mentioned earlier as an example of a pure functional language, tries to provide the best of both worlds on this issue. It does require that variables have types, as in Pascal, to help catch programming errors. But two features make ML's type system more usable than Pascal's. One is the provision of *union types*. It's possible to say that a particular variable must contain either a number or the word done, for example. (Pascal has something like this, called *variants,* but they're less flexible.) Second, the ML compiler uses *type inference,* a technique by which the compiler can often figure out the appropriate type for a variable without an explicit declaration.

Procedures and Functions

In Logo a distinction is made between those procedures that output a value (operations) and those that don't (commands). Pascal has the same categories, but they're called *functions* and *procedures* respectively.

A function is a block just like a procedure block except for the minor changes needed to accommodate the fact that the function produces a value. First of all, the function header has to say what the *type* of the result will be:

```
function whatever (arguments) : integer;
```

The function's type must be a scalar, not an aggregate type. This restriction is in the standard only to make life easier for the compiler, and some versions of Pascal do allow array-valued (or record-valued, etc.) functions.

The other difference is that in the statement part of a function block we have to tell Pascal what the value will be. That is, we need something equivalent to `output` in Logo. Pascal's convention is that somewhere in the block an assignment statement must be executed that has the name of the function as its left hand side. That is, the function name is used in an assignment statement as though it were a variable name. (However, the name must *not* be declared as a variable.) This notation may be a little confusing, because if the same name appears on the *right* side of the assignment statement, it signals a recursive invocation of the function. Perhaps an example will make this clear.

Program `multi` is a Pascal version of the memoized multinomial function from Chapter 3. In the Logo version, $t(n,k)$ was memoized using the property name k on the property list named n. In the Pascal version, since we have multi-dimensional arrays, it is straightforward to use a two-dimensional array and store $t(n,k)$ in `memo[n,k]`.

```
program multi;
 {Multinomial expansion problem}

var memo: array [0..4, 0..7] of integer;
    i,j:  integer;

function t(n,k:integer) : integer;

  function realt(n,k:integer) : integer;
  {without memoization}

    begin {realt}
      if k = 0 then
        realt := 1
      else
        if n = 0 then
          realt := 0
        else
          realt := t(n,k-1)+t(n-1,k)
    end; {realt}
```

```
    begin {t}
      if memo[n,k] < 0 then
        memo[n,k] := realt(n,k);
      t := memo[n,k]
    end; {t}

begin {main program}
  {initialization}
  for i := 0 to 4 do
    for j := 0 to 7 do
      memo[i,j] := -1;

  {How many terms in (a+b+c+d)⁷?}
  writeln(t(4,7));
end.
```

The assignment statements like

```
realt := 0
```

are the ones that control the values returned by the functions. These assignment statements are not exactly like `output` in Logo because they do not cause the function to return immediately. They act just like ordinary assignments, as if there were actually a variable named `realt` or `t`; when the statement part of the function is finished, whatever value was most recently assigned to the function name is the one that's used as the return value. (In fact the functions in program `multi` are written so that only one such assignment is carried out, and there are no more statements to execute after that assignment. That's a pretty common programming style; it's rare to change the assignment to the function name once it's been made.)

Apart from arbitrary syntactic details, Pascal's design with respect to procedures and functions is similar to Logo's, so I can't ask why the two languages made different choices. It's probably just as well, since you shouldn't get the impression that Pascal is the exact opposite of Logo in every way. Instead we could compare these two languages with Lisp, in which there are only operations, or most versions of BASIC, in which there are only commands. But I don't have the space to teach you enough about those languages to make such a comparison meaningful.

Call by Value and Call by Reference

Consider this Logo procedure:

```
to increment :var
make :var (thing :var)+1
end

? make "baz 23
? increment "baz
? print :baz
24
```

The input to increment is the *name* of a variable that you want to increment. A similar technique is used, for example, in the push and pop library procedures, which take the name of a stack variable as input. The reason this technique is necessary is that we want the procedure to be able to modify the variable—to assign it a new value.

The same technique won't work in Pascal. For one thing, the association of a name with a variable only exists at compile time. Once the compiled program is running, the variables have no names, only addresses in computer memory. Also, increment takes advantage of dynamic scope because the variable it wants to modify isn't its own, but rather a variable accessible to the calling procedure.

Here's how you do it in Pascal:

```
procedure increment(var v:integer);
  begin
    v := v+1;
  end;
```

What's new here is the reserved word var in the argument list. This word indicates that v is a *variable parameter;* ordinary ones are called *value parameters.* Increment would be used in a program like this:

```
program whatzit;

var gub:integer;
  begin
  ...
  gub := 5;
  increment(gub);
  ...
  end.
```

Suppose `increment` had been written without the word `var` in its header. In that case, when the statement `increment(gub)` was executed here's what would happen. First, the actual argument to `increment` (namely `gub`) would be evaluated. The value would be 5, since that's the value of the variable `gub`. Then that value would be assigned to the local variable `v` in `increment`. Then the instruction part of `increment` would be run. The assignment statement there would change the value of `v` from 5 to 6. Then `increment` would be finished, and its local variable `v` would disappear. All of this would have no effect on the variable `gub`. This ordinary interpretation of `v` is called *call by value* because what gets associated with the name `v` is the *value* of the actual argument, 5 in this example, regardless of how that 5 was derived. For example, the instruction in the main program could have been

```
increment(2+3);
```

and it wouldn't have mattered.

Making `v` a variable parameter instead of a value parameter changes the operation of the program substantially. When `increment` is invoked, the actual argument *must* be a variable name, not an arbitrary expression. Pascal does not find the value of the actual argument and pass that value along to `increment`; instead, the formal parameter `v` becomes *another name for the same variable* named in the actual argument. In this example, `v` becomes another name for `gub`. So the assignment statement

```
v := v+1
```

isn't really about the local variable `v` at all; it's another way to say

```
gub := gub+1
```

and so it *does* affect the variable in the calling block. This use of variable parameters is called *call by reference* because the formal parameter (`v`) *refers* to another variable.

One way to think about call by reference is that it provides, in effect, a sort of limited dynamic scope. It's a way for a superprocedure to allow a subprocedure access to one selected variable from the superprocedure's lexical environment. Because this permission is given to the subprocedure explicitly, call by reference doesn't give rise to the possible naming bugs that argue against dynamic scope in general. Also, dynamic scope as used in Logo has the problem that you have to be careful not to allow a formal parameter name to be the same as the name of a variable you want to use from the superprocedure's environment. For example, in the Logo version of `increment`, what if you wanted to use `increment` to increment a variable named `var`? If you try to say

```
increment "var
```

it won't work, because `increment` will end up trying to increment its own formal parameter. (This is why the inputs to some of the Berkeley Logo library procedures have such long, obscure names.) But the Pascal `increment` would have no trouble with a variable named `v` in the calling procedure.

On the other hand, call by reference is a little mysterious. If you've understood all of the above, and you know exactly when you should say `var` in a formal parameter list and when you shouldn't, you're doing better than most beginning Pascal students. In Logo there is only one rule about passing inputs to procedures; to make something like `increment` work, you *explicitly* pass the *name* of a variable as input.

Call by reference is generally used when a subprocedure needs to change the value of a variable in a superprocedure. But there is also another situation in which some people use it. Suppose you want to write a procedure that takes a large array as an argument. If you make the array a value parameter, Pascal will allocate space for the array in the subprocedure and will copy each member of the array from the superprocedure's variable into the subprocedure's variable as the first step in invoking the subprocedure. This time-consuming array copying can be avoided by declaring the array as a variable parameter, thereby giving the subprocedure direct access to the superprocedure's array. Pascal enthusiasts consider this use of call by reference cheating, though, because it creates the possibility that the subprocedure could accidentally change something in the superprocedure's array. Call by value is safer, from this point of view.

Parameters in Logo: Call by Binding

Does Logo use call by value or call by reference for passing arguments to procedures? The official textbook answer is "call by value," but I find that misleading, because those two categories really make sense only in a language with a particular idea of what a variable is. A Logo variable is different from a Pascal variable in a subtle way. If you can understand this difference between the two languages, you'll have learned something very valuable.

In Logo, the world is full of data (words, lists, and arrays). These data may or may not be associated with variables. For example, when you enter an instruction like

```
print butlast butfirst [Yes, this is a list evidently.]
```

three different lists are involved: the one you typed explicitly in the instruction and two smaller lists. None of these three lists is the value of any variable. A *variable* is an association (called a *binding*) between a name and a datum. If you enter the instruction

```
make "langs [Logo Lisp APL]
```

we say that the name `langs` *is bound to* the indicated list. If you then do

```
make "mylangs :langs
```

we say that the name `mylangs` is bound to the *same* datum as `langs`. We're dealing with one list that has two names.

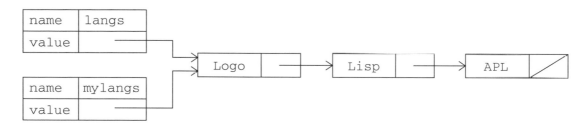

In Pascal a variable is not a binding in this sense. A Pascal variable *is* the datum it contains. If you have two array variables

```
var this,that: array [1..10] of integer;
```

and you do an assignment like

```
this := that;
```

then there are two *separate* arrays that happen to have equal values stored in them. The same thing is true, although it's less obviously meaningful, about scalars. If integer variables `i` and `j` both have the value 10, then there are *two different integers* that happen to have the same value. That's not the way a mathematician uses the word "integer"; to a mathematician, there is only one 10. But to a Pascal programmer, an integer isn't something like 10; an integer is a box, and in the box there might be something like 10.

In Logo, a variable assignment (that is, an invocation of `make`) changes the *binding* of the given variable name so that that name is now associated with a different datum. In Pascal, a variable assignment changes the value of *the datum* that is unalterably associated with the named variable.

The official textbook story is this: A Logo variable is a box, just as a Pascal variable is a box. The difference is that what goes in the box, in Logo, is a *pointer* to the datum of interest. (A binding, officially, is the connection between the variable's name and its box. So there are two levels of indirection in finding what we ordinarily think of as the value of a variable: First the binding gets us from the name to a box—a location in the computer's memory—and then in that box we find a pointer, which gets us to *another* location in memory, which holds the actual information we want. In this model, call by reference can easily be described by saying that two different names are bound to the same box.) From this point of view, it makes sense to say that Logo uses call by value, because the "value" in question is the pointer, which is indeed copied when a procedure is called.

But ordinarily we don't think of the value of a Logo variable as being a pointer; we think that the value of the variable is a word, a list, or an array. From that point of view, parameter passing in Logo acts like call by reference in some ways but like call by value in other ways. For example, call by value makes a copy of the datum being passed. Logo does not copy the actual datum, so in that respect it's like call by reference. On the other hand, assigning a new value to a Logo formal parameter does not change the value of any variables in the calling procedure; in that way, Logo works like call by value. On the third hand, if the datum to which the formal parameter is bound is a *mutable* data structure, such as an array, a Logo subprocedure *can* change the value of a variable in the calling procedure, not by assigning a new value to the formal parameter name (changing the binding), but by invoking `setitem` on the shared datum (altering the bound datum itself).

The chart on the next page is a graphic representation of the ideas in the last paragraph. The three columns represent Pascal call by value, Pascal call by reference, and Logo. In each case the main program has two arrays named `actual` and `other`; it then invokes a procedure `proc` using `actual` as the actual argument providing the value for `proc`'s formal parameter `formal`.

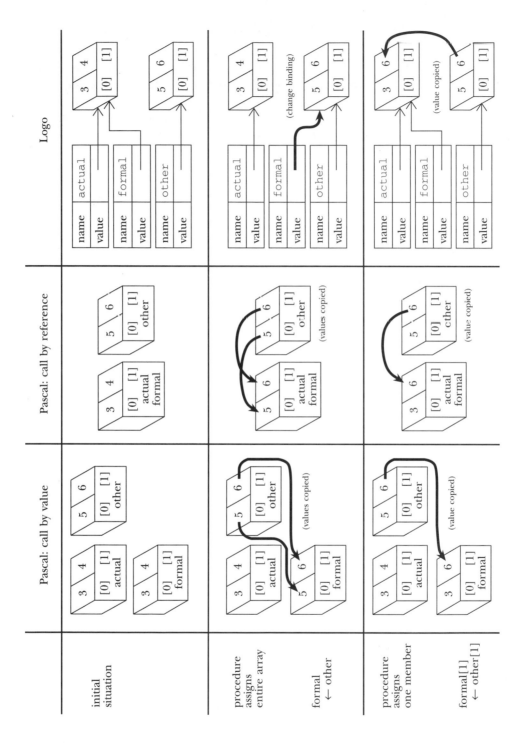

Pascal call by value | Pascal call by reference

```pascal
program pgm;
type pair = array [0..1]
            of integer;
var actual,other: pair;

procedure proc(formal:pair);
  begin
    body
  end

begin
  actual[0] := 3;
  actual[1] := 4;
  other[0] := 5;
  other[1] := 6;
  proc(actual)
end.
```

```pascal
program pgm;
type pair = array [0..1]
            of integer;
var actual,other: pair;

procedure proc(var formal:pair);
  begin
    body
  end

begin
  actual[0] := 3;
  actual[1] := 4;
  other[0] := 5;
  other[1] := 6;
  proc(actual)
end.
```

Logo

```logo
make "actual {3 4}@0
make "other {5 6}@0
proc :actual

to proc :formal
body
end
```

The first row of the figure shows the situation when proc is entered, before its body is executed. The second row shows what happens if proc contains an assignment of other to formal, i.e.,

```
formal := other
```

in either Pascal version or

```
make "formal :other
```

in the Logo version. The third row shows what happens if, instead, proc contains an assignment of just one member of the array, i.e.,

```
formal[1] := other[1]
```

in either Pascal version or

```
setitem 1 :formal (item 1 :other)
```

in the Logo version. Your goal is to see what happens to `actual` in each case when `proc` is finished.

Our final Pascal program example, showing the use of call by reference, is a version of the partition sort from Chapter 3 that uses the technique of exchanging two array members when appropriate to divide the array into two partitions "in place" (without requiring the allocation of extra arrays to hold the partitions). This program is adapted from Jon Bentley's version in *Programming Pearls* (Addison-Wesley, 1986). It's much closer in style to the real quicksort than my list-based version.

In the partition sort program of Chapter 3, I had to put a lot of effort into preventing a situation in which every member of the list being sorted ended up on the same side of the partition value. The quicksort solution starts by choosing some member of the array as the partition value and excluding that member from the partitioning process. As a result, the worst possible case is that the n members of the array are divided into the partitioning member, a partition of size $n - 1$, and a partition of size zero. If we're unlucky enough to hit that case every time, we'll have an $O(n^2)$ running time, but not an infinite loop.

How do we choose the partitioning member? It turns out that just picking one at random is surprisingly successful; sometimes you get a very bad choice, but usually not. But in this program I'm using a popular method that tends to work a little better (that is, to give more balanced partition sizes): The program finds the first member of the unsorted array, the last member, and the one halfway in between, and chooses the *median* of these three values—the one that's neither the largest nor the smallest.

Once the partitioning member has been chosen, the goal is to rearrange the array members into an order like this:

If other members of the array have the same value as the one we've chosen as the partitioning member, it doesn't really matter in which partition they end up. What does matter is that before doing the partitioning, we don't know where in the array the partitioning member will belong, so how can we keep from bumping into it as

Chapter 4   Programming Language Design

we rearrange the other members? The solution is that the partitioning member is temporarily kept in the leftmost possible position; the other members are partitioned, and then the partitioning member is swapped back into its proper position.

The partition works using two *index* variables i and j, which start at the leftmost and rightmost ends of the part of the array that we're sorting. (Remember that this algorithm uses recursive calls to sort each partition, so that might not be all 100 members of the full array.) We move i toward the right, and j toward the left, until we find two members out of place. That is, we look for a situation in which data[i] is greater than the partitioning member and data[j] is smaller than the partitioning member. We then interchange those two members of the array and continue until i and j meet in the middle. Procedure exch has two variable parameters and exchanges their values.

Program psort illustrates a fairly common but not obvious technique: the array data contains 100 "real" members in positions 0 to 99 but also has a "fence" or "sentinel" member (with index 100) just so that the program doesn't have to make a special case check for the index variable i reaching the end of the array. The value of data[100] is guaranteed to be greater than all the numbers that are actually being sorted. Having this extra member in the array avoids the need for an extra comparison of the form

```
if i > upper then ...
```

and thereby helps make the program a little faster.

```
program psort;
  {partition sort demo}

var data: array [0..100] of integer;
    i: integer;

procedure showdata;
  {print the array}

  var i: integer;

  begin {showdata}
    for i := 0 to 99 do
      begin
        if i mod 20 = 0 then writeln;
        write(data[i]:3)
      end;
    writeln;
    writeln
  end; {showdata}
```

```
function median(lower,upper:integer):integer;
  {find the median of three values from the data array}
  var mid: integer;

  begin
    mid := (lower+upper) div 2;
    if (data[lower] <= data[mid]) and (data[mid] <= data[upper]) then
      median := mid
    else if (data[lower] >= data[mid]) and
            (data[mid] >= data[upper]) then
      median := mid
    else if (data[mid] <= data[lower]) and
            (data[lower] <= data[upper]) then
      median := lower
    else if (data[mid] >= data[lower]) and
            (data[lower] >= data[upper]) then
      median := lower
    else median := upper
  end;

procedure sort(lower,upper:integer);
 {sort part of the array}

  var key,i,j:integer;

  procedure exch(var a,b:integer);
    {exchange two integers}

    var temp:integer;

    begin {exch}
      temp := a;
      a := b;
      b := temp
    end; {exch}
```

```
      begin {sort}
        if upper > lower then
          begin
            exch (data[lower],data[median(lower,upper)]);
            key := data[lower];
            i := lower;
            j := upper+1;
            repeat
              i := i+1
            until data[i] >= key;
            repeat
              j := j-1
            until data[j] <= key;
            while (i <= j) do
              begin
                exch(data[i], data[j]);
                repeat
                  i := i+1
                until data[i] >= key;
                repeat
                  j := j-1
                until data[j] <= key
              end;
            exch(data[lower], data[j]);
            sort(lower,j-1);
            sort(i,upper)
          end
      end; {sort}

begin {main program}
  data[100] := 200;
  for i := 0 to 99 do
    data[i] := random(100);
  writeln('Data before sorting:');
  showdata;

  sort(0,99);
  writeln('Data after sorting:');
  showdata
end.
```

5   Programming Language Implementation

Program file for this chapter: `pascal`

We are now ready to turn from the questions of language design to those of compiler implementation. A Pascal compiler is a much larger programming project than most of the ones we've explored so far. You might well ask, "where do we *begin* in writing a compiler?" My goal in this chapter is to show some of the parts that go into a compiler design.

A compiler translates programs from a language like Pascal into the machine language of some particular computer model. My compiler translates into a simplified, simulated machine language; the compiled programs are actually carried out by another Logo program, the simulator, rather than directly by the computer hardware. The advantage of using this simulated machine language is that this compiler will work no matter what kind of computer you have; also, the simplifications in this simulated machine allow me to leave out many confusing details of a practical compiler. Our machine language is, however, realistic enough to give you a good sense of what compiling into a real machine language would be like; it's loosely based on the MIPS microprocessor design. You'll see in a moment that most of the structure of the compiler is independent of the target language, anyway.

Here is a short, uninteresting Pascal program:

```
program test;

procedure doit(n:integer);
   begin
      writeln(n,n*n)
   end;

begin
   doit(3)
end.
```

If you type this program into a disk file and then compile it using `compile` as described in Chapter 4, the compiler will translate the program into this sequence of instructions, contained in a list in the variable named `%test`:

```
[        [add 3 0 0]
         [add 4 0 0]
         [addi 2 0 36]
         [jump "g1]
%doit    [store 1 0(4)]
         [jump "g2]
g2       [rload 7 36(4)]
         [putint 10 7]
         [rload 7 36(4)]
         [rload 8 36(4)]
         [mul 7 7 8]
         [putint 10 7]
         [newline]
         [rload 1 0(4)]
         [add 2 4 0]
         [rload 4 3(2)]
         [jr 1]
g1       [store 5 1(2)]
         [add 5 2 0]
         [addi 2 2 37]
         [store 4 3(5)]
         [store 4 2(5)]
         [addi 7 0 3]
         [store 7 36(5)]
         [add 4 5 0]
         [rload 5 1(4)]
         [jal 1 "%doit]
         [exit]
]
```

I've displayed this list of instructions with some extra spacing thrown in to make it look somewhat like a typical *assembler* listing. (An assembler is a program that translates a notation like `add 3 0 0` into a binary number, the form in which the machine hardware actually recognizes these instructions.) A real assembler listing wouldn't have the square brackets that Logo uses to mark each sublist, but would instead depend on the convention that each instruction occupies one line.

The first three instructions carry out initialization that would be the same for any compiled Pascal program; the fourth is a `jump` instruction that tells the (simulated) computer to skip to the instruction following the *label* `g1` that appears later in the program. (A word that isn't part of a sublist is a label.) In Pascal, the body of the main program comes after the declarations of procedures; this `jump` instruction allows the compiler to translate the parts of the program in the order in which they appear.

(Two instructions later, you'll notice a `jump` to a label that comes right after the jump instruction! The compiler issues this useless instruction just in case some internal procedures were declared within the procedure `doit`. A better compiler would include an *optimizer* that would go through the compiled program looking for ways to eliminate unnecessary instructions such as this one. The optimizer is the most important thing that I've left out of my compiler.)

We're not ready yet to talk in detail about how the compiled instructions represent the Pascal program, but you might be able to guess certain things. For example, the variable n in procedure `doit` seems to be represented as 36(4) in the compiled program; you can see where 36(4) is printed and then multiplied by itself, although it may not yet be clear to you what the numbers 7 and 8 have to do with anything. Before we get into those details, I want to give a broader overview of the organization of the compiler.

The compilation process is divided into three main pieces. First and simplest is *tokenization*. The compiler initially sees the source program as a string of characters: `p`, then `r`, and so on, including spaces and line separators. The first step in compilation is to turn these characters into symbols, so that the later stages of compilation can deal with the word `program` as a unit. The second piece of the compiler is the *parser*, the part that recognizes certain patterns of symbols as representing meaningful units. "Oh," says the parser, "I've just seen the word `procedure` so what comes next must be a procedure header and then a `begin-end` block for the body of the procedure." Finally, there is the process of *code generation*, in which each unit that was recognized by the parser is actually translated into the equivalent machine language instructions.

(I don't mean that parsing and code generation happen separately, one after the other, in the compiler's algorithm. In fact each meaningful unit is translated as it's encountered, and the translation of a large unit like a procedure includes, recursively, the translation of smaller units like statements. But parsing and code generation are conceptually two different tasks, and we'll talk about them separately.)

Formal Syntax Definition

One common starting place is to develop a formal definition for the language we're trying to compile. The regular expressions of Chapter 1 are an example of what I mean by a formal definition. A regular expression tells us unambiguously that certain strings of characters are accepted as members of the category defined by the expression, while other strings aren't. A language like Pascal is too complicated to be described by a regular expression, but other kinds of formal definition can be used.

The formal systems of Chapter 1 just gave a yes-or-no decision for any input string: Is it, or is it not, accepted in the language under discussion? That's not quite good enough for a compiler. We don't just want to know whether a Pascal program is syntactically correct; we want a translation of the program into some executable form. Nevertheless, it turns out to be worthwhile to begin by designing a formal acceptor for Pascal. That part of the compiler—the part that determines the syntactic structure of the source program—is called the *parser*. Later we'll add provisions for *code generation:* the translation of each syntactic unit of the source program into a piece of *object* (executable) program that carries out the meaning (the *semantics*) of that unit.

One common form in which programming languages are described is the *production rule* notation mentioned briefly in Chapter 1. For example, here is part of a specification for Pascal:

program	:	`program` *identifier filenames* ; *block* .
filenames	:	| (*idlist*)
idlist	:	*identifier* | *idlist* , *identifier*
block	:	*varpart procpart compound*
varpart	:	| `var` *varlist*
procpart	:	| *procpart procedure* | *procpart function*
compound	:	`begin` *statements* `end`
statements	:	*statement* | *statements* ; *statement*
procedure	:	`procedure` *identifier args* ; *block* ;
function	:	`function` *identifier args* : *type* ; *block* ;

A program consists of six components. Some of these components are particular words (like `program`) or punctuation marks; other components are defined in terms of even smaller units by other rules.*

---

* The *filenames* component is an optional list of names of files, part of Pascal's input/output capability; my compiler doesn't handle file input or output, so it ignores this list if there is one.

A vertical bar (|) in a rule separates alternatives; an idlist (identifier list) is either a single identifier or a smaller idlist followed by a comma and another identifier. Sometimes one of the alternatives in a rule is empty; for example, a varpart can be empty because a block need not declare any local variables.

The goal in designing a formal specification is to capture the syntactic hierarchy of the language you're describing. For example, you could define a Pascal type as

type   :   `integer` | `real` | `char` | `boolean` | `array` *range* `of integer` |
                `packed array` *range* `of integer` | `array` *range* `of real` |
                . . .

but it's better to say

type   :   *scalar* | `array` *range* `of` *scalar* |
                `packed array` *range* `of` *scalar*

scalar   :   `integer` | `real` | `char` | `boolean`

Try completing the syntactic description of my subset of Pascal along these lines. You might also try a similar syntactic description of Logo. Which is easier?

Another kind of formal description is the *recursive transition network* (RTN). An RTN is like a finite-state machine except that instead of each arrow representing a single symbol in the machine's alphabet, an arrow can be labeled with the name of another RTN; such an arrow represents any string of symbols accepted by that RTN.

On this page and the next I show two RTNs, one for a program and one for a sequence of statements (the body of a compound statement). In the former, the transition from state 5 to state 6 is followed if what comes next in the Pascal program is a string of symbols accepted by the RTN named "block." In these diagrams, a word in `typewriter` style like `program` represents a single symbol, as in a finite-state machine diagram, while a word in *italics* like *block* represents any string accepted by the RTN of that name. The *statements* RTN is recursive; one path through the network involves a transition that requires parsing a smaller *statements* unit.

<u>*program*</u>

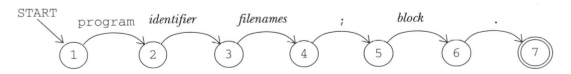

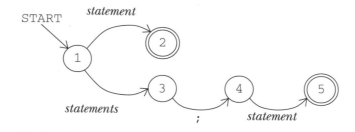

Tokenization

In both the production rules and the RTNs I've treated words like `program` as a single symbol of the "alphabet" of the language. It would be possible, of course, to use single characters as the alphabetic symbols and describe the language in this form:

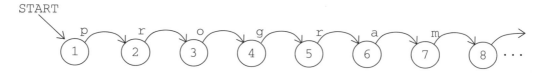

Extending the formal description down to that level, though, makes it hard to see the forest for the trees; the important structural patterns get lost in details about, for instance, where spaces are required between words (as in `program tower`), where they're optional (as in `2 + 3`), and where they're not allowed at all (`prog ram`). A similar complication is that a comment in braces can be inserted anywhere in the program; it would be enormously complicated if every state of every RTN had to have a transition for a left brace beginning a comment.

Most language processors therefore group the characters of the source program into *tokens* used as the alphabet for the formal grammar. A token may be a single character, such as a punctuation mark, or a group of characters, such as a word or a number. Spaces do not ordinarily form part of tokens, although in the Pascal compiler one kind of token is a quoted character string that can include spaces. Comments are also removed during tokenization. Here's what the `tower` program from Chapter 4 looks like in token form:

`program` `tower` `;` `procedure` `hanoi` `(` `number` ...

Tokenization is what the Logo `readlist` operation does when it uses spaces and brackets to turn the string of characters you type into a sequence of words and lists.

Tokenization is also called *lexical analysis.* This term has nothing to do with lexical scope; the word "lexical" is used not to remind us of a dictionary but because the root "lex" means *word* and lexical analysis divides the source program into words.

I've been talking as if the Pascal compiler first went through the entire source file tokenizing it and then went back and parsed the result. That's not actually how it works; instead, the parser just calls a procedure named `token` whenever it wants to see the next token in the source file. I've already mentioned that Pascal was designed to allow the compiler to read straight through the source program without jumping around and re-reading parts of it.

Lookahead

Consider the situation when the parser has recognized the first token (`program`) as the beginning of a program and it invokes `token` to read the second token, the program name. In the `tower` program, the desired token is `tower`. Token reads the letter `t`; since it's a letter, it must be the beginning of an identifier. Any number of letters or digits following the `t` will be part of the identifier, but the first non-alphanumeric character ends the token. (In this case, the character that ends the token will be a semicolon.)

What this means is that `token` has to read one character too many in order to find the end of the word `tower`. The semicolon isn't part of that token; it's part of the *following* token. (In fact it's the entire following token, but in other situations that need not be true.) Ordinarily `token` begins its work by reading a character from the source file, but the next time we call `token` it has to deal with the character it's already read. It would simplify things enormously if `token` could "un-read" the semicolon that ends the token `tower`. It's possible to allow something like un-reading by using a technique called *lookahead.*

```
to getchar
local "char
if namep "peekchar
    [make "char :peekchar
     ern "peekchar
     output :char]
output readchar
end
```

Getchar is the procedure that `token` calls to read the next character from the source file. Ordinarily `getchar` just invokes the primitive `readchar` to read a character from the file.* But if there is a variable named `peekchar`, then `getchar` just outputs whatever is in that variable without looking at the file. Token can now un-read a character by saying

```
make "peekchar :char
```

This technique only allows `token` to un-read a single character at a time. It would be possible to replace `peekchar` with a *list* of pre-read characters to be recycled. But in fact one is enough. When a program "peeks at" characters before they're read "for real," the technique is called *lookahead*. Getchar uses *one-character lookahead* because `peekchar` only stores a single character.

It turns out that, for similar reasons, the Pascal parser will occasionally find it convenient to peek at a *token* and re-read it later. Token therefore provides for one-*token* lookahead using a similar mechanism:

```
to token
local [token char]
if namep "peektoken [make "token :peektoken
                     ern "peektoken   output :token]
make "char getchar
if equalp :char "|{| [skipcomment output token]
if equalp :char char 32 [output token]
if equalp :char char 13 [output token]
if equalp :char char 10 [output token]
if equalp :char "' [output string "']
if memberp :char [+ - * / = ( , ) |[| |]| |;|] [output :char]
if equalp :char "|<| [output twochar "|<| [= >]]
if equalp :char "|>| [output twochar "|>| [=]]
if equalp :char ". [output twochar ". [.]]
if equalp :char ": [output twochar ": [=]]
if numberp :char [output number :char]
if letterp ascii :char [output token1 lowercase :char]
(throw "error sentence [unrecognized character:] :char)
end
```

---

* I'm lying. The real `getchar` is slightly more complicated because it checks for an unexpected end of file and because it prints the characters that it reads onto the screen. The program listing at the end of the chapter tells the whole story.

```
to twochar :old :ok
localmake "char getchar
if memberp :char :ok [output word :old :char]
make "peekchar :char
output :old
end
```

As you can see, `token` is mainly a selection of special cases. `Char 32` is a space; `char 13` or `char 10` is the end-of-line character. `Skipcomment` skips over characters until it sees a right brace. `String` accumulates characters up to and including a single quote (apostrophe), except that two single quotes in a row become one single quote inside the string and don't end the string. `Number` is a little tricky because of decimal points (the string of characters `1.10` is a single token, but the string `1..10` is three tokens!) and exponent notation. I'm not showing you all the details because the compiler is a very large program and we'll never get through it if I annotate every procedure. But I did want to show you `twochar` because it's a good, simple example of character lookahead at work. If the character `<` is seen in the source program, it may be a token by itself or it may be part of the two-character tokens `<=` or `<>`. `Twochar` takes a peek at the next character in the file to decide.

If the character that `token` reads isn't part of any recognizable token, the procedure generates an error. (The error is caught by the toplevel procedure `compile` so that it can close the source file.) This extremely primitive error handling is one of the most serious deficiencies in my compiler; it would be better if the compilation process continued, despite the error, so that any other errors in the program could also be discovered. In a real compiler, more than half of the parsing effort goes into error handling; it's relatively trivial to parse a correct source program.

Parsing

There are general techniques for turning a formal language specification, such as a set of production rules, into an algorithm for parsing the language so specified. These techniques are analogous to the program in Chapter 1 that translates a regular expression into a finite-state machine. A program that turns a formal specification into a parser is called a *parser generator*.

The trouble is that the techniques that work for *any* set of rules are quite slow. The time required to parse a sequence of length n is $O(n^2)$ if the grammar is unambiguous or $O(n^3)$ if it's ambiguous. A grammar is *ambiguous* if the same input sequence can be parsed correctly in more than one way. For example, if the production rule *idlist*   :   *identifier* | *idlist* , *identifier*

is applied to the string

```
Beatles,Who,Zombies,Kinks
```

then the only possible application of the rule to accept the string produces this left-to-right grouping:

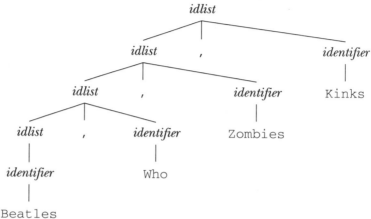

However, if the rule were

idlist   :   *identifier* | *idlist* , *idlist*

this new rule would accept the same strings, but would allow alternative groupings like

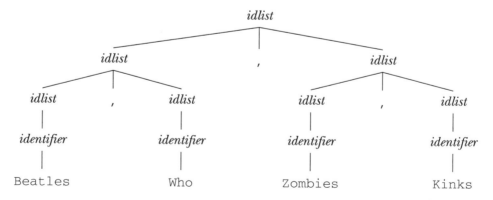

The former rule could be part of an unambiguous grammar; the new rule makes the grammar that contains it ambiguous.

It's usually not hard to devise an unambiguous grammar for any practical programming language, but even a quadratic algorithm is too slow. Luckily, most programming languages have *deterministic grammars,* which is a condition even stricter than being unambiguous. It means that a parser can read a program from left to right, and can figure out what to do with the next token using only a fixed amount of lookahead. A parser for a deterministic grammar can run in linear time, which is a lot better than quadratic.

When I said "figure out what to do with the next token," I was being deliberately vague. A deterministic parser doesn't necessarily know exactly how a token will fit into the complete program—which production rules will be branch nodes in a parse tree having this token as a leaf node—as soon as it reads the token. As a somewhat silly example, pretend that the word `if` is not a "reserved word" in Pascal; suppose it could be the name of a variable. Then, when the parser is expecting the beginning of a new statement and the next token is the word `if`, the parser doesn't know whether it is seeing the beginning of a conditional statement such as `if x > 0 then writeln('positive')` or the beginning of an assignment statement such as `if := 87`. But the parser could still be deterministic. Upon seeing the word `if`, it would enter a state (as in a finite state machine) from which there are two exits. If the next token turned out to be the `:=` assignment operator, the parser would follow one transition; if the next token was a variable or constant value, the parser would choose a different next state.

The real Pascal, though, contains no such syntactic cliffhangers. A Pascal compiler can always tell which production rule the next token requires. That's why the language includes keywords like `var`, `procedure`, and `function`. For the most part, you could figure out which kind of declaration you're reading without those keywords by looking for clues like whether or not there are parentheses after the identifier being declared. (If so, it's a procedure or a function.) But the keywords let you know from the beginning what to expect next. That means we can write what's called a *predictive grammar* for Pascal, even simpler to implement than a deterministic one.

There are general algorithms for parsing deterministic languages, and there are parser generators using these algorithms. One widely used example is the YACC (Yet Another Compiler Compiler) program that translates production rules into a parser in the C programming language.* But because Pascal's grammar is so simple I found it just as easy to do the translation by hand. For each production rule in a formal description of Pascal, the compiler includes a Logo procedure that parses each component part of

---

* A parser generator is also called a *compiler compiler* because it treats the formal specification as a kind of source program and produces a compiler as the object program. But the name isn't quite accurate because, as you know, there's more to a compiler than the parser.

the production rule. A parser written in this way is called a *recursive descent parser*. Here's a sample:

```
to statement
local [token type]
ifbe "begin [compound stop]
ifbe "for [pfor stop]
ifbe "if [pif stop]
ifbe "while [pwhile stop]
ifbe "repeat [prepeat stop]
ifbe "write [pwrite stop]
ifbe "writeln [pwriteln stop]
make "token token
make "peektoken :token
if memberp :token [|;| end until] [stop]
make "type gettype :token
if emptyp :type [(throw "error sentence :token [can't begin statement])]
if equalp :type "procedure [pproccall stop]
if equalp :type "function [pfunset stop]
passign
end

to pif
local [cond elsetag endtag]
make "cond pboolean pexpr
make "elsetag gensym
make "endtag gensym
mustbe "then
code (list "jumpf :cond (word "" :elsetag))
regfree :cond
statement
code (list "jump (word "" :endtag))
code :elsetag
ifbe "else [statement]
code :endtag
end
```

Many of the details of pif have to do with code generation, but never mind those parts now. For the moment, my concern is with the parsing aspect of these procedures: how they decide what to accept.

Statement is an important part of the parser; it is invoked whenever a Pascal statement is expected. It begins by checking the next token from the source file. If that token is begin, for, if, while, or repeat then we're finished with the token and statement turns to a subprocedure to handle the syntax of whatever structured statement type we've found. If the token isn't one of those, then the statement has to be a simple statement and the token has to be an identifier, i.e., the name of a procedure, a function, or a variable. (One other trivial possibility is that this is an *empty* statement, if we're already up to the semicolon, `end`, or `until` that marks the end of a statement.) In any of these cases, the token we've just read is important to the parsing procedure that will handle the simple statement, so `statement` un-reads it before deciding what to do next. `Gettype` outputs the type of the identifier, either a variable type like `real` or else `procedure` or `function`. (The compiler data structures that underlie the work of `gettype` will be discussed later.) If the token is a procedure name, then this is a procedure call statement. If the token is a function name, then this is the special kind of assignment inside a function definition that provides the return value for the function. Otherwise, the token must be a variable name and this is an ordinary assignment statement.

The procedure `pif` parses `if` statements. (The letter `p` in its name stands for "Pascal"; many procedures in the compiler have such names to avoid conflicts with Logo procedures with similar purposes.) The syntax of Pascal `if` is

ifstatement : `if` *boolean* `then` *statement* |
                   `if` *boolean* `then` *statement* `else` *statement*

When `pif` begins, the token `if` has just been read by `statement`. So the first thing that's required is a boolean expression. `Pexpr` parses an expression; that task is relatively complicated and will be discussed in more detail later. `Pboolean` ensures that the expression just parsed does indeed produce a value of type `boolean`.

The next token in the source file *must* be the word `then`. The instruction

```
mustbe "then
```

in `pif` ensures that. Here's `mustbe`:

```
to mustbe :wanted
localmake "token token
if equalp :token :wanted [stop]
(throw "error (sentence "expected :wanted "got :token))
end
```

If `mustbe` returns successfully, `pif` then invokes `statement` recursively to parse the true branch of the conditional. The production rule tells us that there is then an *optional* false branch, signaled by the reserved word `else`. The instruction

```
ifbe "else [statement]
```

handles that possibility. If the next token matches the first input to `ifbe` then the second input, an instruction list, is carried out. Otherwise the token is un-read. There is also an `ifbeelse` that takes a third input, an instruction list to be carried out if the next token isn't equal to the first input. (`Ifbeelse` still un-reads the token in that case, before it runs the third input.) These must be macros so that the instruction list inputs can include `output` or `stop` instructions (as discussed in Volume 2), as in the invocations of `ifbe` in `statement` seen a moment ago.

```
.macro ifbe :wanted :action
localmake "token token
if equalp :token :wanted [output :action]
make "peektoken :token
output []
end

.macro ifbeelse :wanted :action :else
localmake "token token
if equalp :token :wanted [output :action]
make "peektoken :token
output :else
end
```

If there were no code generation involved, `pif` would be written this way:

```
to pif
pboolean pexpr
mustbe "then
statement
ifbe "else [statement]
end
```

This simplified procedure is a straightforward translation of the RTN

pif

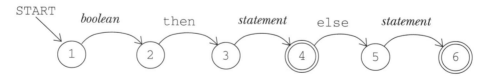

The need to generate object code complicates the parser. But don't let that distract you; in general you can see the formal structure of Pascal syntax reflected in the sequence of instructions used to parse that syntax.

The procedures that handle other structured statements, such as `pfor` and `pwhile`, are a lot like `pif`. Procedure and function declarations (procedures `procedure`, `function`, and `proc1` in the compiler) also use the same straightforward parsing technique, but are a little more complicated because of the need to keep track of type declarations for each procedure's parameters and local variables. Ironically, the hardest thing to compile is the "simple" assignment statement, partly because of operator precedence (multiplication before addition) in expressions (procedure `pexpr` in the compiler) and partly because of the need to deal with the complexity of variables, including special cases such as assignments to `var` parameters and array elements.

I haven't yet showed you `pboolean` because you have to understand how the compiler handles expressions first. But it's worth noticing that Pascal can check *at compile time* whether or not an expression is going to produce a `boolean` value even though the program hasn't been run yet and the variables in the expression don't have values yet. It's the strict variable typing of Pascal that makes this compile-time checking possible. If we were writing a Logo compiler, the checking would have to be postponed until run time because you can't, in general, know what type of datum will be computed by a Logo expression until it's actually evaluated.

Expressions and Precedence

Arithmetic or boolean expressions appear not only on the right side of assignment statements but also as actual parameters, array index values, and as "phrases" in structured statements. One of the classic problems in compiler construction is the translation of these expressions to executable form. The interesting difficulty concerns *operator precedence*—the rule that in a string of alternating operators and operands, multiplications are done before additions, so

```
a + b * c + d
```

means

```
a + (b * c) + d
```

Pascal has four levels of operator precedence. The highest level, number 4, is the *unary* operators +, −, and `not`. (The first two can be used as unary operators (−3) or *binary* ones (6−3); it's only in the unary case that they have this precedence.)* Then

---

* It's unfortunate that the word "binary" is used in computer science both for base-2 numbers and for two-input operations. Kenneth Iverson, in his documentation for the language APL, used

comes multiplication, division, and logical **and** at level 3. Level 2 has binary addition, subtraction, and **or**. And level 1 includes the relational operators like **=**.

The formalization of precedence could be done using the mechanisms we've already seen. For example, here is a production rule grammar for expressions using only the four basic arithmetic operations.

expression   **:**   *term* | *expression* **+** *term* | *expression* **−** *term*
term   **:**   *factor* | *term* * *factor* | *term* / *factor*
factor   **:**   *variable* | *number* | **(** *expression* **)**

This grammar also introduces into the discussion the fact that the precedence of operations can be changed by using parentheses.

This grammar, although formally correct, is not so easy to use in a recursive descent parser. One subtle but important problem is that it's *left recursive:* Some of the alternative forms for an **expression** start with an **expression**. If we tried to translate this into a Logo procedure it would naturally start out

```
to expression
local [left op right]
make "left expression
ifbe "+
  [make "op "+
   make "right term]
  [ifbe "-
     [make "op "-
      make "right term]
     [make "op []] ]
...
```

But this procedure will never get past the first **make**; it's an infinite loop. It will never actually read a token from the source file; instead it keeps invoking itself recursively.

Left association is a problem for automatic compiler compilers, too. There are ways to solve the problem but I don't want to get into that because in fact arithmetic expressions are generally handled by an entirely different scheme, which I'll show you in a moment. The problem wouldn't come up if the order of the operands were reversed, so the rules said

---

the words *monadic* and *dyadic* instead of unary and binary to avoid that ambiguity. But those terms haven't caught on.

$$expression \quad : \quad term \mid term + expression \mid term - expression$$

and so on. Unfortunately this changes the meaning, and the rules of Pascal say that equal-precedence operations are performed left to right.

In any case, the formalization of precedence with production rules gets more complicated as the number of levels of precedence increases. I showed you a grammar with two levels. Pascal, with four levels, might reasonably be done in a similar way, but think about the C programming language, which has 15 levels of precedence!

The Two-Stack Algorithm for Expressions

What we're after is an algorithm that will allow the compiler to read an expression once, left to right, and group operators and operands correctly. The algorithm involves the use of two stacks, one for operations and one for data. For each operation we need to know whether it's unary or binary and what its precedence level is. I'll use the notation "$*_{2,3}$" to represent binary $*$ at precedence level 3. So the expression

```
a + b * - c - d
```

will be represented in this algorithm as

$$\vdash_0 \ a \ +_{2,2} \ b \ *_{2,3} \ -_{1,4} \ c \ -_{2,2} \ d \ \dashv_0$$

The symbols $\vdash$ and $\dashv$ aren't really part of the source expression; they're imaginary markers for the beginning and end of the expression. When we read a token that doesn't make sense as part of an expression, we can un-read that token and pretend we read a $\dashv$ instead. These markers are given precedence level zero because they form a boundary for *any* operators inside them, just as a low-precedence operator like + is a boundary for the operands of a higher-precedence operator like $*$. (For the same reason, you'll see that parentheses are considered precedence zero.)

The two minus signs in this expression have two different meanings. As you read the following algorithm description, you'll see how the algorithm knows whether an operation symbol is unary or binary.

Step 1. We initialize the two stacks this way:

```
operation:  [ ⊢₀ ]

data:       [ ]
```

Step 2. We are now expecting a datum, such as a variable. Read a token. If it's an operation, it must be unary; subscript it accordingly and go to step 4. If it's a datum, push it onto the data stack. (If it's neither an operation nor a datum, something's wrong.)

Step 3. We are now expecting a binary operation. Read a token. If it's an operation, subscript it as binary and go to step 4. If not, we've reached the end of the expression. Un-read the token, and go to step 4 with the token $\dashv_0$.

Step 4. We have an operation in hand at this point and we know its precedence level and how many arguments it needs. Compare its precedence level with that of the topmost (most recently pushed) operation on the stack. If the precedence of the new operation is less than or equal to that of the one on the stack, go to step 5. If it's greater, go to step 6.

Step 5. The topmost operation on the stack has higher precedence than the one we just read, so we should do it right away. (For example, we've just read the + in a*b+c; the multiplication operation and both of its operands are ready on the stacks.) Pop the operation off the stack, pop either one or two items off the data stack depending on the first subscript of the popped operation, then compile machine instructions to perform the indicated computation. Push the result on the data stack as a single quantity. However, if the operation we popped is ⊢, then we're finished. There should be only one thing on the data stack, and it's the completely compiled expression. Otherwise, we still have the new operation waiting to be processed, so return to step 4.

Step 6. The topmost operation on the stack has lower precedence than the one we just read, so we can't do it yet because we're still reading its right operand. (For example, we've just read the * in a+b*c; we're not ready to do either operation until we read the c later.) Push the new operation onto the operation stack, then return to step 2.

Here's how this algorithm works out with the sample expression above. In the data stack, a boxed entry like $\boxed{a+b}$ means the result from translating that subexpression into the object language.

step	operation stack	data stack	token
1	[$\vdash_0$]	[ ]	
2		[a]	a
3			+
4			$+_{2,2}$
6	[$+_{2,2}$ $\vdash_0$]		$+_{2,2}$
2		[b a]	b
3			*
4			$*_{2,3}$

Chapter 5   Programming Language Implementation

	Operation stack	Data stack	
6	[$*_{2,3}$ $+_{2,2}$ $\vdash_0$]		$*_{2,3}$
2			$-$
4			$^-_{1,4}$
6	[$^-_{1,4}$ $*_{2,3}$ $+_{2,2}$ $\vdash_0$]		$^-_{1,4}$
2		[c b a]	c
3			$-$
4			$^-_{2,2}$
5	[$*_{2,3}$ $+_{2,2}$ $\vdash_0$]	[-c b a]	$^-_{2,2}$
4			$^-_{2,2}$
5	[$+_{2,2}$ $\vdash_0$]	[b*-c a]	$^-_{2,2}$
4			$^-_{2,2}$
5	[$\vdash_0$]	[a+b*-c]	$^-_{2,2}$
4			$^-_{2,2}$
6	[$^-_{2,2}$ $\vdash_0$]		$^-_{2,2}$
2		[d a+b*-c]	d
3			$\dashv$
4			$\dashv_0$
5	[$\vdash_0$]	[a+b*-c -d]	$\dashv_0$
5	[ ]	[a+b*-c -d]	$\dashv_0$

The final value on the data stack is the translation of the entire expression.

The algorithm so far does not deal with parentheses. They're handled somewhat like operations, but with slightly different rules. A left parenthesis is stored on the operation stack as $(_0$, like the special marker at the beginning of the expression, but it does not invoke step 5 of the algorithm before being pushed on the stack. A right parenthesis *does* invoke step 5, but only as far down the stack as the first matching left parenthesis; if it were an ordinary operation of precedence zero it would pop everything off the stack. You might try to express precisely how to modify the algorithm to allow for parentheses.

Here are the procedures that embody this algorithm in the compiler. `Pgetunary` and `pgetbinary` output a list like

```
[sub 2 2]
```

for binary − or

```
[minus 1 4]
```

for unary minus. (I'm leaving out some complications having to do with type checking.) They work by looking for a `unary` or `binary` property on the property list of the operation symbol. Procedures with names like `op.prec` are selectors for the members of these lists.

In this algorithm, only step 5 actually generates any instructions in the object program. This is the step in which an operation is removed from the operation stack and actually performed. Step 5 is carried out by the procedure `ppopop` (Pascal pop operation); most of that procedure deals with code generation, but I've omitted that part of the procedure in the following listing because right now we're concerned with the parsing algorithm. We'll return to code generation shortly.

`Pexpr1` invokes `pdata` when it expects to read an operand, which could be a number, a variable, or a function call. `Pdata`, which I'm not showing here, generates code to make the operand available and outputs the location of the result in the simulated computer, in a form that can be used by `pexpr`.

```
to pexpr
local [opstack datastack parenlevel]
make "opstack [[popen 1 0]]                         step 1
make "datastack []
make "parenlevel 0
output pexpr1
end


to pexpr1
local [token op]
make "token token                                   step 2
while [equalp :token "|(|] [popen  make "token token]
make "op pgetunary :token
if not emptyp :op [output pexprop :op]
push "datastack pdata :token
make "token token                                   step 3
while [and (:parenlevel > 0) (equalp :token "|)| )]
   [pclose  make "token token]
make "op pgetbinary :token
if not emptyp :op [output pexprop :op]
make "peektoken :token
pclose
if not emptyp :opstack [(throw "error [too many operators])]
if not emptyp butfirst :datastack [(throw "error [too many operands])]
output pop "datastack
end
```

```
to pexprop :op                              step 4
while [(op.prec :op) < (1 + op.prec first :opstack)] [ppopop]
push "opstack :op                           step 6
output pexpr1
end


to ppopop                                   step 5
local [op function args left right type reg]
make "op pop "opstack
make "function op.instr :op
if equalp :function "plus [stop]
make "args op.nargs :op
make "right pop "datastack
make "left (ifelse equalp :args 2 [pop "datastack] [[[] []]])
make "type pnewtype :op exp.type :left exp.type :right
... code generation omitted ...
push "datastack (list :type "register :reg)
end


to popen
push "opstack [popen 1 0]
make "parenlevel :parenlevel+1
end


to pclose
while [(op.prec first :opstack) > 0] [ppopop]
ignore pop "opstack
make "parenlevel :parenlevel - 1
end
```

The Simulated Machine

We're ready to move from parsing to code generation, but first you must understand what a computer's native language is like. Most computer models in use today have a very similar structure, although there are differences in details. My simulated computer design makes these detail choices in favor of simplicity rather than efficiency. (It wouldn't be very efficient no matter what, compared to real computers. This "computer" is actually an interpreter, written in Logo, which is itself an interpreter. So we have two levels of interpretation involved in each simulated instruction, whereas on a real computer, each instruction is carried out directly by the hardware. Our compiled Pascal programs, as you've probably already noticed, run very slowly. That's not Pascal's fault, and it's not even primarily my compiler's fault, even though the compiler doesn't include optimization techniques. The main slowdown is in the interpretation of the machine instructions.)

Every computer includes a *processor,* which decodes instructions and carries out the indicated arithmetic operations, and a *memory,* in which information (such as the values of variables) is stored. In modern computers, the processor is generally a single *integrated circuit,* nicknamed a *chip,* which is a rectangular black plastic housing one or two inches on a side that contains thousands or even millions of tiny components made of silicon. The memory is usually a *circuit board* containing several memory chips. Computers also include circuitry to connect with input and output devices, but we're not going to have to think about those. What makes one computer model different from another is mainly the processor. If you have a PC, its processor is probably an Intel design with a name like 80486 or Pentium; if you have a Macintosh, the processor might be a Motorola 68040 or a Power PC chip.

It turns out that the wiring connecting the processor to the memory is often the main limiting factor on the speed of a computer. Things happen at great speed within the processor, and within the memory, but only one value at a time can travel from one to the other. Computer designers have invented several ways to get around this problem, but the important one for our purposes is that every modern processor includes a little bit of memory within the processor chip itself. By "a little bit" I mean that a typical processor has enough memory in it to hold 32 values, compared to several million values that can be stored in the computer's main memory. The 32 memory slots within the processor are called *registers.**

Whenever you want to perform an arithmetic operation, the operands must already be within the processor, in registers. So, for example, the Pascal instruction

```
c := a + b
```

isn't compiled into a single machine instruction. First we must *load* the values of a and b from memory into registers, then add the two registers, then *store* the result back into memory:

```
rload 8 a
rload 9 b
add 10 8 9
store 10 c
```

------

* One current topic in computer architecture research is the development of *parallel* computers with many processors working together. In some of these designs, each processor includes its own medium-size memory within the processor chip.

The first `rload` instruction loads the value from memory location `a` into register 8.* The `add` instruction adds the numbers in registers 8 and 9, putting the result into register 10. (In practice, you'll see that the compiler would be more likely to conserve registers by reusing one of the operand registers for the result, but for this first example I wanted to keep things simple.) Finally we store the result into the variable `c` in memory.

The instructions above are actually not machine language instructions, but rather *assembly language* instructions, a kind of shorthand. A program called an *assembler* translates assembly language into machine language, in which each instruction is represented as a number. For example, if the instruction code for `add` is `0023`, then the `add` instruction above might be translated into `0023100809`, with four digits for the instruction code and two digits for each of the three register numbers. (In reality the encoding would use binary numbers rather than the decimal numbers I've shown in this example.) Since a machine language instruction is just a number, the instructions that make up a computer program are stored in memory along with the program's data values. But one of the simplifications I've made in my simulated computer is that the simulator deals directly with assembly language instructions, and those instructions are stored in a Logo list, separate from the program's data memory.

The simulated computer has 32 processor registers plus 3000 locations of main memory; it's a very small computer, but big enough for my sample Pascal programs. (You can change these sizes by editing procedure `opsetup` in the compiler.) The registers are numbered from 0 to 31, and the memory locations are numbered from 0 to 2999. The number of a memory location is called its *address*. Each memory location can hold one numeric value.** A Pascal array will be represented by a contiguous block of memory locations, one for each member of the array. Each register, too, can hold one numeric value. In this machine, as in some real computers, register number 0 is special; it always contains the value zero.

The simulated computer understands 50 instruction codes, fewer than most real computers. The first group we'll consider are the 14 binary arithmetic instructions: `add`, `sub`, `mul`, `div` (real quotient), `quo` (integer quotient), `rem` (remainder), `land` (logical

---

* Really I should have called this instruction `load`, but my machine simulator uses Logo procedures to carry out the machine instructions, and I had to pick a name that wouldn't conflict with the Logo `load` primitive.

** This, too, is a simplification. In real computers, different data types require different amounts of memory. A character value, for example, fits into eight *bits* (binary digits) of memory, whereas an integer requires 32 bits in most current computers. Instead of a single `load` instruction, a real computer has a separate one for each datum size.

and), `lor` (logical or), `eql` (compare two operands for equality), `neq` (not equal), `less`, `gtr` (greater than), `leq` (less than or equal), and `geq` (greater than or equal). The result of each of the six comparison operators is 0 for false or 1 for true. The machine also has four unary arithmetic instructions: `lnot` (logical not), `sint` (truncate to integer), `sround` (round to integer), and `srandom`. Each of these 18 arithmetic instructions takes its operands from registers and puts its result into a register.

All but the last three of these are typical instructions of real computers.* (Not every computer has all of them; for example, if a computer has `eql` and `lnot`, then it doesn't really need a `neq` instruction because the same value can be computed by a sequence of two instructions.) The operations `sint`, `sround`, and `srandom` are less likely to be machine instructions on actual computers. On the other hand, most real computers have a *system call* mechanism, which is a machine instruction that switches the computer from the user's program to a part of the operating system that performs some task on behalf of the user. System calls are used mainly for input and output, but we can pretend that there are system calls to compute these Pascal library functions. (The letter `s` in the instruction names stands for "system call" to remind us.)

The simulated computer also has another set of 18 *immediate* instructions, with the letter `i` added to the instruction name: `addi`, `subi`, and so on. In these instructions, the rightmost operand in the instruction is the actual value desired, rather than the number of a register containing the operand. For example,

```
add 10 8 9
```

means, "add the number in register 8 and the number in register 9, putting the result into register 10." But

```
addi 10 8 9
```

means, "add the number in register 8 to the value 9, putting the result in register 10."

It's only the right operand that can be made immediate. So, for example, the Pascal assignment

```
y := x - 5
```

---

* One important simplification is that in the simulated computer, the same instructions are used for all kinds of numbers. A typical computer has three `add` instructions: one for integers, one for short reals (32 bits), and one for long reals (64 bits).

can be translated into

```
rload 8 x
subi 8 8 5
store 8 y
```

but the Pascal assignment

```
y := 5 - x
```

must be translated as

```
addi 8 0 5
rload 9 x
sub 8 8 9
store 8 y
```

This example illustrates one situation in which it's useful to have register 0 guaranteed to contain the value 0.

Our simulated machine has six more system call instructions having to do with printing results. One of them, `newline`, uses no operands and simply prints a newline character, moving to the beginning of a new line on the screen. Four more are for printing the value in a register; the instruction used depends on the data type of the value in the register. The instructions are `putch` for a character, `puttf` for a boolean (true or false) value, `putint` for an integer, and `putreal` for a real number. Each takes two operands; the first, an immediate value, gives the minimum width in which to print the value, and the second is a register number. So the instruction

```
putint 10 8
```

means, "print the integer value in register 8, using at least 10 character positions on the line." The sixth printing instruction, `putstr`, is used only for constant character strings in the Pascal program; its first operand is a width, as for the others, but its second is a Logo list containing the string to print:

```
putstr 1 [The shuffled deck:]
```

This is, of course, unrealistic; in a real computer the second operand would have to be the memory address of the beginning of the array of characters to print. But the way I handle printing isn't very realistic in any case; I wanted to do the simplest possible thing, because worrying about printing really doesn't add anything to your understanding of the process of compilation, which is the point of this chapter.

The next group of instructions has to do with the flow of control in the computer program. Ordinarily the computer carries out its instructions in sequence, that is, in the order in which they appear in the program. But in order to implement conditionals (such as `if`), loops (such as `while`), and procedure calls, we must be able to jump out of sequence. The `jump` instruction takes a single operand, a *label* that appears somewhere in the program. When the computer carries out a jump instruction, it looks for the specified label and starts reading instructions just after where that label appears in the program. (We saw an example of labels at the beginning of this chapter.)

The `jump` instruction is used for unconditional jumps. In order to implement conditionals and loops, we need a way to jump if some condition is true. The instruction `jumpt` (jump if true) has two operands, a register number and a label. It jumps to the specified label if and only if the given register contains a true value. (Since registers hold only numbers, we use the value 1 to represent true, and 0 to represent false.) Similarly, `jumpf` jumps if the value in the given register is false.

For procedure and function calls, we need a different mechanism. The jump is unconditional, but the computer must remember where it came from, so that it can continue where it left off once the called procedure or function returns. The instruction `jal` (jump and link) takes two operands, a register and a label. It puts into the register the address of the instruction following the `jal` instruction.* Then it jumps to the specified label. To return from the called procedure, we use the `jr` (jump register) instruction. It has one operand, a register number; it jumps to the instruction whose address is in the register.

One final instruction that affects the flow of control is the `exit` system call. It requires no operands; it terminates the running of the program. In this simulated computer, it returns to a Logo prompt; in a real computer, the operating system would start running another user program.

The only remaining instructions are `rload` and `store`. You already know what these do, but I've been showing them in oversimplified form so far. The second operand can't just be a variable name, because that variable might not be in the same place in memory every time the procedure is called. Think, for example, about a recursive

---

* In a real computer, each instruction is stored in a particular memory location, so the address of an instruction is the address of the memory location in which it's stored. In this simulated computer, I keep the program in the form of a Logo list, and so I cheat and put the sublist starting at the next instruction into the register. This isn't quite as much of a cheat as it may seem, though, since you know from Chapter 3 that Logo represents a list with the memory address of the first pair of the list.

procedure. Several invocations may be in progress at once, all of them carrying out the same compiled instructions, but each referring to a separate set of local variables. The solution to this problem is that the compiler arranges to load into a register the address of a block of memory containing all the local variables for a given procedure call. If the variable c, for example, is in the sixth memory location of that block, an instruction to load or store that variable must be able to say "the memory location whose address is the contents of register 4 (let's say) plus five." So each load and store instruction contains an *index register* in parentheses following an *offset* to be added to the contents of that register. We'd say

```
store 8 5(4)
```

to store the contents of register 8 into the variable c, provided that register 4 points to the correct procedure invocation's local variables and that c is in the sixth position in the block. (The first position in the block would have offset 0, and so on.)

Stack Frames

The first step in invoking a procedure or function is to set aside, or *allocate,* a block of memory locations for use by that invocation. This block will include the procedure's local variables, its arguments, and room to save the values of registers as needed. The compiler's data structures include, for each procedure, how much memory that procedure needs when it's invoked. That block of memory is called a *frame.*

In most programming languages, including Pascal and Logo (but not, as it turns out, Lisp), the frame allocated when a procedure invocation begins can be released, or *deallocated,* when that invocation returns to its caller. In other words, the procedure's local variables no longer exist once the invocation is finished. In these languages, the frames for all the active procedure invocations can be viewed as a *stack,* a data structure to which new elements are added by a Push operation, and elements are removed using a Pop operation that removes the most recently pushed element. (In this case, the elements are the frames.) That is, suppose that procedure A invokes B, which invokes C, which invokes D. For each of these invocations a new frame is pushed onto the stack. Which procedure finishes first? It has to be D, the last one invoked. When D returns, its frame can be popped off the stack. Procedure C returns next, and its frame is popped, and so on. The phrase *stack frame* is used to refer to frames that behave like elements of a stack.

My Pascal compiler allocates memory starting at location 0 and working upward. At the beginning of the program, a *global frame* is allocated to hold the program's global variables. Register 3, the *global pointer,* always contains the address of the beginning of the global frame, so that every procedure can easily make use of global variables. (Since the global frame is the first thing in memory, its address is always zero, so the value in register 3 is always 0. But in a more realistic implementation the program itself would appear in memory before the global frame, so its address would be greater than zero.)

At any point in the program, register 4, the *frame pointer,* contains the address of the beginning of the current frame, that is, the frame that was created for the current procedure invocation. Register 2, the *stack pointer,* contains the address of the first currently unused location in memory.

My compiler is a little unusual in that when a procedure is called, the stack frame for the new invocation is allocated by the caller, not by the called procedure. This simplifies things because the procedure's arguments can be stored in its own frame; if each procedure allocates its own frame, then the caller must store argument values in its (the caller's) frame, because the callee's frame doesn't exist yet. So, in my compiler, the first step in a procedure call is to set register 5, the *new frame pointer,* to point to the first free memory location, and change the stack pointer to allocate the needed space. If N memory locations are needed for the new frame, the calling procedure will contain the following instructions:

```
add 5 2 0
addi 2 2 N
```

The first instruction copies the value from register 2 (the first free memory location) into register 5; the second adds N to register 2. (I've left out a complication, which is that the old value in register 5 must be saved somewhere before putting this new value into it. You can read the code generation instructions at the beginning of **pproccall1**, in the program listing at the end of the chapter, for all the details.) The current frame pointer is also saved in location 3 of the new frame:

```
store 4 3(5)
```

The compiler uses data abstraction to refer to these register numbers and frame slots; for example, the procedure **reg.frameptr** takes no arguments and always outputs 4, while **frame.prevframe** outputs 3.

The next step is to put the argument values into the new frame. During this process, the calling procedure must use register 4 to refer to its own variables, and register 5 to refer to the callee's variables. The final step, just before calling the procedure, is to make the frame pointer (register 4) point to the new frame:

```
add 4 5 0
```

Once the caller has set up the new frame and saved the necessary registers, it can call the desired procedure, putting the return address in register 1:

```
jal 1 "proclabel
```

The first step in the called procedure is to save the return address in location zero of its frame:

```
store 1 0(4)
```

The procedure then carries out the instructions in its body. When it's ready to return, it must load the saved return address back into register 1, then restore the old stack pointer and frame pointer to deallocate its frame, and finally return to the caller:

```
rload 1 0(4)
add 2 4 0
rload 4 3(2)
jr 1
```

(Procedure `proc1` in the compiler generates these instructions for each procedure.)

One final complication about stack frames comes from Pascal's block structure. Suppose we have a program with internal procedures arranged in this structure:

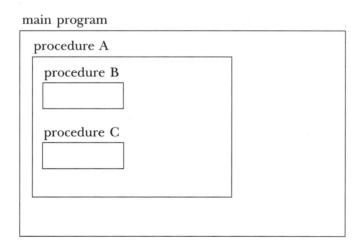

Then suppose that the main program calls procedure A, which calls B, which calls C, which calls itself recursively. The current (inner) invocation of C has access to its own variables, those of procedure A, and the global variables, but not to procedure B's variables. How does procedure C know where procedure A's stack frame is located? The answer is that every frame, in addition to saving a pointer to the previous frame, must include a pointer to the *lexically enclosing* frame. The calling procedure sets this up; it can do this because it knows its own lexical depth and that of the called procedure. For example, when procedure B calls procedure C, C's lexically enclosing frame will be the same as B's (namely, the frame for the invocation of A), because B and C are at the same lexical depth. (They are both declared inside A.) But when procedure A calls procedure B, which is declared within itself, A must store its own frame pointer as B's lexically enclosing frame. Here is a picture of what's where in memory:

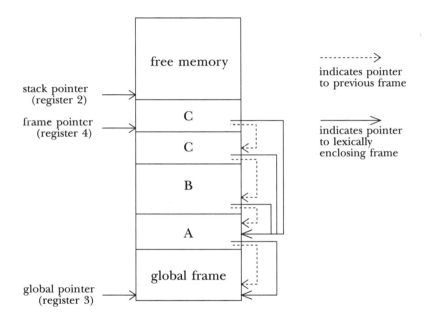

If all these pointers between frames confuse you, it might help to keep in mind that the two kinds of pointers have very different purposes. The pointer to the previous frame is used only when a procedure returns, to help in putting everything back the way it was before the procedure was called (in particular, restoring the old value of register 4). The pointer to the lexically enclosing frame is used while the procedure is running, whenever the procedure makes reference to a variable that belongs to some outer procedure (for example, a reference in procedure B or C to a variable that belongs to procedure A).*

---

* If procedures used the previous-frame pointers to make variable references, we would be compiling a dynamically scoped language! In this example, because Pascal is lexically scoped, procedure C can't refer to procedure B's variables, even though B called C.

Data Structures

In this section I'll describe the main data structures used during compilation (abstract data types for identifiers and for expressions) and during the running of the program (registers and frames).

The main body of information that the compiler must maintain is the list of Pascal identifiers (variable, procedure, and function names). Since Pascal is lexically scoped, some attention is necessary to ensure that each compiled Pascal procedure has access to precisely the variables that it should. At any point during the compilation, the value of `:idlist` is a list of just those identifiers that may be used in the part of the program being compiled. We'll see in a moment how that's accomplished.

There are two main categories of identifier: procedure names (including the main program and functions in this category) and variable names. The information maintained for a procedure name looks like this example:

```
[myproc procedure %myproc [2 46]]
```

The first member of this list is the Pascal name of the program, procedure, or function. The second member is the type indicator, which will be one of the words `program`, `procedure`, or `function`. The third member is the procedure's "Logo name," the unique name used within the compiler to represent this program or procedure. The program's Logo name is used as the variable name whose value will be the compiled program; the Logo names for procedures and functions are used as the labels in the compiled program at which each procedure or function begins. The fourth member of the list contains the frame information for the procedure; it's a list of two numbers, the lexical depth and the frame size. The lexical depth is 0 for the main program, 1 for a procedure declared inside the main program, 2 for a procedure declared inside a depth-1 procedure, and so on. The frame size indicates how many memory locations must be allocated for each invocation of the procedure. (For the main program, the frame size indicates the size of the global frame.)

Because of the Pascal scope rules, there can be two procedures with the same name, each declared within a different region of the program. But there is no scoping of labels in the compiled program; each label must be unique. The simplest solution would be to use a distinct program-generated name for every Pascal procedure; the Pascal `doit` would become the Logo `g14`. In fact I chose to modify this approach somewhat. When an identifier `symbol` is declared in the source program, the compiler looks to see whether another identifier with the same name has appeared anywhere in the program. If not, the Logo name `%symbol` is used; if so, a generated symbol is used. This rule makes the compiled program a little easier to read, while preserving the rule that all Logo names must be unique. The percent sign in `%symbol` ensures that this Logo name doesn't conflict with any names used in the compiler itself. Procedure `newlname` in the compiler takes a Pascal identifier as input and generates a new Logo name to correspond.

The selectors `id.type`, `id.lname`, and `id.frame` are used for the second through fourth members of these lists. There's no selector for the first member, the Pascal name, because the compiler never extracts this information explicitly. Instead, the Pascal name is used by procedure `getid`, which takes a Pascal name as its input and returns the corresponding identifier list.

For variable names, the identifier information looks a little different:

```
[i integer [1 41] false]
```

The first two members of this list are the Pascal name and the type, the same as for a procedure. The third member is the *pointer* information for the variable: its lexical depth and the offset within a frame where it should be kept. The compiler will use this information to issue instructions to load or store the value of the variable. The fourth member of the list is `true` if this variable is a `var` (call by reference) parameter, `false` otherwise.

The variable `i` above has a scalar type, so its type indicator is a word. Had it been an array, the type indicator would be a list such as

```
[integer [0 6] [5 3]]
```

for a variable declared as `array [0..5, 5..7] of integer`.

For each dimension of the array, the first number in the list is the smallest possible index, while the second number is the number of possible index values in this dimension. That is, the range `[3..7]` is represented by the list `[3 5]` because there are five possible values starting from 3. Notice that there is no "Logo name" for a variable; in the compiled program, a variable is represented as an offset and an index register, such as `41(4)`.

For variables, the selectors used are `id.type`, `id.pointer`, and `id.varp`.

The information about currently accessible identifiers is kept in the list `idlist`. This variable holds a list of lists; each Pascal identifier is represented by a list as indicated above. `Idlist` is a local variable in the compiler procedures `program`, `procedure`, and `function`. That is, there is a separate version for each block of the Pascal source program. Each local version starts out with the same value as the higher-level version; identifiers declared within a block are added to the local version but not to the outer one. When the compiler finishes a block, the (Logo) procedure in charge of that block stops and the outer `idlist` becomes current again.

This arrangement may or may not seem strange to you. Recall that we had to invent this `idlist` mechanism because Pascal's lexical scope is different from Logo's dynamic scope. The reason we have these different versions of `idlist` is to keep track of which identifiers are lexically available to which blocks. And yet we are using Logo's dynamic scope to determine which `idlist` is available at any point in the compilation. The reason this works is that *the dynamic environment at compile time reflects the lexical environment at run time.* For example, in the `tower` program, the fact that `tower` *contains* `hanoi`, which in turn contains `movedisk`, is reflected in the fact that `program` (compiling `tower`) *invokes* `procedure` (compiling `hanoi`), which in turn *invokes* `procedure` recursively (compiling `movedisk`). Earlier I said that lexical scope is easier for a compiler than dynamic scope; this paragraph may help you see why that's true. Even dynamically scoped Logo naturally falls into providing lexical scope for a Pascal compiler.

Here is how procedure and function declarations are compiled:

```
to procedure
proc1 "procedure framesize.proc
end

to function
proc1 "function framesize.fun
end

to proc1 :proctype :framesize
localmake "procname token
localmake "lexical.depth :lexical.depth+1
localmake "frame (list :lexical.depth 0)
push "idlist (list :procname :proctype (newlname :procname) :frame)
localmake "idlist :idlist
  ...
end
```

(I'm leaving out the code generation part for now.) What I want to be sure you understand is that the `push` instruction adds the new procedure name to the *outer* `idlist`; after that, it creates a new `idlist` whose initial value is the same as the old one. It's very important that the instruction

```
localmake "idlist :idlist
```

comes where it does and not at the beginning of the procedure. `Proc1` needs access to the outer `idlist` when it starts, and then later it "shadows" that variable with its own local version. This example shows that Logo's `local` command really is an executable command and not a declaration like Pascal's `var` declaration. In Pascal it would be unthinkable to declare a new local variable in the middle of a block.

Getid depends on Logo's dynamic scope to give it access to the right version of `idlist`. Think about writing a Pascal compiler in Pascal. There would be a large block for `program` with many other procedures inside it. Two of those inner procedures would be the ones for `procedure` and `function`. (Of course they couldn't have those names, because they're Pascal reserved words. They'd be called `compileprocedure` or some such thing. But I think this will be easier to follow if I stick with the names used in the Logo version of the compiler.) Those two procedures should be at the same level of block structure; neither should be lexically within the other. That's because a Pascal procedure block can include a function definition or vice versa. Now, where in the lexical structure does `getid` belong? It needs access to the local `idlist` of either `procedure` or `function`, whichever is currently active. Similarly, things like `statement` need to be lexically within both `procedure` and `function`, and actually also within `program` because the outermost program block has statements too. It would theoretically be possible to solve the problem by writing three identical versions of each of these subprocedures, but that solution is too horrible to contemplate. Instead a more common technique is to have only one `idlist` variable, a global one, and write the compiler so that it explicitly maintains a stack of old values of that variable. The Pascal programmer has to do the work that the programming language should be doing automatically. This is an example in which dynamic scope, while not absolutely essential, makes the program much easier to write and more straightforward to understand.

For every procedure or function in the Pascal source program, the compiler creates a global Logo variable with the same name as the corresponding label—that is, either a percent-prefix name or a generated symbol. The value of this variable is a list of types, one for each argument to the procedure or function. (For a function, the first member of the list is the type of the function itself; the butfirst is the list of types of its arguments.) The compiler examines this "type signature" variable when a procedure or function is invoked, to make sure that the types of the actual arguments match the types of the formal parameters.

The other important compile-time data structure is the one that represents a compiled expression. When the compiler calls `pexpr`, its job is to parse an expression from the Pascal source program and generate code to compute (when the compiled program runs!) the value of the expression. The generated code leaves the computed value in some register. What `pexpr` returns to its caller is a data structure indicating which register and what type the expression has, like this:

```
[real register 8]
```

The first member of this list is the type of the expression. Most of the time, the second member is the word `register` and the third member is the register number in which the expression's value can be found. The only exception is for a constant expression; if the expression is, for example, 15 then `pexpr` will output

```
[integer immediate 15]
```

For the most part, these immediate expressions are useful only within recursive calls to `pexpr`. In compiling the Pascal assignment

```
x := 15
```

we're going to have to get the value 15 into a register anyway in order to be able to store it into `x`; the generated code will be something like

```
addi 7 0 15
store 7 48(4)
```

An immediate expression is most useful in compiling something like

```
x := a+15
```

in which we can avoid loading the value 15 into a register, but can directly add it to the register containing `a`:

```
rload 7 53(4)
addi 7 7 15
store 7 48(4)
```

The members of an expression list are examined using the selectors `exp.type`, `exp.mode` (the word `register` or `immediate`), and `exp.value` (the register number or immediate value).

In this compiler an "expression" is always a *scalar* type; although the formal definition of Pascal allows for array expressions, there are no operations that act on arrays the way operations like + act on scalars, and so an array expression can only be the name of an array variable. (*Members* of arrays can, of course, be part of a scalar expression.) `Passign`, the compiler procedure that handles assignment statements, first checks for the special case of an array assignment and then, only if the left side of the assignment is a scalar, invokes `pexpr` to parse a scalar expression.

In order to understand the code generated by the compiler, you should also know about the *runtime* data structures used by compiled programs. First, certain registers are reserved for special purposes:

number	name	purpose
0	`reg.zero`	always contains zero
1	`reg.retaddr`	return address from procedure call
2	`reg.stackptr`	first free memory address
3	`reg.globalptr`	address of global frame
4	`reg.frameptr`	address of current frame
5	`reg.newfp`	address of frame being made for procedure call
6	`reg.retval`	return value from function
7	`reg.firstfree`	first register available for expressions

We've already seen most of these while discussing stack frames. A Pascal function returns its result in register 6; the caller immediately copies the return value into some other register so that it won't be lost if the program calls another function, for a case like

```
x := f(3)+f(4)
```

Whenever a register is needed to hold some computed value, the compiler calls the Logo procedure `newregister`, which finds the first register number starting from 7 that isn't currently in use. When the value in a register is no longer needed, the compiler calls `regfree` to indicate that that register can be reassigned by `newregister`.

The other noteworthy runtime data structure is the use of slots within each frame for special purposes:

number	name	purpose
0	`frame.retaddr`	address from which this procedure was called
1	`frame.save.newfp`	saved register 3 while filling this new frame
2	`frame.outerframe`	the frame lexically enclosing this one
3	`frame.prevframe`	the frame from which this one was called
4–35	`frame.regsave`	space for saving registers
36	`frame.retval`	function return value

Why is there both a register and a frame slot for a function's return value? Remember that the way you indicate the return value in a Pascal function is by assigning to the function's name as if it were a variable. Such an assignment is not necessarily the last instruction in the function; it may do more work after computing the return value. The compiler notices as assignment to the function name and generates code to save the computed value in slot 36 of the current frame. Then, when the function actually returns, the compiler generates the instruction

```
rload 6 36(4)
```

to copy the return value into register 6. The function's frame is about to be freed, so the caller can't look there for the return value; that's why a register is used.

Each frame includes a block of space for saving registers when another procedure is called. That's because each procedure allocates register numbers independently; each starts with register 7 as the first free one. So if the registers weren't saved before a procedure call and restored after the call, the values in the registers would be lost. (Although the frame has enough room to save all 32 registers, to make things simple, not all 32 are actually saved. The compiler knows which registers contain active expression values at the moment of the procedure call, and it generates code to save and restore only the necessary ones.)

You might think it would be easier to have each procedure use a separate set of registers, so saving wouldn't be necessary. But this doesn't work for two reasons. First, there are only a few registers, and in a large program we'd run out. Even more important, the compiled code for a *recursive* procedure is going to use the same registers in each invocation, so we certainly can't avoid saving registers in that situation.

Code Generation

Let's look again at how the compiler handles a Pascal `if` statement:

```
to pif
local [cond elsetag endtag]
make "cond pboolean pexpr
make "elsetag gensym
make "endtag gensym
mustbe "then
code (list "jumpf :cond (word "" :elsetag))
regfree :cond
statement
code (list "jump (word "" :endtag))
code :elsetag
ifbe "else [statement]
code :endtag
end
```

I showed you this procedure while talking about parsing, asking you to ignore the parts about code generation. Now we'll come back to that part of the process.

The format of the if statement is either of these:

if *condition* then *statement*
if *condition* then *statement* else *statement*

(There is probably a semicolon after the statement, but it's not officially part of the if; it's part of the compound statement that contains the if.) When we get to pif, the compiler has already read the token if; the next thing to read is an expression, which must be of type boolean, providing the condition part of the statement.

In the instruction

```
make "cond pboolean pexpr
```

the call to pexpr generates code for the expression and returns an expression list, in the format shown earlier. The procedure pboolean does three things: First, it checks the mode of the expression; if it's immediate, the value is loaded into a register. Second, it checks the type of the expression to ensure that it really is boolean. Third, pboolean returns just the register number, which will be used in code generated by pif.

```
to pboolean :expr [:pval noimmediate :expr]
if equalp exp.type :pval "boolean [output exp.value :pval]
(throw "error sentence exp.type :pval [not true or false])
end

to noimmediate :value
if equalp exp.mode :value "immediate ~
   [localmake "reg newregister
    code (list "addi :reg reg.zero exp.value :value)
    output (list exp.type :value "register :reg)]
output :value
end
```

Overall, the code compiled for the if statement will look like this:

```
... get condition into register cond ...
jumpf cond "g5
... code for then statement ...
jump "g6
g5
... code for else statement ...
g6
```

The labels g5 and g6 in this example are generated symbols; they'll be different each time. The labels are generated by the instructions

```
make "elsetag gensym
make "endtag gensym
```

in pif. After we call pexpr to generate the code for the conditional expression, we explicitly generate the jumpf instruction:

```
code (list "jumpf :cond (word "" :elsetag))
regfree :cond
```

Notice that once we've generated the jumpf instruction, we no longer need the value in register :cond, and we call regfree to say so. The rest of this code generation process should be easy to work out. All of the structured statements (for, while, and repeat) are similarly simple.

The code generation for expressions is all in ppopop. Most of the complexity of dealing with expressions is in the parsing, not in the code generation; by the time we get to ppopop, we know that we want to carry out a single operation on two values, both of which are either in registers or immediate values. The simple case is that both are in registers; suppose, for example, that we are given the subtraction operation and the two operands are in registers 8 and 9. Then we just generate the instruction

```
sub 8 8 9
```

and declare register 9 free. Ppopop is a little long, because it has to check for special cases such as immediate operands. Also, a unary minus is turned into a subtraction from register zero, since there is no unary minus operation in our simulated machine.

Ironically, it's the "simple" statements that are hardest to compile: assignment and procedure calling. For procedure (or function) calling, the difficulty is in matching actual argument expressions with formal parameters. Procedure pproccall1 generates the instructions to manipulate frame pointers, as described earlier, and procedure procargs fills the newly-created frame with the actual argument values. (If an argument is an array passed by value, each member of the array must be copied into the new frame.) Assignment, handled by procedure passign in the compiler, is similar to argument passing; a value must be computed and then stored into a frame. I wouldn't be too upset if you decide to stop here and take code generation for memory references on faith.

Suppose we are compiling the assignment

x := *expression*

Passign reads the name x and uses getid to find the information associated with that name. If the assignment is to an array member, then passign must also read the array indices, but let's say that we are assigning to a scalar variable, to keep it simple.

```
to passign
local [name id type index value pointer target]
make "name token
make "index []
ifbe "|[| [make "index commalist [pexpr] mustbe "|]|]
mustbe "|:=|
make "id getid :name
make "pointer id.pointer :id
make "type id.type :id
passign1
end
```

Procedure passign1 contains the steps that are in common between ordinary assignment (handled by passign) and assignment to the name of the current function, to set the return value (handled by pfunset, which you can read in the complete listing at the end of the chapter).

```
to passign1
if and (listp :type) (emptyp :index) [parrayassign :id  stop]
setindex "false
make "value check.type :type pexpr
codestore :value (id.pointer :id) (id.varp :id) :index
regfree :value
end
```

We call pexpr to generate the code to compute the expression. Check.type is like pboolean, which you saw earlier, except that it takes the desired type as an argument. It returns the number of the register that contains the expression value.

The real work is done by codestore, which takes four inputs. The first is the register number whose value should be stored; the other three inputs indicate where in memory the value should go. First comes the pointer from the identifier list; this, you'll recall, tells us the lexical depth at which the variable was declared and the offset within its frame where the variable is kept. Next is a true or false value indicating whether or not this variable is a var parameter; if so, then its value is a pointer to the variable whose value we *really* want to change. Finally, the *index* input will be zero for a scalar variable, or the number of a register containing the array index for an array member. (Procedure `lindex`, whose name stands for "linear index," has been called to generate code to convert the possible multi-dimensional indices, with possibly varying starting values, into a single number indicating the position within the array, starting from zero for the first member.)

```
to codestore :reg :pointer :varflag :index
localmake "target memsetup :pointer :varflag :index
code (list "store :reg targetaddr)
regfree last :target
end
```

(There is a similar procedure `codeload` used to generate the code to load a variable's value into a register.) `Codestore` invokes a subprocedure `memsetup` whose job is to work out an appropriate operand for an `rload` or `store` machine instruction. That operand must be an offset and an index register, such as `41(4)`. What `memsetup` returns is a list of the two numbers, in this case `[41 4]`. Procedure `targetaddr` turns that into the right notation for use in the instruction.

`Memsetup` is the most complicated procedure in the compiler, because there are so many special cases. I'll describe the easy cases here. Suppose that we are dealing with a scalar variable that isn't a `var` parameter. Then there are three cases. If the lexical depth of that variable is equal to the current lexical depth, then this variable is declared in the same block that we're compiling. In that case, we use register 4 (the current frame pointer) as the index register, and the variable's frame slot as the offset. If the variable's lexical depth is zero, then it's a global variable. In that case, we use register 3 (the global frame pointer) as the index register, and the variable's frame slot as the offset. If the variable's depth is something other than zero or the current depth, then we have to find a pointer to the variable's own frame by looking in the current frame's `frame.outerframe` slot, and perhaps in *that* frame's `frame.outerframe` slot, as many times as the difference between the current depth and the variable's depth.

If the variable is a `var` parameter, then we go through the same cases just described, and then load the value of that variable (which is a pointer to the variable we really want) into a register. We use that new register as the index register, and zero as the offset.

If the variable is an array member, then we must add the linear index (which is already in a register) to the offset as computed so far.

Perhaps an example will help sort this out. Here is the compiled version of the `tower` program, with annotations:

```
[                 [add 3 0 0]                  set up initial pointers
                  [add 4 0 0]
                  [addi 2 0 36]
                  [jump "g1]                   jump to main program

%hanoi            [store 1 0(4)]               save return value
                  [jump "g2]                   jump to body of hanoi

%movedisk         [store 1 0(4)]
                  [jump "g3]

g3                [putstr 1 [Move disk ]]      body of movedisk
                  [rload 7 36(4)]
                  [putint 1 7]                 write(number:1)
                  [putstr 1 [ from ]]
                  [rload 7 37(4)]
                  [putch 1 7]                  write(from:1)
                  [putstr 1 [ to ]]
                  [rload 7 38(4)]
                  [putch 1 7]                  write(to:1)
                  [newline]
                  [rload 1 0(4)]               reload return address
                  [add 2 4 0]                  free stack frame
                  [rload 4 3(2)]
                  [jr 1]                        return to caller
```

```
g2      [rload 7 36(4)]          body of hanoi
        [neqi 7 7 0]             if number <> 0
        [jumpf 7 "g4]
        [store 5 1(2)]           allocate new frame
        [add 5 2 0]
        [addi 2 2 40]
        [store 4 3(5)]           set previous frame
        [rload 7 2(4)]
        [store 7 2(5)]           set enclosing frame
        [rload 7 36(4)]
        [subi 7 7 1]
        [store 7 36(5)]          first arg is number-1
        [rload 7 37(4)]
        [store 7 37(5)]          next arg is from
        [rload 7 39(4)]
        [store 7 38(5)]          next arg is other
        [rload 7 38(4)]
        [store 7 39(5)]          next arg is onto
        [add 4 5 0]              switch to new frame
        [rload 5 1(4)]
        [jal 1 "%hanoi]          recursive call

        [store 5 1(2)]           set up for movedisk
        [add 5 2 0]
        [addi 2 2 39]
        [store 4 3(5)]
        [store 4 2(5)]           note different enclosing frame
        [rload 7 36(4)]
        [store 7 36(5)]          copy args
        [rload 7 37(4)]
        [store 7 37(5)]
        [rload 7 38(4)]
        [store 7 38(5)]
        [add 4 5 0]
        [rload 5 1(4)]
        [jal 1 "%movedisk]       call movedisk
```

```
            [store 5 1(2)]                  second recursive call
            [add 5 2 0]
            [addi 2 2 40]
            [store 4 3(5)]
            [rload 7 2(4)]
            [store 7 2(5)]
            [rload 7 36(4)]
            [subi 7 7 1]
            [store 7 36(5)]
            [rload 7 39(4)]
            [store 7 37(5)]
            [rload 7 38(4)]
            [store 7 38(5)]
            [rload 7 37(4)]
            [store 7 39(5)]
            [add 4 5 0]
            [rload 5 1(4)]
            [jal 1 "%hanoi]
            [jump "g5]                       end of if...then


g4
g5          [rload 1 0(4)]                   return to caller
            [add 2 4 0]
            [rload 4 3(2)]
            [jr 1]


g1          [store 5 1(2)]                   body of main program
            [add 5 2 0]                      prepare to call hanoi
            [addi 2 2 40]
            [store 4 3(5)]
            [store 4 2(5)]
            [addi 7 0 5]                     constant argument 5
            [store 7 36(5)]
            [addi 7 0 97]                    ASCII code for 'a'
            [store 7 37(5)]
            [addi 7 0 98]                    ASCII code for 'b'
            [store 7 38(5)]
            [addi 7 0 99]                    ASCII code for 'c'
            [store 7 39(5)]
            [add 4 5 0]
            [rload 5 1(4)]
            [jal 1 "%hanoi]                  call hanoi
            [exit]
]
```

Program Listing

```
to compile :file
if namep "peekchar [ern "peekchar]
if namep "peektoken [ern "peektoken]
if not namep "idlist [opsetup]
if not emptyp :file [openread :file]
setread :file
ignore error
catch "error [program]
localmake "error error
if not emptyp :error [print first butfirst :error]
setread []
if not emptyp :file [close :file]
end


;; Global setup

to opsetup
make "numregs 32
make "memsize 3000
pprop "|=| "binary [eql 2 [boolean []] 1]
pprop "|<>| "binary [neq 2 [boolean []] 1]
pprop "|<| "binary [less 2 [boolean []] 1]
pprop "|>| "binary [gtr 2 [boolean []] 1]
pprop "|<=| "binary [leq 2 [boolean []] 1]
pprop "|>=| "binary [geq 2 [boolean []] 1]
pprop "|+| "binary [add 2 [[] []] 2]
pprop "|-| "binary [sub 2 [[] []] 2]
pprop "or "binary [lor 2 [boolean boolean] 2]
pprop "|*| "binary [mul 2 [[] []] 3]
pprop "|/| "binary [quo 2 [real []] 3]
pprop "div "binary [div 2 [integer integer] 3]
pprop "mod "binary [rem 2 [integer integer] 3]
pprop "and "binary [land 2 [boolean boolean] 3]
pprop "|+| "unary [plus 1 [[] []] 4]
pprop "|-| "unary [minus 1 [[] []] 4]
pprop "not "unary [lnot 1 [boolean boolean] 4]
make "idlist '[[trunc function int [1 ,[framesize.fun+1]]]
               [round function round [1 ,[framesize.fun+1]]]
               [random function random [1 ,[framesize.fun+1]]]]
make "int [integer real]
make "round [integer real]
make "random [integer integer]
end
```

```
;; Block structure

to program
mustbe "program
localmake "progname token
ifbe "|(| [ignore commalist [id]  mustbe "|)|]
mustbe "|;|
localmake "lexical.depth 0
localmake "namesused []
localmake "needint "false
localmake "needround "false
localmake "needrandom "false
localmake "idlist :idlist
localmake "frame [0 0]
localmake "id (list :progname "program (newlname :progname) :frame)
push "idlist :id
localmake "codeinto word "% :progname
make :codeinto []
localmake "framesize framesize.proc
program1
mustbe ".
code [exit]
foreach [int round random] "plibrary
make :codeinto reverse thing :codeinto
end


to program1
localmake "regsused (array :numregs 0)
for [i reg.firstfree :numregs-1] [setitem :i :regsused "false]
ifbe "var [varpart]
.setfirst butfirst :frame :framesize
if :lexical.depth = 0 [code (list "add reg.globalptr reg.zero reg.zero)
                       code (list "add reg.frameptr reg.zero reg.zero)
                       code (list "addi reg.stackptr reg.zero :framesize)]
localmake "bodytag gensym
code (list "jump (word "" :bodytag))
tryprocpart
code :bodytag
mustbe "begin
blockbody "end
end


to plibrary :func
if not thing (word "need :func) [stop]
code :func
code (list "rload reg.firstfree (memaddr framesize.fun reg.frameptr))
code (list (word "s :func) reg.retval reg.firstfree)
code (list "add reg.stackptr reg.frameptr reg.zero)
code (list "rload reg.frameptr (memaddr frame.prevframe reg.stackptr))
code (list "jr reg.retaddr)
end
```

```
;; Variable declarations

to varpart
local [token namelist type]
make "token token
make "peektoken :token
if reservedp :token [stop]
vargroup
foreach :namelist [newvar ? :type]
mustbe "|;|
varpart
end

to vargroup
make "namelist commalist [id]
mustbe ":
ifbe "packed []
make "type token
ifelse equalp :type "array [make "type arraytype] [typecheck :type]
end

to id
localmake "token token
if letterp ascii first :token [output :token]
make "peektoken :token
output []
end

to arraytype
local [ranges type]
mustbe "|[|
make "ranges commalist [range]
mustbe "|]|
mustbe "of
make "type token
typecheck :type
output list :type :ranges
end

to range
local [first last]
make "first range1
mustbe "..
make "last range1
if :first > :last ~
   [(throw "error (sentence [array bounds not increasing:]
                              :first ".. :last))]
output list :first (1 + :last - :first)
end
```

```
to range1
localmake "bound token
if equalp first :bound "' [output ascii first butfirst :bound]
if equalp :bound "|-| [make "bound minus token]
if equalp :bound int :bound [output :bound]
(throw "error sentence [array bound not ordinal:] :bound)
end

to typecheck :type
if memberp :type [real integer char boolean] [stop]
(throw "error sentence [undefined type] :type)
end

to newvar :pname :type
if reservedp :pname [(throw "error sentence :pname [reserved word])]
push "idlist (list :pname :type (list :lexical.depth :framesize) "false)
make "framesize :framesize + ifelse listp :type [arraysize :type] [1]
end

to arraysize :type
output reduce "product map [last ?] last :type
end

;; Procedure and function declarations

to tryprocpart
ifbeelse "procedure ~
        [procedure tryprocpart] ~
        [ifbe "function [function tryprocpart]]
end

to procedure
proc1 "procedure framesize.proc
end

to function
proc1 "function framesize.fun
end
```

```
to proc1 :proctype :framesize
localmake "procname token
localmake "lexical.depth :lexical.depth+1
localmake "frame (list :lexical.depth 0)
push "idlist (list :procname :proctype (newlname :procname) :frame)
localmake "idlist :idlist
make lname :procname []
ifbe "|(| [arglist]
if equalp :proctype "function ~
   [mustbe ":
    localmake "type token
    typecheck :type
    make lname :procname fput :type thing lname :procname]
mustbe "|;|
code lname :procname
code (list "store reg.retaddr (memaddr frame.retaddr reg.frameptr))
program1
if equalp :proctype "function ~
   [code (list "rload reg.retval (memaddr frame.retval reg.frameptr))]
code (list "rload reg.retaddr (memaddr frame.retaddr reg.frameptr))
code (list "add reg.stackptr reg.frameptr reg.zero)
code (list "rload reg.frameptr (memaddr frame.prevframe reg.stackptr))
code (list "jr reg.retaddr)
mustbe "|;|
end


to arglist
local [token namelist type varflag]
make "varflag "false
ifbe "var [make "varflag "true]
vargroup
foreach :namelist [newarg ? :type :varflag]
ifbeelse "|;| [arglist] [mustbe "|)|]
end


to newarg :pname :type :varflag
if reservedp :pname [(throw "error sentence :pname [reserved word])]
localmake "pointer (list :lexical.depth :framesize)
push "idlist (list :pname :type :pointer :varflag)
make "framesize :framesize + ifelse (and listp :type not :varflag) ~
                                     [arraysize :type] [1]
queue lname :procname ifelse :varflag [list "var :type] [:type]
end


;; Statement part

to blockbody :endword
statement
ifbeelse "|;| [blockbody :endword] [mustbe :endword]
end
```

```
to statement
local [token type]
ifbe "begin [compound stop]
ifbe "for [pfor stop]
ifbe "if [pif stop]
ifbe "while [pwhile stop]
ifbe "repeat [prepeat stop]
ifbe "write [pwrite stop]
ifbe "writeln [pwriteln stop]
make "token token
make "peektoken :token
if memberp :token [|;| end until] [stop]
make "type gettype :token
if emptyp :type [(throw "error sentence :token [can't begin statement])]
if equalp :type "procedure [pproccall stop]
if equalp :type "function [pfunset stop]
passign
end


;; Compound statement

to compound
blockbody "end
end


;; Structured statements

to pif
local [cond elsetag endtag]
make "cond pboolean pexpr
make "elsetag gensym
make "endtag gensym
mustbe "then
code (list "jumpf :cond (word "" :elsetag))
regfree :cond
statement
code (list "jump (word "" :endtag))
code :elsetag
ifbe "else [statement]
code :endtag
end


to prepeat
local [cond looptag]
make "looptag gensym
code :looptag
blockbody "until
make "cond pboolean pexpr
code (list "jumpf :cond (word "" :looptag))
regfree :cond
end
```

```
to pfor
local [var init step final looptag endtag testreg]
make "var token
mustbe "|:=|
make "init pinteger pexpr
make "step 1
ifbeelse "downto [make "step -1] [mustbe "to]
make "final pinteger pexpr
mustbe "do
make "looptag gensym
make "endtag gensym
code :looptag
localmake "id getid :var
codestore :init (id.pointer :id) (id.varp :id) 0
make "testreg newregister
code (list (ifelse :step<0 ["less] ["gtr]) :testreg :init :final)
code (list "jumpt :testreg (word "" :endtag))
regfree :testreg
statement
code (list "addi :init :init :step)
code (list "jump (word "" :looptag))
code :endtag
regfree :init
regfree :final
end

to pwhile
local [cond looptag endtag]
make "looptag gensym
make "endtag gensym
code :looptag
make "cond pboolean pexpr
code (list "jumpf :cond (word "" :endtag))
regfree :cond
mustbe "do
statement
code (list "jump (word "" :looptag))
code :endtag
end

;; Simple statements: procedure call

to pproccall
localmake "pname token
localmake "id getid :pname
localmake "lname id.lname :id
localmake "vartypes thing :lname
pproccall1 framesize.proc
end
```

```
to pproccall1 :offset
code (list "store reg.newfp (memaddr frame.save.newfp reg.stackptr))
code (list "add reg.newfp reg.stackptr reg.zero)
code (list "addi reg.stackptr reg.stackptr (last id.frame :id))
code (list "store reg.frameptr (memaddr frame.prevframe reg.newfp))
localmake "newdepth first id.frame :id
ifelse :newdepth > :lexical.depth ~
     [code (list "store reg.frameptr
                    (memaddr frame.outerframe reg.newfp))] ~
     [localmake "tempreg newregister
      code (list "rload :tempreg (memaddr frame.outerframe reg.frameptr))
      repeat (:lexical.depth - :newdepth)
            [code (list "rload :tempreg
                           (memaddr frame.outerframe :tempreg))]
      code (list "store :tempreg (memaddr frame.outerframe reg.newfp))
      regfree :tempreg]
if not emptyp :vartypes [mustbe "|(|  procargs :vartypes :offset]
for [i reg.firstfree :numregs-1] ~
   [if item :i :regsused
        [code (list "store :i (memaddr frame.regsave+:i reg.frameptr))]]
code (list "add reg.frameptr reg.newfp reg.zero)
code (list "rload reg.newfp (memaddr frame.save.newfp reg.frameptr))
code (list "jal reg.retaddr (word "" :lname))
for [i reg.firstfree :numregs-1] ~
   [if item :i :regsused
        [code (list "rload :i (memaddr frame.regsave+:i reg.frameptr))]]
end


to procargs :types :offset
if emptyp :types [mustbe "|)|  stop]
localmake "next procarg first :types :offset
if not emptyp butfirst :types [mustbe ",]
procargs butfirst :types :offset+:next
end


to procarg :type :offset
if equalp first :type "var [output procvararg last :type]
if listp :type [output procarrayarg :type]
localmake "result check.type :type pexpr
code (list "store :result (memaddr :offset reg.newfp))
regfree :result
output 1
end
```

```
to procvararg :ftype
local [pname id type index]
make "pname token
make "id getid :pname
make "type id.type :id
ifelse wordp :ftype ~
        [setindex "true] ~
        [make "index 0]
if not equalp :type :ftype ~
   [(throw "error sentence :pname [arg wrong type])]
localmake "target memsetup (id.pointer :id) (id.varp :id) :index
localmake "tempreg newregister
code (list "addi :tempreg (last :target) (first :target))
code (list "store :tempreg (memaddr :offset reg.newfp))
regfree last :target
regfree :tempreg
output 1
end


to procarrayarg :type
localmake "pname token
localmake "id getid :pname
if not equalp :type (id.type :id) ~
   [(throw "error (sentence "array :pname [wrong type for arg]))]
localmake "size arraysize :type
localmake "rtarget memsetup (id.pointer :id) (id.varp :id) 0
localmake "pointreg newregister
code (list "addi :pointreg reg.newfp :offset)
localmake "ltarget (list 0 :pointreg)
copyarray
output :size
end


;; Simple statements: write and writeln

to pwrite
mustbe "|(|
pwrite1
end


to pwrite1
pwrite2
ifbe "|)| [stop]
ifbeelse ", [pwrite1] [(throw "error [missing comma])]
end
```

```
to pwrite2
localmake "result pwrite3
ifbe ": [.setfirst (butfirst :result) token]
code :result
if not equalp first :result "putstr [regfree last :result]
end


to pwrite3
localmake "token token
if equalp first :token "' ~
   [output (list "putstr 1 (list butlast butfirst :token))]
make "peektoken :token
localmake "result pexpr
if equalp first :result "char [output (list "putch 1 pchar :result)]
if equalp first :result "boolean [output (list "puttf 1 pboolean :result)]
if equalp first :result "integer [output (list "putint 10 pinteger :result)]
output (list "putreal 20 preal :result)
end


to pwriteln
ifbe "|(| [pwrite1]
code [newline]
end


;; Simple statements: assignment statement (including function value)

to passign
local [name id type index value pointer target]
make "name token
make "index []
ifbe "|[| [make "index commalist [pexpr] mustbe "|]|]
mustbe "|:=|
make "id getid :name
make "pointer id.pointer :id
make "type id.type :id
passign1
end


to pfunset
local [name id type index value pointer target]
make "name token
make "index []
if not equalp :name :procname ~
   [(throw "error sentence [assign to wrong function] :name)]
mustbe "|:=|
make "pointer (list :lexical.depth frame.retval)
make "type first thing lname :name
make "id (list :name :type :pointer "false)
passign1
end
```

```
to passign1
if and (listp :type) (emptyp :index) [parrayassign :id  stop]
setindex "false
make "value check.type :type pexpr
codestore :value (id.pointer :id) (id.varp :id) :index
regfree :value
end


to noimmediate :value
if not equalp exp.mode :value "immediate [output :value]
localmake "reg newregister
code (list "addi :reg reg.zero exp.value :value)
output (list exp.type :value "register :reg)
end


to check.type :type :result
if equalp :type "real [output preal :result]
if equalp :type "integer [output pinteger :result]
if equalp :type "char [output pchar :result]
if equalp :type "boolean [output pboolean :result]
end


to preal :expr [:pval noimmediate :expr]
if equalp exp.type :pval "real [output exp.value :pval]
output pinteger :pval
end


to pinteger :expr [:pval noimmediate :expr]
localmake "type exp.type :pval
if memberp :type [integer boolean char] [output exp.value :pval]
(throw "error sentence exp.type :pval [isn't ordinal])
end


to pchar :expr [:pval noimmediate :expr]
if equalp exp.type :pval "char [output exp.value :pval]
(throw "error sentence exp.type :pval [not character value])
end


to pboolean :expr [:pval noimmediate :expr]
if equalp exp.type :pval "boolean [output exp.value :pval]
(throw "error sentence exp.type :pval [not true or false])
end
```

```
to parrayassign :id
localmake "right token
if equalp first :right "' ~
   [pstringassign :type (butlast butfirst :right)  stop]
localmake "rid getid :right
if not equalp (id.type :id) (id.type :rid) ~
   [(throw "error (sentence "arrays :name "and :right [unequal types]))]
localmake "size arraysize id.type :id
localmake "ltarget memsetup (id.pointer :id) (id.varp :id) 0
localmake "rtarget memsetup (id.pointer :rid) (id.varp :rid) 0
copyarray
end


to pstringassign :type :string
if not equalp first :type "char [stringlose]
if not emptyp butfirst last :type [stringlose]
if not equalp (last first last :type) (count :string) [stringlose]
localmake "ltarget memsetup (id.pointer :id) (id.varp :id) 0
pstringassign1 newregister (first :ltarget) (last :ltarget) :string
regfree last :ltarget
end


to pstringassign1 :tempreg :offset :reg :string
if emptyp :string [regfree :tempreg  stop]
code (list "addi :tempreg reg.zero ascii first :string)
code (list "store :tempreg (memaddr :offset :reg))
pstringassign1 :tempreg :offset+1 :reg (butfirst :string)
end


to stringlose
(throw "error sentence :name [not string array or wrong size])
end


;; Multiple array indices to linear index computation

to setindex :parseflag
ifelse listp :type ~
      [if :parseflag
         [mustbe "|[|  make "index commalist [pexpr]  mustbe "|]| ]
        make "index lindex last :type :index
        make "type first :type] ~
      [make "index 0]
end


to lindex :bounds :index
output lindex1 (offset pinteger noimmediate first :index
                     first first :bounds) ~
            butfirst :bounds butfirst :index
end
```

```
to lindex1 :sofar :bounds :index
if emptyp :bounds [output :sofar]
output lindex1 (nextindex :sofar
                          last first :bounds
                          pinteger noimmediate first :index
                          first first :bounds) ~
              butfirst :bounds butfirst :index
end

to nextindex :old :factor :new :offset
code (list "muli :old :old :factor)
localmake "newreg offset :new :offset
code (list "add :old :old :newreg)
regfree :newreg
output :old
end

to offset :indexreg :lowbound
if not equalp :lowbound 0 [code (list "subi :indexreg :indexreg :lowbound)]
output :indexreg
end

;; Memory interface: load and store instructions

to codeload :reg :pointer :varflag :index
localmake "target memsetup :pointer :varflag :index
code (list "rload :reg targetaddr)
regfree last :target
end

to codestore :reg :pointer :varflag :index
localmake "target memsetup :pointer :varflag :index
code (list "store :reg targetaddr)
regfree last :target
end

to targetaddr
output memaddr (first :target) (last :target)
end

to memaddr :offset :index
output (word :offset "\( :index "\))
end
```

```
to memsetup :pointer :varflag :index
localmake "depth first :pointer
localmake "offset last :pointer
local "newreg
ifelse equalp :depth 0 ~
        [make "newreg reg.globalptr] ~
        [ifelse equalp :depth :lexical.depth
                [make "newreg reg.frameptr]
                [make "newreg newregister
                 code (list "rload :newreg
                            (memaddr frame.outerframe reg.frameptr))
                 repeat (:lexical.depth - :depth) - 1
                        [code (list "rload :newreg
                                    (memaddr frame.outerframe :newreg))]]]
if :varflag ~
   [ifelse :newreg = reg.frameptr
           [make "newreg newregister
            code (list "rload :newreg (memaddr :offset reg.frameptr))]
           [code (list "rload :newreg (memaddr :offset :newreg))]
    make "offset 0]
if not equalp :index 0 ~
   [code (list "add :index :index :newreg)
    regfree :newreg
    make "newreg :index]
output list :offset :newreg
end


to copyarray
localmake "looptag gensym
localmake "sizereg newregister
code (list "addi :sizereg reg.zero :size)
code :looptag
localmake "tempreg newregister
code (list "rload :tempreg (memaddr (first :rtarget) (last :rtarget)))
code (list "store :tempreg (memaddr (first :ltarget) (last :ltarget)))
code (list "addi (last :rtarget) (last :rtarget) 1)
code (list "addi (last :ltarget) (last :ltarget) 1)
code (list "subi :sizereg :sizereg 1)
code (list "gtr :tempreg :sizereg reg.zero)
code (list "jumpt :tempreg (word "" :looptag))
regfree :sizereg
regfree :tempreg
regfree last :ltarget
regfree last :rtarget
end
```

```
;; Expressions

to pexpr
local [opstack datastack parenlevel]
make "opstack [[popen 1 0]]
make "datastack []
make "parenlevel 0
output pexpr1
end

to pexpr1
local [token op]
make "token token
while [equalp :token "|(|] [popen  make "token token]
make "op pgetunary :token
if not emptyp :op [output pexprop :op]
push "datastack pdata :token
make "token token
while [and (:parenlevel > 0) (equalp :token "|)| )] ~
      [pclose  make "token token]
make "op pgetbinary :token
if not emptyp :op [output pexprop :op]
make "peektoken :token
pclose
if not emptyp :opstack [(throw "error [too many operators])]
if not emptyp butfirst :datastack [(throw "error [too many operands])]
output pop "datastack
end

to pexprop :op
while [(op.prec :op) < (1 + op.prec first :opstack)] [ppopop]
push "opstack :op
output pexpr1
end

to popen
push "opstack [popen 1 0]
make "parenlevel :parenlevel + 1
end

to pclose
while [(op.prec first :opstack) > 0] [ppopop]
ignore pop "opstack
make "parenlevel :parenlevel - 1
end

to pgetunary :token
output gprop :token "unary
end
```

```
to pgetbinary :token
output gprop :token "binary
end


to ppopop
local [op function args left right type reg]
make "op pop "opstack
make "function op.instr :op
if equalp :function "plus [stop]
make "args op.nargs :op
make "right pop "datastack
make "left (ifelse equalp :args 2 [pop "datastack] [[[] []]])
make "type pnewtype :op exp.type :left exp.type :right
if equalp exp.mode :left "immediate ~
   [localmake "leftreg newregister
    code (list "addi :leftreg reg.zero exp.value :left)
    make "left (list exp.type :left "register :leftreg)]
ifelse equalp exp.mode :left "register ~
        [make "reg exp.value :left] ~
        [ifelse equalp exp.mode :right "register
                [make "reg exp.value :right]
                [make "reg newregister]]
if equalp :function "minus ~
   [make "left (list exp.type :right "register reg.zero)
    make "function "sub
    make "args 2]
if equalp exp.mode :right "immediate ~
   [make "function word :function "i]
ifelse equalp :args 2 ~
        [code (list :function :reg exp.value :left exp.value :right)] ~
        [code (list :function :reg exp.value :right)]
if not equalp :reg exp.value :left [regfree exp.value :left]
if (and (equalp exp.mode :right "register)
        (not equalp :reg exp.value :right)) ~
   [regfree exp.value :right]
push "datastack (list :type "register :reg)
end


to pnewtype :op :ltype :rtype
localmake "type op.types :op
if emptyp :ltype [make "ltype :rtype]
if not emptyp last :type [pchecktype last :type :ltype :rtype]
if and (equalp :ltype "real) (equalp :rtype "integer) [make "rtype "real]
if and (equalp :ltype "integer) (equalp :rtype "real) [make "ltype "real]
if not equalp :ltype :rtype [(throw "error [type clash])]
if emptyp last :type ~
   [if not memberp :rtype [integer real]
       [(throw "error [nonarithmetic type])]]
if emptyp first :type [output :rtype]
output first :type
end
```

```
to pchecktype :want :left :right
if not equalp :want :left [(throw "error (sentence :left "isn't :want))]
if not equalp :want :right [(throw "error (sentence :right "isn't :want))]
end


;; Expression elements

to pdata :token
if equalp :token "true [output [boolean immediate 1]]
if equalp :token "false [output [boolean immediate 0]]
if equalp first :token "' [output pchardata :token]
if numberp :token [output (list numtype :token "immediate :token)]
localmake "id getid :token
if emptyp :id [(throw "error sentence [undefined symbol] :token)]
localmake "type id.type :id
if equalp :type "function [output pfuncall :token]
local "index
setindex "true
localmake "reg newregister
codeload :reg (id.pointer :id) (id.varp :id) :index
output (list :type "register :reg)
end


to pchardata :token
if not equalp count :token 3 ~
   [(throw "error sentence :token [not single character])]
output (list "char "immediate ascii first butfirst :token)
end


to numtype :number
if memberp ". :number [output "real]
if memberp "e :number [output "real]
output "integer
end


to pfuncall :pname
localmake "id getid :pname
localmake "lname id.lname :id
if namep (word "need :lname) [make (word "need :lname) "true]
localmake "vartypes thing :lname
localmake "returntype first :vartypes
make "vartypes butfirst :vartypes
pproccall1 framesize.fun
localmake "reg newregister
code (list "add :reg reg.retval reg.zero)
output (list :returntype "register :reg)
end
```

```
;; Parsing assistance

to code :stuff
if emptyp :stuff [stop]
push :codeinto :stuff
end

to commalist :test [:sofar []]
local [result token]
make "result run :test
if emptyp :result [output :sofar]
ifbe ", [output (commalist :test (lput :result :sofar))]
output lput :result :sofar
end

.macro ifbe :wanted :action
localmake "token token
if equalp :token :wanted [output :action]
make "peektoken :token
output []
end

.macro ifbeelse :wanted :action :else
localmake "token token
if equalp :token :wanted [output :action]
make "peektoken :token
output :else
end

to mustbe :wanted
localmake "token token
if equalp :token :wanted [stop]
(throw "error (sentence "expected :wanted "got :token))
end

to newregister
for [i reg.firstfree :numregs-1] ~
    [if not item :i :regsused [setitem :i :regsused "true  output :i]]
(throw "error [not enough registers available])
end

to regfree :reg
setitem :reg :regsused "false
end
```

```
to reservedp :word
output memberp :word [and array begin case const div do downto else end ~
                     file for forward function goto if in label mod nil ~
                     not of packed procedure program record repeat set ~
                     then to type until var while with]
end


;; Lexical analysis

to token
local [token char]
if namep "peektoken [make "token :peektoken
                     ern "peektoken    output :token]
make "char getchar
if equalp :char "|{| [skipcomment output token]
if equalp :char char 32 [output token]
if equalp :char char 13 [output token]
if equalp :char char 10 [output token]
if equalp :char "' [output string "']
if memberp :char [+ - * / = ( , ) |[| |]| |;|] [output :char]
if equalp :char "|<| [output twochar "|<| [= >]]
if equalp :char "|>| [output twochar "|>| [=]]
if equalp :char ". [output twochar ". [.]]
if equalp :char ": [output twochar ": [=]]
if numberp :char [output number :char]
if letterp ascii :char [output token1 lowercase :char]
(throw "error sentence [unrecognized character:] :char)
end


to skipcomment
if equalp getchar "|}| [stop]
skipcomment
end


to string :string
localmake "char getchar
if not equalp :char "' [output string word :string :char]
make "char getchar
if equalp :char "' [output string word :string :char]
make "peekchar :char
output word :string "'
end


to twochar :old :ok
localmake "char getchar
if memberp :char :ok [output word :old :char]
make "peekchar :char
output :old
end
```

```
to number :num
localmake "char getchar
if equalp :char ". ~
   [make "char getchar ~
    ifelse equalp :char ". ~
            [make "peektoken ".. output :num] ~
            [make "peekchar :char output number word :num ".]]
if equalp :char "e [output number word :num twochar "e [+ -]]
if numberp :char [output number word :num :char]
make "peekchar :char  output :num
end


to token1 :token
localmake "char getchar
if or letterp ascii :char numberp :char ~
   [output token1 word :token lowercase :char]
make "peekchar :char  output :token
end


to letterp :code
if and (:code > 64) (:code < 91) [output "true]
output and (:code > 96) (:code < 123)
end


to getchar
local "char
if namep "peekchar [make "char :peekchar  ern "peekchar  output :char]
ifelse eofp [output char 1] [output rc1]
end


to rc1
localmake "result readchar
type :result  output :result
end


;; Data abstraction: ID List

to newlname :word
if memberp :word :namesused [output gensym]
if namep word "% :word [output gensym]
push "namesused :word
output word "% :word
end


to lname :word
localmake "result getid :word
if not emptyp :result [output item 3 :result]
(throw "error sentence [unrecognized identifier] :word)
end
```

```
to gettype :word
localmake "result getid :word
if not emptyp :result [output item 2 :result]
(throw "error sentence [unrecognized identifier] :word)
end

to getid :word [:list :idlist]
if emptyp :list [output []]
if equalp :word first first :list [output first :list]
output (getid :word butfirst :list)
end

to id.type :id                    to id.varp :id
output item 2 :id                 output item 4 :id
end                               end

to id.pointer :id                 to id.frame :id
output item 3 :id                 output item 4 :id
end                               end

to id.lname :id
output item 3 :id
end

;; Data abstraction: Operators

to op.instr :op                   to op.types :op
output first :op                  output item 3 :op
end                               end

to op.nargs :op                   to op.prec :op
output first bf :op               output last :op
end                               end

;; Data abstraction: Expressions

to exp.type :exp
output first :exp
end

to exp.mode :exp
output first butfirst :exp
end

to exp.value :exp
output last :exp
end
```

```
;; Data abstraction: Frame slots

to frame.retaddr                to frame.regsave
output 0                        output 4
end                             end

to frame.save.newfp             to framesize.proc
output 1                        output 4+:numregs
end                             end

to frame.outerframe             to frame.retval
output 2                        output 4+:numregs
end                             end

to frame.prevframe              to framesize.fun
output 3                        output 5+:numregs
end                             end

;; Data abstraction: Registers

to reg.zero                     to reg.frameptr
output 0                        output 4
end                             end

to reg.retaddr                  to reg.newfp
output 1                        output 5
end                             end

to reg.stackptr                 to reg.retval
output 2                        output 6
end                             end

to reg.globalptr                to reg.firstfree
output 3                        output 7
end                             end

;; Runtime (machine simulation)

to prun :progname
localmake "prog thing word "% :progname
localmake "regs (array :numregs 0)
local filter "wordp :prog
foreach :prog [if wordp ? [make ? ?rest]]
localmake "memory (array :memsize 0)
setitem 0 :regs 0
if not procedurep "add [runsetup]
prun1 :prog
end
```

```
to prun1 :pc
if emptyp :pc [stop]
if listp first :pc [run first :pc]
prun1 butfirst :pc
end


to rload :reg :offset :index
setitem :reg :regs (item (item :index :regs)+:offset :memory)
end


to store :reg :offset :index
setitem (item :index :regs)+:offset :memory (item :reg :regs)
end


to runsetup
foreach [[add sum] [sub difference] [mul product] [quo quotient]
        [div [int quotient]] [rem remainder] [land product]
        [lor [tobool lessp 0 sum]] [eql [tobool equalp]]
        [neq [tobool not equalp]] [less [tobool lessp]]
        [gtr [tobool greaterp]] [leq [tobool not greaterp]]
        [geq [tobool not lessp]]] ~
        [define first ?
                '[[dest src1 src2]
                  [setitem :dest :regs ,@[last ?] (item :src1 :regs)
                                                  (item :src2 :regs)]]
          define word first ? "i
                '[[dest src1 immed]
                  [setitem :dest :regs ,@[last ?] (item :src1 :regs)
                                                  :immed]]]
foreach [[lnot [difference 1]] [sint int] [sround round] [srandom random]] ~
        [define first ?
                '[[dest src]
                  [setitem :dest :regs ,@[last ?] (item :src :regs)]]
          define word first ? "i
                '[[dest immed]
                  [setitem :dest :regs ,@[last ?] :immed]]]
end


to tobool :tf
output ifelse :tf [1] [0]
end


to jump :label
make "pc fput :label thing :label
end


to jumpt :reg :label
if (item :reg :regs)=1 [jump :label]
end
```

```
to jumpf :reg :label
if (item :reg :regs)=0 [jump :label]
end

to jr :reg
make "pc item :reg :regs
end

to jal :reg :label
setitem :reg :regs :pc
jump :label
end

to putch :width :reg
spaces :width 1
type char (item :reg :regs)
end

to putstr :width :string
spaces :width (count first :string)
type :string
end

to puttf :width :bool
spaces :width 1
type ifelse (item :bool :regs)=0 ["F] ["T]
end

to putint :width :reg
localmake "num (item :reg :regs)
spaces :width count :num
type :num
end

to putreal :width :reg
putint :width :reg
end

to spaces :width :count
if :width > :count [repeat :width - :count [type "| |]]
end

to newline
print []
end

to exit
make "pc [exit]
end
```

6   Artificial Intelligence

Program file for this chapter: `student`

Can a computer be intelligent? What would it mean for a computer to be intelligent?
John McCarthy, one of the founders of artificial intelligence research, once defined the
field as "getting a computer to do things which, when done by people, are said to involve
intelligence." The point of the definition was that he felt perfectly comfortable about
carrying on his research without first having to defend any particular philosophical view
of what the word "intelligence" means.

There have always been two points of view among AI researchers about what their
purpose is. One point of view is that AI programs contribute to our understanding of
human psychology; when researchers take this view they try to make their programs reflect
the actual mechanisms of intelligent human behavior. For example, Allen Newell and
Herbert A. Simon begin their classic AI book *Human Problem Solving* with the sentence,
"The aim of this book is to advance our understanding of how humans think." In one
of their research projects they studied cryptarithmetic problems, in which digits are
replaced with letters in a multi-digit addition or multiplication. First they did a careful
observation and analysis of how a human subject attacked such a problem, then they
pointed out specific problem-solving techniques that the person used, and used those
techniques as the basis for designing a computer simulation. The other point of view
is that AI programs provide a more abstract model for intelligence in general; just as
one can learn about the properties of computers by studying finite-state machines, even
though no real computer operates precisely as a formal finite-state machine does, we can
learn about the properties of any possible intelligent being by simulating intelligence in a
computer program, whether or not the mechanisms of that program are similar to those
used by people.

In the early days of AI research these two points of view were not sharply divided.
Sometimes the same person would switch from one to the other, sometimes trying to
model human thought processes and sometimes trying to solve a given problem by

whatever methods could be made to work. More recently, researchers who hold one or the other point of view consistently have begun to define two separate fields. One is *cognitive science,* in which computer scientists join with psychologists, linguists, biologists, and others to study human cognitive psychology, using computer programs as a concrete embodiment of theories about the human mind. The other is called *expert systems* or *knowledge engineering,* in which programming techniques developed by AI researchers are put to practical use in programs that solve real-world business problems such as the diagnosis and repair of malfunctioning equipment.

Microworlds: Student

In this chapter I'm going to concentrate on one particular area of AI research: teaching a computer to understand English. Besides its inherent interest, this area has the advantage that it doesn't require special equipment, as do some other parts of AI such as machine vision and the control of robot manipulators.

In the 1950s many people were very optimistic about the use of computers to translate from one language to another. IBM undertook a government-sponsored project to translate scientific journals from Russian to English. At first they thought that this translation could be done very straightforwardly, with a Russian-English dictionary and a few little kludges to rearrange the order of words in a sentence to account for differences in the grammatical structure of the two languages. This simple approach was not successful. One problem is that the same word can have different meanings, and even different parts of speech, in different contexts. (According to one famous anecdote, the program translated the Russian equivalent of "The spirit is willing but the flesh is weak" into "The vodka is strong but the meat is rotten.")

A decade later, several AI researchers had the idea that ambiguities in the meanings of words could be resolved by trying to understand English only in some limited context. If you know in advance that the sentence you're trying to understand is about baseball statistics, or about relationships in a family tree, or about telling a robot arm to move blocks on a table (these are actual examples of work done in that period) then only certain narrowly defined types of sentences are meaningful at all. You needn't think about metaphors or about the many assumptions about commonsense knowledge that people make in talking with one another. Such a limited context for a language understanding program is called a *microworld.*

This chapter includes a Logo version of Student, a program written by Daniel G. Bobrow for his 1964 Ph.D. thesis, *Natural Language Input for a Computer Problem Solving System,* at MIT. Student is a program that solves algebra word problems:

? student [The price of a radio is $69.70. If this price is 15 percent less than the marked price, find the marked price.]

The marked price is 82 dollars

(In this illustration I've left out some of Student's display of intermediate results.) The program has two parts: one that translates the word problem into the form of equations and another that solves the equations. The latter part is complex (about 40 Logo procedures) but straightforward; it doesn't seem surprising to most people that a computer can manipulate mathematical equations. It is Student's understanding of English sentences that furthered the cause of artificial intelligence.

> The aim of the research reported here was to discover how one could build a computer program which could communicate with people in a natural language within some restricted problem domain. In the course of this investigation, I wrote a set of computer programs, the Student system, which accepts as input a comfortable but restricted subset of English which can be used to express a wide variety of algebra story problems...

> In the following discussion, I shall use phrases such as "the computer understands English." In all such cases, the "English" is just the restricted subset of English which is allowable as input for the computer program under discussion. In addition, for purposes of this report I have adopted the following operational definition of understanding. A computer *understands* a subset of English if it accepts input sentences which are members of this subset, and answers questions based on information contained in the input. The Student system understands English in this sense. [Bobrow, 1964.]

How does the algebra microworld simplify the understanding problem? For one thing, Student need not know anything about the meanings of noun phrases. In the sample problem above, the phrase **The price of a radio** is used as a variable name. The problem could just as well have been

The weight of a giant size detergent box is 69.70 ounces. If this weight is 15 percent less than the weight of an enormous size box, find the weight of an enormous size box.

For Student, either problem boils down to

variable1 = 69.70 *units*

variable1 = 0.85 * *variable2*

Find *variable2*.

Student understands particular words only to the extent that they have a *mathematical* meaning. For example, the program knows that `15 percent less than` means the same as `0.85 times`.

How Student Translates English to Algebra

Student translates a word problem into equations in several steps. In the following paragraphs, I'll mention in parentheses the names of the Logo procedures that carry out each step I describe, but don't read the procedures yet. First read through the description of the process without worrying about the programming details of each step. Later you can reread this section while examining the complete listing at the end of the chapter.

In translating Student to Logo, I've tried not to change the capabilities of the program in any way. The overall structure of my version is similar to that of Bobrow's original implementation, but I've changed some details. I've used iteration and mapping tools to make the program easier to read; I've changed some aspects of the fine structure of the program to fit more closely with the usual Logo programming style; in a few cases I've tried to make exceptionally slow parts of the program run faster by finding a more efficient algorithm to achieve the same goal.

The top-level procedure `student` takes one input, a list containing the word problem. (The disk file that accompanies this project includes several variables containing sample problems. For example,

`? student :radio`

will carry out the steps I'm about to describe.) Student begins by printing the original problem:

`? student :radio`

`The problem to be solved is`

`The price of a radio is $69.70. If this price is 15 percent less than the marked price, find the marked price.`

The first step is to separate punctuation characters from the attached words. For example, the word "`price,`" in the original problem becomes the two words "`price ,`" with the comma on its own. Then (`student1`) certain *mandatory substitutions* are applied (`idioms`). For example, the phrase `percent less than` is translated into the single word `perless`. The result is printed:

`With mandatory substitutions the problem is`

```
The price numof a radio is 69.70 dollars . If this price is 15 perless
the marked price , find the marked price .
```

(The word of in an algebra word problem can have two different meanings. Sometimes it means "times," as in the phrase "one half of the population." Other times, as in this problem, "of" is just part of a noun phrase like "the price of a radio." The special word numof is a flag to a later part of the program and will then be further translated either into times or back into of. The original implementation of Student used, instead of a special word like numof, a "tagged" word represented as a list like [of / op]. Other examples of tagging are [Bill / person] and [has / verb].)

The next step is to separate the problem into simple sentences (bracket):

```
The simple sentences are

The price numof a radio is 69.70 dollars .

This price is 15 perless the marked price .

Find the marked price .
```

Usually this transformation of the problem is straightforward, but the special case of "age problems" is recognized at this time, and special transformations are applied so that a sentence like

```
Mary is 24 years old.
```

is translated into

```
Mary s age is 24 .
```

An age problem is one that contains any of the phrases as old as, age, or years old.

The next step is to translate each simple sentence into an equation or a variable whose value is desired as part of the solution (senform).

```
The equations to be solved are

Equal [price of radio] [product 69.7 [dollars]]

Equal [price of radio] [product 0.85 [marked price]]
```

The third simple sentence is translated, not into an equation, but into a request to solve these equations for the variable marked price.

The translation of simple sentences into equations is the most "intelligent" part of the program; that is, it's where the program's knowledge of English grammar and vocabulary come into play and many special cases must be considered. In this example, the second simple sentence starts with the phrase `this price`. The program recognizes the word `this` (procedure `nmtest`) and replaces the entire phrase with the left hand side of the previous equation (procedure `this`).

Pattern Matching

Student analyzes a sentence by comparing it to several *patterns* (`senform1`). For example, one sentence form that Student understands is exemplified by these sentences:

```
Joe weighs 163 pounds .
The United States Army has 8742 officers .
```

The general pattern is

something   verb   number   unit .

Student treats such sentences as if they were rearranged to match

`The number of` *unit something verb* `is` *number* .

and so it generates the equations

```
Equal [number of pounds Joe weighs] 163
```

```
Equal [number of officers United States Army has] 8742
```

The original version of Student was written in a pattern matching language called Meteor, which Bobrow wrote in Lisp. In Meteor, the instruction that handles this sentence type looks like this:

```
(*    ($ ($1 / verb) (fn nmtest) $1 $ ($1 / dlm)) 0
      (/ (*s shelf (*k equal (fn opform (*k the number of 4 1 2))
                            (fn opform (*k 3 5 6)))))            return)
```

The top line contains the pattern to be matched. In the pattern, a dollar sign represents zero or more words; the notation $1 represents a single word. The zero at the end of the line means that the text that matches the pattern should be deleted and nothing should replace it. The rest of the instruction pushes a new equation onto a stack named `shelf`; that equation is formed out of the pieces of the matched pattern according to the numbers in the instruction. That is, the number 4 represents the fourth component of the pattern, which is $1.

Here is the corresponding instruction in the Logo version:

```
if match [^one !verb1:verb !factor:numberp #stuff1 !:dlm] :sent
   [output (list (list "equal
                       opform (sentence [the number of]
                                        :stuff1 :one :verb1)
                       opform (list :factor) ))]
```

The pattern matcher I used for Student is the same as the one in *Advanced Techniques,* the second volume of this series.* Student often relies on the fact that Meteor's pattern matcher finds the *first substring* of the text that matches the pattern, rather than requiring the entire text to match. Many patterns in the Logo version therefore take the form

[^beg *interesting part* #end]

where the "interesting part" is all that appeared in the Meteor pattern.

Here is a very brief summary of the Logo pattern matcher included in this program. For a fuller description with examples, please refer to Volume 2. `Match` is a predicate with two inputs, both lists. The first input is the *pattern* and the second input is the *sentence.* `Match` outputs `true` if the sentence *matches* the pattern. A word in the pattern that does not begin with one of the special *quantifier* characters listed below matches the identical word in the sentence. A word in the pattern that does begin with a quantifier matches zero or more words in the sentence, as follows:

#	zero or more words	!	exactly one word
&	one or more words	@	zero or more words (test as group)
?	zero or one word	^	zero or more words (as few as possible)

All quantifiers match as many consecutive words as possible while still allowing the remaining portion of the pattern to be matched, except for ^. A quantifier may be used alone, or it can be followed by a variable name, a predicate name, or both:

```
#
#var
#:pred
#var:pred
```

---

* The version in this project is modified slightly; the `match` procedure first does a fast test to try to reject an irrelevant pattern in $O(n)$ time before calling the actual pattern matcher, which could take as much as $O(2^n)$ time to reject a pattern, and which has been renamed `rmatch` (for "real match") in this project.

If a variable name is used, the word or words that match the quantifier will be stored in that variable if the match is successful. (The value of the variable if the match is not successful is not guaranteed.) If a predicate is used, it must take one word as input; in order for a word in the sentence to be accepted as (part of) a match for the quantifier, the predicate must output `true` when given that word as input. For example, the word

```
!factor:numberp
```

in the pattern above requires exactly one matching word in the sentence; that word must be a number, and it is remembered in the variable `factor`. If the quantifier is @ then the predicate must take a *list* as input, and it must output `true` for all the candidate matching words taken together as a list. For example, if you define a procedure

```
to threep :list
output equalp count :list 3
end
```

then the pattern word

```
@:threep
```

will match exactly three words in the sentence. (Student does not use this last feature of the pattern matcher. In fact, predicates are applied only to the single-word quantifiers ? and !.)

Pattern matching is also heavily used in converting words and phrases with mathematical meaning into the corresponding arithmetic operations (`opform`). An equation is a list of three members; the first member is the word `equal` and the other two are expressions formed by applying operations to variables and numbers. Each operation that is required is represented as a list whose first member is the name of the Logo procedure that carries out the operation and whose remaining members are expressions representing the operands. For example, the equation

$$y = 3x^2 + 6x - 1$$

would be represented by the list

```
[equal [y] [sum [product 3 [square [x]]] [product 6 [x]] [minus 1]]]
```

The variables are represented by lists like `[x]` rather than just the words because in Student a variable can be a multi-word phrase like `price of radio`. The difference between two expressions is represented by a `sum` of one expression and `minus` the other, rather than as the `difference` of the expressions, because this representation turns out to make the process of simplifying and solving the equations easier.

In word problems, as in arithmetic expressions, there is a precedence of operations. Operations like `squared` apply to the variables right next to them; ones like `times` are intermediate, and ones like `plus` apply to the largest possible subexpressions. Student looks first for the lowest-priority ones like `plus`; if one is found, the entire rest of the clause before and after the operation word provide the operands. Those operands are recursively processed by `opform`; when all the low-priority operations have been found, the next level of priority will be found by matching the pattern

```
[^left !op:op1 #right]
```

Solving the Equations

Student uses the substitution technique to solve the equations. That is, one equation is rearranged so that the left hand side contains only a single variable and the right hand side does not contain that variable. Then, in some other equation, every instance of that variable is replaced by the right hand side of the first equation. The result is a new equation from which one variable has been eliminated. Repeating this process enough times should eventually yield an equation with only a single variable, which can be solved to find the value of that variable.

When a problem gives rise to several linear equations in several variables, the traditional technique for computer solution is to use matrix inversion; this technique is messy for human beings because there is a lot of arithmetic involved, but straightforward for computers because the algorithm can be specified in a simple way that doesn't depend on the particular equations in each problem. Bobrow chose to use the substitution method because some problems give rise to equations that are linear in the variable for which a solution is desired but nonlinear in other variables. Consider this problem:

`? student :tom`

The problem to be solved is

If the number of customers Tom gets is twice the square of 20 per cent of the number of advertisements he runs, and the number of advertisements he runs is 45, what is the number of customers Tom gets?

With mandatory substitutions the problem is

```
If the number numof customers Tom gets is 2 times the square 20 percent
numof the number numof advertisements he runs , and the number numof
advertisements he runs is 45 , what is the number numof customers
Tom gets ?


The simple sentences are

The number numof customers Tom gets is 2 times the square 20 percent
numof the number numof advertisements he runs .

The number numof advertisements he runs is 45 .

What is the number numof customers Tom gets ?


The equations to be solved are

Equal [number of customers Tom gets]
      [product 2 [square [product 0.2 [number of advertisements
                                       he runs]]]]

Equal [number of advertisements he runs] 45


The number of customers Tom gets is 162

The problem is solved.
```

The first equation that Student generates for this problem is linear in the number of customers Tom gets, but nonlinear in the number of advertisements he runs. (That is, the equation refers to the *square* of the latter variable. An equation is *linear* in a given variable if that variable isn't multiplied by anything other than a constant number.) Using the substitution method, Student can solve the problem by substituting the value 45, found in the second equation, for the number of advertisements variable in the first equation.

(Notice, in passing, that one of the special `numof` words in this problem was translated into a multiplication rather than back into the original word `of`.)

The actual sequence of steps required to solve a set of equations is quite intricate. I recommend taking that part of Student on faith the first time you read the program, concentrating instead on the pattern matching techniques used to translate the English sentences into equations. But here is a rough guide to the solution process. Both `student1` and `student2` call `trysolve` with four inputs: a list of the equations to solve, a list of the variables for which values are wanted, and two lists of *units*. A unit is a word or phrase like `dollars` or `feet` that may be part of a solution. Student treats units like variables while constructing the equations, so the combination of a number and a unit is represented as a product, like

```
[product 69.7 [dollars]]
```

for $69.70 in the first sample problem. While constructing the equations, Student generates two lists of units. The first, stored in the variable `units`, contains any word or phrase that appears along with a number in the problem statement, like the word `feet` in the phrase `3 feet` (`nmtest`). The second, in the variable `aunits`, contains units mentioned explicitly in the `find` or `how many` sentences that tell Student what variables should be part of the solution (`senform1`). If the problem includes a sentence like

```
How many inches is a yard?
```

then the variable `[inches]`, and *only* that variable, is allowed to be part of the answer. If there are no `aunits`-type variables in the problem, then any of the `units` variables may appear in the solution (`trysolve`).

Trysolve first calls `solve` to solve the equations and then uses `pranswers` to print the results. `Solve` calls `solver` to do most of the work and then passes its output through `solve.reduce` for some final cleaning up. `Solver` works by picking one of the variables from the list `:wanted` and asking `solve1` to find a solution for that variable in terms of *all* the other variables—the other wanted variables as well as the units allowed in the ultimate answer. If `solve1` succeeds, then `solver` invokes itself, adding the newly-found expression for one variable to an *association list* (in the variable `alis`) so that, from then on, any occurrence of that variable will be replaced with the equivalent expression. In effect, the problem is simplified by eliminating one variable and eliminating one equation, the one that was solved to find the equivalent expression.

Solve1 first looks for an equation containing the variable for which it is trying to find a solution. When it finds such an equation, the next task is to eliminate from that equation any variables that aren't part of the wanted-plus-units list that `solver` gave `solve1` as an input. To eliminate these extra variables, `solve1` invokes `solver` with the extras as the list of wanted variables. This mutual recursion between `solver` and `solve1` makes the structure of the solution process difficult to follow. If `solver` manages to eliminate the extra variables by expressing them in terms of the originally wanted ones, then `solve1` can go on to substitute those expressions into its originally chosen equation and then use `solveq` to solve that one equation for the one selected variable in terms of all the other allowed variables. `Solveq` manipulates the equation more or less the way students in algebra classes do, adding the same term to both sides, multiplying both sides by the denominator of a polynomial fraction, and so on.

Here is how `solve` solves the radio problem. The equations, again, are

```
Equal [price of radio] [product 69.7 [dollars]]

Equal [price of radio] [product 0.85 [marked price]]
```

`Trysolve` evaluates the expression

```
(1) solve [[marked price]]
          [[equal [price of radio] [product 69.7 [dollars]]]
           [equal [price of radio] [product 0.85 [marked price]]] ]
          [[dollars]]
```

(I'm numbering these expressions so that I can refer to them later in the text.) The first input to `solve` is the list of variables wanted in the solution; in this case there is only one such variable. The second input is the list of two equations. The third is the list of unit variables that are allowed to appear in the solution; in this case only [`dollars`] is allowed. `Solve` evaluates

```
(2) solver [[marked price]] [[dollars]] [] []
```

(There is a fifth input, the word `insufficient`, but this is used only as an error flag if the problem can't be solved. To simplify this discussion I'm going to ignore that input for both `solver` and `solve1`.) `Solver` picks the first (in this case, the only) wanted variable as the major input to `solve1`:

```
(3) solve1 [marked price]
           [[dollars]]
           []
           [[equal [price of radio] [product 69.7 [dollars]]]
            [equal [price of radio] [product 0.85 [marked price]]] ]
           []
```

Notice that the first input to `solve1` is a single variable, not a list of variables. `Solve1` examines the first equation in the list of equations making up its fourth input. The desired variable does not appear in this equation, so `solve1` rejects that equation and invokes itself recursively:

```
(4) solve1 [marked price]
           [[dollars]]
           []
           [[equal [price of radio] [product 0.85 [marked price]]]]
           [[equal [price of radio] [product 69.7 [dollars]]]]
```

This time, the first (and now only) equation on the list of candidates does contain the desired variable. Solve1 removes that equation, not from its own list of equations (:eqns), but from solve's overall list (:eqt). The equation, unfortunately, can't be solved directly to express [marked price] in terms of [dollars], because it contains the extra, unwanted variable [price of radio]. We must eliminate this variable by solving the remaining equations for it:

(5) solver [[price of radio]] [[marked price] [dollars]] [] []

As before, solver picks the first (again, in this case, the only) wanted variable and asks solve1 to solve it:

```
(6) solve1 [price of radio]
           [[marked price] [dollars]]
           []
           [[equal [price of radio] [product 69.7 [dollars]]]]
           []
```

Solve1 does find the desired variable in the first (and only) equation, and this time there are no extra variables. Solve1 can therefore ask solveq to solve the equation:

```
(7) solveq [price of radio]
           [equal [price of radio] [product 69.7 [dollars]]]
```

It isn't part of solveq's job to worry about which variables may or may not be part of the solution; solve1 doesn't call solveq until it's satisfied that the equation is okay.

In this case, solveq has little work to do because the equation is already in the desired form, with the chosen variable alone on the left side and an expression not containing that variable on the right.

solveq (7) *outputs* [[price of radio] [product 69.7 [dollars]]]
           to solve1 (6)

Solve1 appends this result to the previously empty association list.

solve1 (6) *outputs* [[[price of radio] [product 69.7 [dollars]]]]
           to solver (5)

Solver only had one variable in its :wanted list, so its job is also finished.

solver (5) *outputs* [[[price of radio] [product 69.7 [dollars]]]]
           to solve1 (4,3)

This outer invocation of `solve1` was trying to solve for `[marked price]` an equation that also involved `[price of radio]`. It is now able to use the new association list to substitute for this unwanted variable an expression in terms of wanted variables only; this modified equation is then passed on to `solveq`:

```
(8) solveq [marked price]
            [equal [product 69.7 [dollars]] [product 0.85 [marked price]]]
```

This time `solveq` has to work a little harder, exchanging the two sides of the equation and dividing by 0.85.

```
solveq (8) outputs [[marked price] [product 82 [dollars]]]
           to solve1 (4,3)
```

`Solve1` appends this result to the association list:

```
solve1 (4,3) outputs [[[price of radio] [product 69.7 [dollars]]]
                       [[marked price] [product 82 [dollars]]] ]
            to solver (2)
```

Since `solver` has no other wanted variables, it outputs the same list to `solve`, and `solve` outputs the same list to `trysolve`. (In this example, `solve.reduce` has no effect because all of the expressions in the association list are in terms of allowed units only. If the equations had been different, the expression for `[price of radio]` might have included `[marked price]` and then `solve.reduce` would have had to substitute and simplify (`subord`).)

It'll probably take tracing a few more examples and beating your head against the wall a bit before you really understand the structure of `solve` and its subprocedures. Again, don't get distracted by this part of the program until you've come to understand the language processing part, which is our main interest in this chapter.

Age Problems

The main reason why Student treats age problems specially is that the English form of such problems is often expressed as if the variables were people, like "Bill," whereas the real variable is "Bill's age." The pattern matching transformations look for proper names (`personp`) and insert the words `s age` after them (`ageify`). The first such age variable in the problem is remembered specially so that it can be substituted for pronouns (`agepron`). A special case is the phrase `their ages`, which is replaced (`ageprob`) with a list of all the age variables in the problem.

`? `**`student :uncle`**

The problem to be solved is

Bill's father's uncle is twice as old as Bill's father. 2 years from now Bill's father will be 3 times as old as Bill. The sum of their ages is 92 . Find Bill's age.

With mandatory substitutions the problem is

Bill s father s uncle is 2 times as old as Bill s father . 2 years from now Bill s father will be 3 times as old as Bill . sum their ages is 92 . Find Bill s age .

The simple sentences are

Bill s father s uncle s age is 2 times Bill s father s age .

Bill s father s age pluss 2 is 3 times Bill s age pluss 2 .

Sum Bill s age and Bill s father s age and Bill s father s uncle s age is 92 .

Find Bill s age .

The equations to be solved are

Equal [Bill s father s uncle s age] [product 2 [Bill s father s age]]

Equal [sum [Bill s father s age] 2] [product 3 [sum [Bill s age] 2]]

Equal [sum [Bill s age]
           [sum [Bill s father s age] [Bill s father s uncle s age]]] 92

Bill s age is 8

The problem is solved.

(Note that in the original problem statement there is a space between the number 92 and the following period. I had to enter the problem in that form because of an inflexibility in Logo's input parser, which assumes that a period right after a number is part of the number, so that "92." is reformatted into 92 without the dot.)

Student represents the possessive word Bill's as the two words Bill s because this representation allows the pattern matcher to manipulate the possessive marker as a separate element to be matched. A phrase like `as old as` is just deleted (`ageprob`) because the transformation from people to ages makes it redundant.

The phrase `2 years from now` in the original problem is first translated to `in 2 years`. This phrase is further processed according to where it appears in a sentence. When it is attached to a particular variable, in a phrase like `Bill s age in 2 years`, the entire phrase is translated into the arithmetic operation `Bill s age pluss 2 years` (`agewhen`). (The special word `pluss` is an addition operator, just like `plus`, except for its precedence; `opform` treats it as a tightly binding operation like `squared` instead of a loosely binding one like the ordinary `plus`.) When a phrase like `in 2 years` appears at the beginning of a sentence, it is remembered (`agesen`) as an implicit modifier for *every* age variable in that sentence that isn't explicitly modified. In this example, `in 2 years` modifies both `Bill s father s age` and `Bill s age`. The special precedence of `pluss` is needed in this example so that the equation will be based on the grouping

```
3 times [ Bill s age pluss 2 ]
```

rather than

```
[ 3 times Bill s age ] plus 2
```

as it would be with the ordinary `plus` operator. You can also see how the substitution for `their ages` works in this example.

Here is a second sample age problem that illustrates a different kind of special handling:

```
? student :ann
```

```
The problem to be solved is
```

```
Mary is twice as old as Ann was when Mary was as old as Ann is now. If
Mary is 24 years old, how old is Ann?
```

```
With mandatory substitutions the problem is
```

```
Mary is 2 times as old as Ann was when Mary was as old as Ann is now . If
Mary is 24 years old , what is Ann ?
```

```
The simple sentences are
```

```
Mary s age is 2 times Ann s age minuss g1 .
```

```
Mary s age minuss g1 is Ann s age .
```

```
Mary s age is 24 .

What is Ann s age ?
```

```
The equations to be solved are

Equal [Mary s age] [product 2 [sum [Ann s age] [minus [g1]]]]

Equal [sum [Mary s age] [minus [g1]]] [Ann s age]

Equal [Mary s age] 24
```

```
Ann s age is 18

The problem is solved.
```

What is new in this example is Student's handling of the phrase `was when` in the sentence

```
Mary is 2 times as old as Ann was when Mary was as old as Ann is now .
```

Sentences like this one often cause trouble for human algebra students because they make *implicit* reference to a quantity that is not explicitly present as a variable. The sentence says that Mary's age *now* is twice Ann's age *some number* of years ago, but that number is not explicit in the problem. Student makes this variable explicit by using a *generated symbol* like the word `g1` in this illustration. Student replaces the phrase `was when` with the words

```
was g1 years ago . g1 years ago
```

This substitution (in `ageprob`) happens *before* the division of the problem statement into simple sentences (`bracket`). As a result, this one sentence in the original problem becomes the two sentences

```
Mary s age is 2 times Ann s age g1 years ago .

G1 years ago Mary s age was Ann s age now .
```

The phrase `g1 years ago` in each of these sentences is further processed by `agesen` and `agewhen` as discussed earlier; the final result is

```
Mary s age is 2 times Ann s age minuss g1 .

Mary s age minuss g1 is Ann s age .
```

A new generated symbol is created each time this situation arises, so there is no conflict from trying to use the same variable name for two different purposes. The phrase `will be when` is handled similarly, except that the translated version is

```
in g2 years . in g2 years
```

AI and Education

> These decoupling heuristics are useful not only for the Student program but for people trying to solve age problems. The classic age problem about Mary and Ann, given above, took an MIT graduate student over 5 minutes to solve because he did not know this heuristic. With the heuristic he was able to set up the appropriate equations much more rapidly. As a crude measure of Student's relative speed, note that Student took less than one minute to solve this problem.

This excerpt from Bobrow's thesis illustrates the idea that insights from artificial intelligence research can make a valuable contribution to the education of human beings. An intellectual problem is solved, at least in many cases, by dividing it into pieces and developing a technique for each subproblem. The subproblems are the same whether it is a computer or a person trying to solve the problem. If a certain technique proves valuable for the computer, it may be helpful for a human problem solver to be aware of the computer's methods. Bobrow's suggestion to teach people one specific heuristic for algebra word problems is a relatively modest example of this general theme. (A *heuristic* is a rule that gives the right answer most of the time, as opposed to an *algorithm,* a rule that always works.) Some researchers in cognitive science and education have proposed the idea of *intelligent CAI* (computer assisted instruction), in which a computer would be programmed as a "tutor" that would observe the efforts of a student in solving a problem. The tutor would know about some of the mistaken ideas people can have about a particular class of problem and would notice a student falling into one of those traps. It could then offer advice tailored to the needs of that individual student.

The development of the Logo programming language (and so also, indirectly, this series of books) is another example of the relationship between AI and education. Part of the idea behind Logo is that the process of programming a computer resembles, in some ways, the process of teaching a person to do something. (This can include teaching oneself.) For example, when a computer program doesn't work, the experienced programmer doesn't give up in despair, but instead *debugs* the program. Yet many students are willing to give up and say "I just don't get it" if their understanding of some problem isn't perfect on the first try.

The critic is afraid that children will adopt the computer as model and eventually come to "think mechanically" themselves. Following the opposite tack, I have invented ways to take educational advantage of the opportunities to master the art of *deliberately* thinking like a computer, according, for example, to the stereotype of a computer program that proceeds in a step-by-step, literal, mechanical fashion. There are situations where this style of thinking is appropriate and useful. Some children's difficulties in learning formal subjects such as grammar or mathematics derive from their inability to see the point of such a style.

A second educational advantage is indirect but ultimately more important. By deliberately learning to imitate mechanical thinking, the learner becomes able to articulate what mechanical thinking is and what it is not. The exercise can lead to greater confidence about the ability to choose a cognitive style that suits the problem. Analysis of "mechanical thinking" and how it is different from other kinds and practice with problem analysis can result in a new degree of intellectual sophistication. By providing a very concrete, down-to-earth model of a particular style of thinking, work with the computer can make it easier to understand that there is such a thing as a "style of thinking." And giving children the opportunity to choose one style or another provides an opportunity to develop the skill necessary to choose between styles. Thus instead of inducing mechanical thinking, contact with computers could turn out to be the best conceivable antidote to it. And for me what is most important in this is that through these experiences these children would be serving their apprenticeships as epistemologists, that is to say learning to think articulately about thinking. [Seymour Papert, *Mindstorms*, Basic Books, 1980, p. 27.]

Combining Sentences Into One Equation

In age problems, as we've just seen, a single sentence may give rise to two equations. Here is an example of the opposite, several sentences that together contribute a single equation.

? **student :nums**

The problem to be solved is

A number is multiplied by 6 . This product is increased by 44 . This result is 68 . Find the number.

With mandatory substitutions the problem is

```
A number ismulby 6 . This product is increased by 44 . This result is
68 . Find the number .
```

The simple sentences are

```
A number ismulby 6 .
```

```
This product is increased by 44 .
```

```
This result is 68 .
```

```
Find the number .
```

The equations to be solved are

```
Equal [sum [product [number] 6] 44] 68
```

The number is 4

The problem is solved.

Student recognizes problems like this by recognizing the phrases "is multiplied by," "is divided by," and "is increased by" (`senform1`). A sentence containing one of these phrases is not translated into an equation; instead, a *partial* equation is saved until the next sentence is read. That next sentence is expected to start with a phrase like "this result" or "this product." The same procedure (`this`) that in other situations uses the left hand side of the last equation as the expression for the `this`-phrase notices that there is a remembered partial equation and uses that instead. In this example, the sentence

```
A number ismulby 6 .
```

remembers the algebraic expression

```
[product [number] 6]
```

The second sentence uses that remembered expression as part of a new, larger expression to be remembered:

```
[sum [product [number] 6] 44]
```

The third sentence does not contain one of the special "is increased by" phrases, but is instead a standard "A is B" sentence. That sentence, therefore, does give rise to an equation, as shown above.

Perhaps the most interesting thing to notice about this category of word problem is how narrowly defined Student's criterion for recognizing the category is. Student gets away with it because algebra word problems are highly *stereotyped;* there are just a few categories, with traditional, standard wordings. In principle there could be a word problem starting

```
Robert has a certain number of jelly beans.  This number is twice the
number of jelly beans Linda has.
```

These two sentences are together equivalent to

```
The number of jelly beans Robert has is twice the number of jelly beans
Linda has.
```

But Student would not recognize the situation because the first sentence doesn't talk about "is increased by." We could teach Student to understand a word problem in this form by adding the instruction

```
if match [^one !verb1:verb a certain number of #stuff1 !:dlm] :sent
    [push "ref opform (se [the number of] :stuff1 :one :verb1)
      op []]
```

along with the other known sentence forms in `senform1`. (Compare this to the pattern matching instruction shown earlier for a similar sentence but with an explicitly specified number.)

Taking advantage of the stereotyped nature of word problems is an example of how the microworld strategy helped make the early AI programs possible. If word problems were expressed with all the flexibility of language in general, Student would need many more sentence patterns than it actually has. (How many different ways can you think of to express the same idea about Robert and Linda? How many of those ways can Student handle?)

Allowing Flexible Phrasing

In the examples we've seen so far, Student has relied on the repetition of identical or near-identical phrases such as "the marked price" or "the number of advertisements he runs." (The requirement is not quite strictly identical phrases because articles are removed from the noun phrases to make variable names.) In real writing, though, such phrases are often abbreviated when they appear for a second time. Student will translate such a problem into a system of equations that can't be solved, because what should be one variable is instead a different variable in each equation. But Student can recognize this situation and apply heuristic rules to guess that two similar variable names are meant, in fact, to represent the same variable. (Some early writers on AI considered the use of heuristic methods one of the defining characteristics of the field. Computer scientists outside of AI were more likely to insist on fully reliable algorithms. This distinction still has some truth to it, but it isn't emphasized so much as a critical issue these days.) Student doesn't try to equate different variables until it has first tried to solve the equations as they are originally generated. If the first attempt at solution fails, Student has recourse to less certain techniques (`student2` calls `vartest`).

`? `**`student :sally`**

```
The problem to be solved is

The sum of Sally's share of some money and Frank's share is $4.50.
Sally's share is twice Frank's. Find Frank's and Sally's share.


With mandatory substitutions the problem is

sum Sally s share numof some money and Frank s share is 4.50 dollars .
Sally s share is 2 times Frank s . Find Frank s and Sally s share .


The simple sentences are

Sum Sally s share numof some money and Frank s share is 4.50 dollars .

Sally s share is 2 times Frank s .

Find Frank s and Sally s share .


The equations to be solved are

Equal [sum [Sally s share of some money] [Frank s share]]
      [product 4.50 [dollars]]

Equal [Sally s share] [product 2 [Frank s]]


The equations were insufficient to find a solution.

Assuming that
[Frank s] is equal to [Frank s share]

Assuming that
[Sally s share] is equal to [Sally s share of some money]

Frank s is 1.5 dollars
```

Chapter 6   Artificial Intelligence

```
Sally s share is 3 dollars
```

```
The problem is solved.
```

In this problem Student has found two pairs of similar variable names. When it finds such a pair, Student adds an equation of the form

```
[equal variable1 variable2]
```

to the previous set of equations. In both of the pairs in this example, the variable that appears later in the problem statement is entirely contained within the one that appears earlier.

Another point of interest in this example is that the variable [`dollars`] is included in the list of units that may be part of the answer. The word problem does not explicitly ask "How many dollars is Sally's share," but because one of the sentences sets an expression equal to "4.50 dollars" Student takes that as implicit permission to express the answer in dollars.

The only other condition under which Student will consider two variables equal is if their names are identical except that some phrase in the one that appears earlier is replaced with a pronoun in the one that appears later. That is, a variable like [`the number of ice cream cones the children eat`] will be considered equal to a later variable [`the number of ice cream cones they eat`]. Here is a problem in which this rule is applied:

```
? student :guns
```

```
The problem to be solved is
```

```
The number of soldiers the Russians have is one half of the number of
guns they have. They have 7000 guns. How many soldiers do they have?
```

```
With mandatory substitutions the problem is
```

```
The number numof soldiers the Russians have is 0.5 numof the number numof
guns they have . They have 7000 guns . howm soldiers do they have ?
```

```
The simple sentences are
```

```
The number numof soldiers the Russians have is 0.5 numof the number numof
guns they have .
```

```
They have 7000 guns .
```

```
Howm soldiers do they have ?

The equations to be solved are

Equal [number of soldiers Russians have]
      [product 0.5 [number of guns they have]]

Equal [number of guns they have] 7000


The equations were insufficient to find a solution.

Assuming that
[number of soldiers they have] is equal to
  [number of soldiers Russians have]

The number of soldiers they have is 3500

The problem is solved.
```

Using Background Knowledge

In some word problems, not all of the necessary information is contained within the problem statement itself. The problem requires the student to supply some piece of general knowledge about the world in order to determine the appropriate equations. This knowledge may be about unit conversions (one foot is 12 inches) or about relationships among physical quantities (distance equals speed times time). Student "knows" some of this *background* information and can apply it (`geteqns`) if the equations determined by the problem statement are insufficient.

```
? student :jet

The problem to be solved is

The distance from New York to Los Angeles is 3000 miles. If the average
speed of a jet plane is 600 miles per hour, find the time it takes to
travel from New York to Los Angeles by jet.


With mandatory substitutions the problem is

The distance from New York to Los Angeles is 3000 miles . If the average
speed numof a jet plane is 600 miles per hour , find the time it takes to
travel from New York to Los Angeles by jet .


The simple sentences are
```

The distance from New York to Los Angeles is 3000 miles .

The average speed numof a jet plane is 600 miles per hour .

Find the time it takes to travel from New York to Los Angeles by jet .

The equations to be solved are

Equal [distance from New York to Los Angeles] [product 3000 [miles]]

Equal [average speed of jet plane]
      [quotient [product 600 [miles]] [product 1 [hours]]]

The equations were insufficient to find a solution.

Using the following known relationships

Equal [distance] [product [speed] [time]]

Equal [distance] [product [gas consumption]
                          [number of gallons of gas used]]

Assuming that
[speed] is equal to [average speed of jet plane]

Assuming that
[time] is equal to [time it takes to travel
                    from New York to Los Angeles by jet]

Assuming that
[distance] is equal to [distance from New York to Los Angeles]

The time it takes to travel from New York
  to Los Angeles by jet is 5 hours

The problem is solved.

Student's library of known relationships is indexed according to the first word of the name of each variable involved in the relationship. (If a variable starts with the words **number of** it is indexed under the following word.) The relationships, in the form of equations, are stored in the property lists of these index words.

Property lists are also used to keep track of irregular plurals and the corresponding singulars. Student tries to keep all units in plural form internally, so that if a problem refers to both 1 **foot** and 2 **feet** the same variable name will be used for both. (That is, the first of these will be translated into

```
[product 1 [feet]]
```

in Student's internal representation. Then the opposite translation is needed if the product of 1 and some unit appears in an answer to be printed.

The original Student also used property lists to remember the parts of speech of words and the precedence of operators, but because of differences in the syntax of the Meteor pattern matcher and my Logo pattern matcher I've found it easier to use predicate operations for that purpose.

The original Student system included a separately invoked `remember` procedure that allowed all these kinds of global information to be entered in the form of English sentences. You'd say

```
Feet is the plural of foot
```

or

```
Distance equals speed times time
```

and `remember` would use patterns much like those used in understanding word problems to translate these sentences into `pprop` instructions. Since Lisp programs, like Logo programs, can themselves be manipulated as lists, `remember` could even accept information of a kind that's stored in the Student program itself, such as the wording transformations in `idioms`, and modify the program to reflect this information. I haven't bothered to implement that part of the Student system because it takes up extra memory and doesn't exhibit any new techniques.

As the above example shows, it's important that Student's search for relevant known relationships comes before the attempt to equate variables with similar names. The general relationship that uses a variable named simply [`distance`] doesn't help unless Student can identify it as relevant to the variable named [`distance from New York to Los Angeles`] in the specific problem under consideration.

Here is another example in which known relationships are used:

```
? student :span

The problem to be solved is

If 1 span is 9 inches, and 1 fathom is 6 feet,
  how many spans is 1 fathom?

With mandatory substitutions the problem is
```

If 1 span is 9 inches , and 1 fathom is 6 feet , howm spans is 1 fathom ?

The simple sentences are

1 span is 9 inches .

1 fathom is 6 feet .

Howm spans is 1 fathom ?

The equations to be solved are

Equal [product 1 [spans]] [product 9 [inches]]

Equal [product 1 [fathoms]] [product 6 [feet]]

Equal g2 [product 1 [fathoms]]

The equations were insufficient to find a solution.

Using the following known relationships

Equal [product 1 [yards]] [product 3 [feet]]

Equal [product 1 [feet]] [product 12 [inches]]

1 fathom is 8 spans

The problem is solved.

    Besides the use of known relationships, this example illustrates two other features of Student. One is the use of an explicitly requested unit in the answer. Since the problem asks

How many spans is 1 fathom?

Student knows that the answer must be expressed in spans. Had there been no explicit request for a particular unit, all the units that appear in phrases along with a number would be eligible to appear in the answer: inches, feet, and fathoms. Student might then blithely inform us that

1 fathom is 1 fathom

The problem is solved.

The other new feature demonstrated by this example is the use of a generated symbol to represent the desired answer. In the statement of this problem, there is no explicit variable representing the unknown. [Fathoms] is a *unit,* not a variable for which a value could be found. The problem asks for the value of the expression

```
[product 1 [fathoms]]
```

in terms of spans. Student generates a variable name (g2) to represent the unknown and produces an equation

```
[equal g2 [product 1 [fathoms]]
```

to add to the list of equations. A generated symbol will be needed whenever the "Find" or "What is" sentence asks for an expression rather than a simple variable name. For example, an age problem that asks "What is the sum of their ages" would require the use of a generated symbol. (The original Student *always* used a generated symbol for the unknowns, even if there was already a single variable in the problem representing an unknown. It therefore had equations like

```
[equal g3 [marked price]]
```

in its list, declaring one variable equal to another. I chose to check for this case and avoid the use of a generated symbol because the time spent in the actual solution of the equations increases quadratically with the number of equations.)

Optional Substitutions

We have seen many cases in which Student replaces a phrase in the statement of a problem with a different word or phrase that fits better with the later stages of processing, like the substitution of 2 times for twice or a special keyword like perless for percent less than. Student also has a few cases of *optional* substitutions that may or may not be made (tryidiom).

There are two ways in which optional substitutions can happen. One is exemplified by the phrase the perimeter of the rectangle. Student first attempts the problem without any special processing of this phrase. If a solution is not found, Student then replaces the phrase with twice the sum of the length and width of the rectangle and processes the resulting new problem from the beginning. Unlike the use of known relationships or similarity of variable names, which Student handles by adding to the already-determined equations, this optional substitution requires the entire translation process to begin again. For example, the word `twice` that begins the replacement phrase will be further translated to 2 `times`.

The second category of optional substitution is triggered by the phrase `two numbers`. This phrase must always be translated to something, because it indicates that two different variables are needed. But the precise translation depends on the wording of the rest of the problem. Student tries two alternative translations: `one of the numbers` and `the other number` and `one number` and `the other number`. Here is an example in which the necessary translation is the one Student tries second:

```
? student :sumtwo
```

The problem to be solved is

The sum of two numbers is 96, and one number is 16 larger than the other number. Find the two numbers.

The problem with an idiomatic substitution is

The sum of one of the numbers and the other number is 96 , and one number is16 larger than the other number . Find the one of the numbers and the other number .

With mandatory substitutions the problem is

sum one numof the numbers and the other number is 96 , and one number is 16 plus the other number . Find the one numof the numbers and the other number .

The simple sentences are

Sum one numof the numbers and the other number is 96 .

One number is 16 plus the other number .

Find the one numof the numbers and the other number .

The equations to be solved are

Equal [sum [one of numbers] [other number]] 96

Equal [one number] [sum 16 [other number]]

The equations were insufficient to find a solution.

The problem with an idiomatic substitution is

The sum of one number and the other number is 96 , and one number is 16
larger than the other number . Find the one number and the other number .

With mandatory substitutions the problem is

sum one number and the other number is 96 , and one number is 16 plus the
other number . Find the one number and the other number .

The simple sentences are

Sum one number and the other number is 96 .

One number is 16 plus the other number .

Find the one number and the other number .

The equations to be solved are

Equal [sum [one number] [other number]] 96

Equal [one number] [sum 16 [other number]]

The one number is 56

The other number is 40

The problem is solved.

There is no essential reason why Student uses one mechanism rather than another
to deal with a particular problematic situation. The difficulties about perimeters and
about the phrase "two numbers" might have been solved using mechanisms other than
this optional substitution one. For example, the equation

```
[equal [perimeter] [product 2 [sum [length] [width]]]]
```

might have been added to the library of known relationships. The difficulty about
alternate phrasings for "two numbers" could be solved by adding

```
[[one of the !word:pluralp] ["one singular :word]]
```

to the list of idiomatic substitutions in idiom.

Not all the mechanisms are equivalent, however. The "two numbers" problem
couldn't be solved by adding equations to the library of known relationships, because

that phrase appears as part of a larger phrase like "the sum of two numbers," and Student's understanding of thc word **sum** doesn't allow it to be part of a variable name. The word **sum** only makes sense to Student in the context of a phrase like **the sum of** *something* and *something else*. (See procedure **tst.sum**.)

If All Else Fails

Sometimes Student fails to solve a problem because the problem is beyond either its linguistic capability or its algebraic capability. For example, Student doesn't know how to solve quadratic equations. But sometimes a problem that Student could solve in principle stumps it because it happens to lack a particular piece of common knowledge. When a situation like that arises, Student is capable of asking the user for help (**student2**).

```
? student :ship
```

The problem to be solved is

The gross weight of a ship is 20000 tons. If its net weight is 15000 tons, what is the weight of the ships cargo?

With mandatory substitutions the problem is

The gross weight numof a ship is 20000 tons . If its net weight is 15000 tons , what is the weight numof the ships cargo ?

The simple sentences are

The gross weight numof a ship is 20000 tons .

Its net weight is 15000 tons .

What is the weight numof the ships cargo ?

The equations to be solved are

Equal [gross weight of ship] [product 20000 [tons]]

Equal [its net weight] [product 15000 [tons]]

The equations were insufficient to find a solution.

Do you know any more relationships among these variables?

Weight of ships cargo

```
Its net weight

Tons

Gross weight of ship
```

The weight of a ships cargo is the gross weight minus the net weight

```
Assuming that
[net weight] is equal to [its net weight]

Assuming that
[gross weight] is equal to [gross weight of ship]

The weight of the ships cargo is 5000 tons

The problem is solved.
```

Limitations of Pattern Matching

Student relies on certain stereotyped forms of sentences in the problems it solves. It's easy to make up problems that will completely bewilder it:

```
Suppose you have 14 jelly beans.  You give 2 each to Tom, Dick, and
Harry.  How many do you have left?
```

The first mistake Student makes is that it thinks the word **and** following a comma separates two clauses; it generates simple sentences

```
You give 2 each to Tom , Dick .

Harry .
```

This is quite a fundamental problem; Student's understanding of the difference between a phrase and a clause is extremely primitive and prone to error. Adding another pattern won't solve this one; the trouble is that Student pays no attention to the words in between the key words like **and**.

There are several other difficulties with this problem, some worse than others. Student doesn't recognize the word **suppose** as having a special function in the sentence, so it makes up a noun phrase **suppose you** just like **the russians**. This could be fixed with an idiomatic substitution that just ignored **suppose**. Another relatively small problem is that the sentence starting **how many** doesn't say how many of what; Student needs a way to understand that the relevant noun phrase is **jelly beans** and not, for example, **Tom**. The words **give** (representing subtraction) and **each** (representing counting a set and then multiplying) have special mathematical meanings comparable to `percent less`. A much more subtle problem in knowledge representation is that in this problem there are two different quantities that could be called `the number of jelly beans you have`: the number you have at the beginning of the problem and the number you have at the end. Student has a limited understanding of this passage-of-time difficulty when it's doing an age problem, but not in general.

How many more difficulties can you find in this problem? For how many of them can you invent improvements to Student to get around them?

Some difficulties seem to require a "more of the same" strategy: adding some new patterns to Student that are similar to the ones already there. Other difficulties seem to require a more fundamental redesign. Can that redesign be done using a pattern matcher as the central tool, or are more powerful tools needed? How powerful *is* pattern matching, anyway?

Answering questions like these is the job of automata theory. From that point of view, the answer is that it depends exactly what you mean by "pattern matching." The pattern matcher used in Student is equivalent to a finite-state machine. The important thing to note about the patterns used in Student is that they only apply predicates to one word at a time, not to groups of words. In other words, they don't use the @ quantifier. Here is a typical `student` pattern:

```
[^ what !:in [is are] #one !:dlm]
```

For the purposes of this discussion, you can ignore the fact that the pattern matcher can set variables to remember which words matched each part of the pattern. In comparing a pattern matcher to a finite-state machine, the question we're asking is what categories of strings can the pattern matcher accept. This particular pattern is equivalent to the following machine:

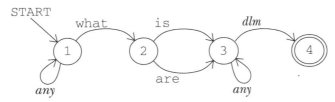

The arrow that I've labeled *dlm* is actually several arrows connecting the same states, one for each symbol that the predicate `dlm` accepts, i.e., period, question mark, and semicolon. Similarly, the arrows labeled *any* are followed for any symbol at all. This machine is nondeterministic, but you'll recall that that doesn't matter; we can turn it into a deterministic one if necessary.

To be sure you understand the equivalence of patterns and finite-state machines, see if you can draw a machine equivalent to this pattern:

```
[I see !:in [the a an] ?:numberp &:adjective !:noun #:adverb]
```

This pattern uses all the quantifiers that test words one at a time.

If these patterns are equivalent to finite-state machines, you'd expect them to have trouble recognizing sentences that involve *embedding* of clauses within clauses, since these pose the same problem as keeping track of balancing of parentheses. For example, a sentence like "The book that the boy whom I saw yesterday was reading is interesting" would strain the capabilities of a finite-state machine. (As in the case of parentheses, we could design a FSM that could handle such sentences up to some fixed depth of embedding, but not one that could handle arbitrarily deep embedding.)

Context-Free Languages

If we allow the use of the @ quantifier in patterns, and if the predicates used to test substrings of the sentences are true functions without side effects, then the pattern matcher is equivalent to an RTN or a production rule grammar. What makes an RTN different from a finite-state machine is that the former can include arrows that match several symbols against another (or the same) RTN. Equivalently, the @ quantifier matches several symbols against another (or the same) pattern.

A language that can be represented by an RTN is called a *context-free* language. The reason for the name is that in such a language a given string consistently matches or doesn't match a given predicate regardless of the rest of the sentence. That's the point of what I said just above about side effects; the output from a test predicate can't depend on anything other than its input. Pascal is a context-free language because

```
this := that
```

is always an assignment statement regardless of what other statements might be in the program with it.

What *isn't* a context-free language? The classic example in automata theory is the language consisting of the strings

```
abc
aabbcc
aaabbbccc
aaaabbbbcccc
```

and so on, with the requirement that the number of as be equal to the number of bs and also equal to the number of cs. That language can't be represented as RTNs or production rules. (Try it. Don't confuse it with the language that accepts any number of as followed by any number of bs and so on; even a finite-state machine can represent that one. The equal number requirement is important.)

The classic formal system that can represent *any* language for which there are precise rules is the Turing machine. Its advantage over the RTN is precisely that it can "jump around" in its memory, looking at one part while making decisions about another part.

There is a sharp theoretical boundary between context-free and context-sensitive languages, but in practice the boundary is sometimes fuzzy. Consider again the case of Pascal and that assignment statement. I said that it's recognizably an assignment statement because it matches a production rule like

```
assignment    :  identifier := expression
```

(along with a bunch of other rules that determine what qualifies as an expression). But that production rule doesn't really express *all* the requirements for a legal Pascal assignment statement. For example, the identifier and the expression must be of the same type. The actual Pascal compiler (any Pascal compiler, not just mine) includes instructions that represent the formal grammar plus extra instructions that represent the additional requirements.

The type agreement rule is an example of context sensitivity. The types of the relevant identifiers were determined in **var** declarations earlier in the program; those declarations are part of what determines whether the given string of symbols is a legal assignment.

Augmented Transition Networks

One could create a clean formal description of Pascal, type agreement rules and all, by designing a Turing machine to accept Pascal programs. However, Turing machines aren't easy to work with for any practical problem. It's much easier to set up a context-free grammar for Pascal and then throw in a few side effects to handle the context-sensitive aspects of the language.

Much the same is true of English. It's possible to set up an RTN (or a production rule grammar) for noun phrases, for example, and another one for verb phrases. It's tempting then to set up an RTN for a sentence like this:

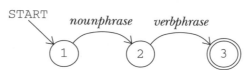

This machine captures some, but not all, of the rules of English. It's true that a sentence requires a noun phrase (the subject) and a verb phrase (the predicate). But there are *agreement* rules for person and number (I *run* but he *runs*) analogous to the type agreement rules of Pascal.

Some artificial intelligence researchers, understanding all this, parse English sentences using a formal description called an *augmented transition network* (ATN). An ATN is just like an RTN except that each transition arrow can have associated with it not only the name of a symbol or another RTN but also some *conditions* that must be met in order to follow the arrow and some *actions* that the program should take if the arrow is followed. For example, we could turn the RTN just above into an ATN by adding an action to the first arrow saying "store the number (singular or plural) of the noun phrase in the variable `number`" and adding a condition to the second arrow saying "the number of the verb phrase must be equal to the variable `number`."

Subject-predicate agreement is not the only rule in English grammar best expressed as a side effect in a transition network. On the next page is an ATN for noun phrases taken from *Language as a Cognitive Process, Volume 1: Syntax* by Terry Winograd (page 598). I'm not going to attempt to explain the notation or the detailed rules here, but just to give one example, the condition labeled "h16p" says that the transition for apostrophe-s can be followed if the head of the phrase is an ordinary noun ("the book's") but not if it's a pronoun ("you's").

The ATN is equivalent in power to a Turing machine; there is no known mechanism that is more flexible in carrying out algorithms. The flexibility has a cost, though. The time required to parse a string with an ATN is not bounded by a polynomial function. (Remember, the time for an RTN is $O(n^3)$.) It can easily be exponential, $O(2^n)$. One reason is that a context-sensitive procedure can't be subject to memoization. If two invocations of the same procedure with the same inputs can give different results because of side effects, it does no good to remember what result we got the last time. Turning an ATN into a practical program is often possible, but not a trivial task.

In thinking about ATNs we've brought together most of the topics in this book: formal systems, algorithms, language parsing, and artificial intelligence. Perhaps that's a good place to stop.

The NP network

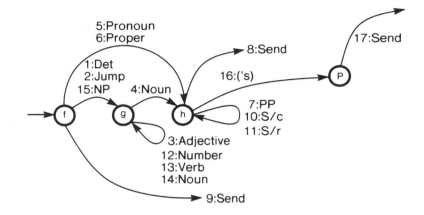

Roles: Determiner (Det), Head, Describers, Qualifiers

Feature Dimensions:

   Number: Sing, Pl; *default,* –empty–.   Person (Per): 1, 2, 3; *default,* 3.
   Ques: Yes, No; *default,* No. Case: Subj, Obj, Poss; *default,* –empty–.

Initializations, Conditions, and Actions:

f1g.   **A:** [Num←*.Num; Ques←*.Ques; Det←*]

f2g.   *No initializations, conditions, or actions*

g3g.   **A:** [Desc⇐*]

g4h.   **C:** [*.Num=Num or Num=∅]   **A:** [Num←*.Num; Head←*]

f5h.   **A:** [Num←*.Num; Per←*.Per; Ques←*.Ques; Head←*]

f6h.   **A:** [Num←*.Num; Head←*]

h7h.   **A:** [Qual⇐*]

h8.   **A:** [Case←Head.Case]

f9.   **C:** [Hold is an NP]   **A:** [Empty and return Hold]

h10h.   **I:** [Subj←*COPY*; Mood←Rel; MV←dummy Verb(*be*)]   **A:** [Qual⇐*]

h11h.   **I:** [Hold←*COPY*; Mood←WhRel]   **A:** [Qual⇐*]

g12g.   **A:** [Desc⇐*]

g13g.   **C:** [*.Form=Pres-Part or Past-Part]   **A:** [Desc⇐*]

g14g.   **C:** [*.Num=Sing]   **A:** [Desc⇐*]

f15g.   **C:** [*.Case=Poss]   **A:** [Det←*]

h16p.   **C:** [Head is not a Pronoun]

p17.   **A:** [Case←Poss]

Program Listing

```
to student :prob [:orgprob :prob]
say [The problem to be solved is] :prob
make "prob map.se [depunct ?] :prob
student1 :prob [[[the perimeter of ! rectangle]
                 [twice the sum of the length and width of the rectangle]]
                [[two numbers] [one of the numbers and the other number]]
                [[two numbers] [one number and the other number]]]
end


to student1 :prob :idioms
local [simsen shelf aunits units wanted ans var lasteqn
       ref eqt1 beg end idiom reply]
make "prob idioms :prob
if match [^ two numbers #] :prob ~
   [make "idiom find [match (sentence "^beg first ? "#end) :orgprob] :idioms ~
     tryidiom stop]
while [match [^beg the the #end] :prob] [make "prob (sentence :beg "the :end)]
say [With mandatory substitutions the problem is] :prob
ifelse match [# @:in [[as old as] [age] [years old]] #] :prob ~
       [ageprob] [make "simsen bracket :prob]
lsay [The simple sentences are] :simsen
foreach [aunits wanted ans var lasteqn ref units] [make ? []]
make "shelf filter [not emptyp ?] map.se [senform ?] :simsen
lsay [The equations to be solved are] :shelf    make "units remdup :units
if trysolve :shelf :wanted :units :aunits [print [The problem is solved.] stop]
make "eqt1 remdup geteqns :var
if not emptyp :eqt1 [lsay [Using the following known relationships] :eqt1]
student2 :eqt1
end


to student2 :eqt1
make "var remdup sentence (map.se [varterms ?] :eqt1) :var
make "eqt1 sentence :eqt1 vartest :var
if not emptyp :eqt1 ~
   [if trysolve (sentence :shelf :eqt1) :wanted :units :aunits
       [print [The problem is solved.] stop]]
make "idiom find [match (sentence "^beg first ? "#end) :orgprob] :idioms
if not emptyp :idiom [tryidiom stop]
lsay [Do you know any more relationships among these variables?] :var
make "reply map.se [depunct ?] readlist
if equalp :reply [yes] [print [Tell me.] make "reply readlist]
if equalp :reply [no] [print [] print [I can't solve this problem.] stop]
if dlm last :reply [make "reply butlast :reply]
if not match [^beg is #end] :reply [print [I don't understand that.] stop]
make "shelf sentence :shelf :eqt1
student2 (list (list "equal opform :beg opform :end))
end
```

```
;; Mandatory substitutions

to depunct :word
if emptyp :word [output []]
if equalp first :word "$ [output sentence "$ depunct butfirst :word]
if equalp last :word "% [output sentence depunct butlast :word "percent]
if memberp last :word [. ? |;| ,] ~
   [output sentence depunct butlast :word last :word]
if emptyp butfirst :word [output :word]
if equalp last2 :word "'s [output sentence depunct butlast butlast :word "s]
output :word
end


to idioms :sent
local "number
output changes :sent ~
    [[[the sum of] ["sum]] [[square of] ["square]] [[of] ["numof]]
     [[how old] ["what]] [[is equal to] ["is]]
     [[years younger than] [[less than]]] [[years older than] ["plus]]
     [[percent less than] ["perless]] [[less than] ["lessthan]]
     [[these] ["the]] [[more than] ["plus]]
     [[first two numbers] [[the first number and the second number]]]
     [[three numbers]
      [[the first number and the second number and the third number]]]
     [[one half] [0.5]] [[twice] [[2 times]]]
     [[$ !number] [sentence :number "dollars]] [[consecutive to] [[1 plus]]]
     [[larger than] ["plus]] [[per cent] ["percent]] [[how many] ["howm]]
     [[is multiplied by] ["ismulby]] [[is divided by] ["isdivby]]
     [[multiplied by] ["times]] [[divided by] ["divby]]]
end


to last2 :word
output word (last butlast :word) (last :word)
end


to changes :sent :list
localmake "keywords map.se [findkey first ?] :list
output changes1 :sent :list :keywords
end


to findkey :pattern
if equalp first :pattern "!:in [output first butfirst :pattern]
if equalp first :pattern "?:in ~
   [output sentence (item 2 :pattern) (item 3 :pattern)]
output first :pattern
end
```

```
to changes1 :sent :list :keywords
if emptyp :sent [output []]
if memberp first :sent :keywords [output changes2 :sent :list :keywords]
output fput first :sent changes1 butfirst :sent :list :keywords
end


to changes2 :sent :list :keywords
changes3 :list :list
output fput first :sent changes1 butfirst :sent :list :keywords
end


to changes3 :biglist :nowlist
if emptyp :nowlist [stop]
if changeone first :nowlist [changes3 :biglist :biglist stop]
changes3 :biglist butfirst :nowlist
end


to changeone :change
local "end
if not match (sentence first :change [#end]) :sent [output "false]
make "sent run (sentence "sentence last :change ":end)
output "true
end


;; Division into simple sentences

to bracket :prob
output bkt1 finddelim :prob
end


to finddelim :sent
output finddelim1 :sent [] []
end


to finddelim1 :in :out :simples
if emptyp :in ~
   [ifelse emptyp :out [output :simples]
                       [output lput (sentence :out ".) :simples]]
if dlm first :in ~
   [output finddelim1 (nocap butfirst :in) []
                      (lput (sentence :out first :in) :simples)]
output finddelim1 (butfirst :in) (sentence :out first :in) :simples
end


to nocap :words
if emptyp :words [output []]
if personp first :words [output :words]
output sentence (lowercase first :words) butfirst :words
end
```

```
to bkt1 :problist
local [first word rest]
if emptyp :problist [output []]
if not memberp ", first :problist ~
   [output fput first :problist bkt1 butfirst :problist]
if match [if ^first , !word:qword #rest] first :problist ~
   [output bkt1 fput (sentence :first ".)
                     fput (sentence :word :rest) butfirst :problist]
if match [^first , and #rest] first :problist ~
   [output fput (sentence :first ".) (bkt1 fput :rest butfirst :problist)]
output fput first :problist bkt1 butfirst :problist
end


;; Age problems

to ageprob
local [beg end sym who num subj ages]
while [match [^beg as old as #end] :prob] [make "prob sentence :beg :end]
while [match [^beg years old #end] :prob] [make "prob sentence :beg :end]
while [match [^beg will be when #end] :prob] ~
     [make "sym gensym
      make "prob (sentence :beg "in :sym [years . in] :sym "years :end)]
while [match [^beg was when #end] :prob] ~
     [make "sym gensym
      make "prob (sentence :beg :sym [years ago .] :sym [years ago] :end)]
while [match [^beg !who:personp will be in !num years #end] :prob] ~
     [make "prob (sentence :beg :who [s age in] :num "years #end)]
while [match [^beg was #end] :prob] [make "prob (sentence :beg "is :end)]
while [match [^beg will be #end] :prob] [make "prob (sentence :beg "is :end)]
while [match [^beg !who:personp is now #end] :prob] ~
     [make "prob (sentence :beg :who [s age now] :end)]
while [match [^beg !num years from now #end] :prob] ~
     [make "prob (sentence :beg "in :num "years :end)]
make "prob ageify :prob
ifelse match [^ !who:personp ^end s age #] :prob ~
       [make "subj sentence :who :end] [make "subj "someone]
make "prob agepron :prob
make "end :prob
make "ages []
while [match [^ !who:personp ^beg age #end] :end] ~
       [push "ages (sentence "and :who :beg "age)]
make "ages butfirst reduce "sentence remdup :ages
while [match [^beg their ages #end] :prob] [make "prob (sentence :beg :ages :end)]
make "simsen map [agesen ?] bracket :prob
end
```

```
to ageify :sent
if emptyp :sent [output []]
if not personp first :sent [output fput first :sent ageify butfirst :sent]
catch "error [if equalp first butfirst :sent "s
                [output fput first :sent ageify butfirst :sent]]
output (sentence first :sent [s age] ageify butfirst :sent)
end


to agepron :sent
if emptyp :sent [output []]
if not pronoun first :sent [output fput first :sent agepron butfirst :sent]
if posspro first :sent [output (sentence :subj "s agepron butfirst :sent)]
output (sentence :subj [s age] agepron butfirst :sent)
end


to agesen :sent
local [when rest num]
make "when []
if match [in !num years #rest] :sent ~
   [make "when sentence "pluss :num make "sent :rest]
if match [!num years ago #rest] :sent ~
   [make "when sentence "minuss :num make "sent :rest]
output agewhen :sent
end


to agewhen :sent
if emptyp :sent [output []]
if not equalp first :sent "age [output fput first :sent agewhen butfirst :sent]
if match [in !num years #rest] butfirst :sent ~
   [output (sentence [age pluss] :num agewhen :rest)]
if match [!num years ago #rest] butfirst :sent ~
   [output (sentence [age minuss] :num agewhen :rest)]
if equalp "now first butfirst :sent ~
   [output sentence "age agewhen butfirst butfirst :sent]
output (sentence "age :when agewhen butfirst :sent)
end


;; Translation from sentences into equations

to senform :sent
make "lasteqn senform1 :sent
output :lasteqn
end
```

```
to senform1 :sent
local [one two verb1 verb2 stuff1 stuff2 factor]
if emptyp :sent [output []]
if match [^ what are ^one and ^two !:dlm] :sent ~
   [output fput (qset :one) (senform (sentence [what are] :two "?))]
if match [^ what !:in [is are] #one !:dlm] :sent ~
   [output (list qset :one)]
if match [^ howm !one is #two !:dlm] :sent ~
   [push "aunits (list :one) output (list qset :two)]
if match [^ howm ^one do ^two have !:dlm] :sent ~
   [output (list qset (sentence [the number of] :one :two "have))]
if match [^ howm ^one does ^two have !:dlm] :sent ~
   [output (list qset (sentence [the number of] :one :two "has))]
if match [^ find ^one and #two] :sent ~
   [output fput (qset :one) (senform sentence "find :two)]
if match [^ find #one !:dlm] :sent [output (list qset :one)]
make "sent filter [not article ?] :sent
if match [^one ismulby #two] :sent ~
   [push "ref (list "product opform :one opform :two) output []]
if match [^one isdivby #two] :sent ~
   [push "ref (list "quotient opform :one opform :two) output []]
if match [^one is increased by #two] :sent ~
   [push "ref (list "sum opform :one opform :two) output []]
if match [^one is #two] :sent ~
   [output (list (list "equal opform :one opform :two))]
if match [^one !verb1:verb ^factor as many ^stuff1 as
            ^two !verb2:verb ^stuff2 !:dlm] ~
         :sent ~
   [if emptyp :stuff2 [make "stuff2 :stuff1]
    output (list (list "equal ~
                   opform (sentence [the number of] :stuff1 :one :verb1) ~
                   opform (sentence :factor [the number of]
                                    :stuff2 :two :verb2)))]
if match [^one !verb1:verb !factor:numberp #stuff1 !:dlm] :sent ~
   [output (list (list "equal ~
                   opform (sentence [the number of] :stuff1 :one :verb1) ~
                   opform (list :factor)))]
say [This sentence form is not recognized:] :sent
throw "error
end


to qset :sent
localmake "opform opform filter [not article ?] :sent
if not operatorp first :opform ~
   [queue "wanted :opform queue "ans list :opform oprem :sent output []]
localmake "gensym gensym
queue "wanted :gensym
queue "ans list :gensym oprem :sent
output (list "equal :gensym opform (filter [not article ?] :sent))
end
```

Program Listing

```
to oprem :sent
output map [ifelse equalp ? "numof ["of] [?]] :sent
end


to opform :expr
local [left right op]
if match [^left !op:op2 #right] :expr [output optest :op :left :right]
if match [^left !op:op1 #right] :expr [output optest :op :left :right]
if match [^left !op:op0 #right] :expr [output optest :op :left :right]
if match [#left !:dlm] :expr [make "expr :left]
output nmtest filter [not article ?] :expr
end


to optest :op :left :right
output run (list (word "tst. :op) :left :right)
end


to tst.numof :left :right
if numberp last :left [output (list "product opform :left opform :right)]
output opform (sentence :left "of :right)
end


to tst.divby :left :right
output (list "quotient opform :left opform :right)
end


to tst.tothepower :left :right
output (list "expt opform :left opform :right)
end


to expt :num :pow
if :pow < 1 [output 1]
output :num * expt :num :pow - 1
end


to tst.per :left :right
output (list "quotient ~
        opform :left ~
        opform (ifelse numberp first :right [:right] [fput 1 :right]))
end


to tst.lessthan :left :right
output opdiff opform :right opform :left
end


to opdiff :left :right
output (list "sum :left (list "minus :right))
end
```

```
to tst.minus :left :right
if emptyp :left [output list "minus opform :right]
output opdiff opform :left opform :right
end


to tst.minuss :left :right
output tst.minus :left :right
end


to tst.sum :left :right
local [one two three]
if match [^one and ^two and #three] :right ~
   [output (list "sum opform :one opform (sentence "sum :two "and :three))]
if match [^one and #two] :right ~
   [output (list "sum opform :one opform :two)]
say [sum used wrong:] :right  throw "error
end


to tst.squared :left :right
output list "square opform :left
end


to tst.difference :left :right
local [one two]
if match [between ^one and #two] :right [output opdiff opform :one opform :two]
say [Incorrect use of difference:] :right  throw "error
end


to tst.plus :left :right
output (list "sum opform :left opform :right)
end


to tst.pluss :left :right
output tst.plus :left :right
end


to square :x
output :x * :x
end


to tst.square :left :right
output list "square opform :right
end


to tst.percent :left :right
if not numberp last :left ~
   [say [Incorrect use of percent:] :left throw "error]
output opform (sentence butlast :left ((last :left) / 100) :right)
end
```

```
to tst.perless :left :right
if not numberp last :left ~
   [say [Incorrect use of percent:] :left  throw "error]
output (list "product ~
            (opform sentence butlast :left ((100 - (last :left)) / 100)) ~
            opform :right)
end


to tst.times :left :right
if emptyp :left [say [Incorrect use of times:] :right throw "error]
output (list "product opform :left opform :right)
end


to nmtest :expr
if match [& !:numberp #] :expr [say [argument error:] :expr throw "error]
if and (equalp first :expr 1) (1 < count :expr) ~
   [make "expr (sentence 1 plural (first butfirst :expr)
                                    (butfirst butfirst :expr))]
if and (numberp first :expr) (1 < count :expr) ~
   [push "units (list first butfirst :expr) ~
    output (list "product (first :expr) (opform butfirst :expr))]
if numberp first :expr [output first :expr]
if memberp "this :expr [output this :expr]
if not memberp :expr :var [push "var :expr]
output :expr
end


to this :expr
if not emptyp :ref [output pop "ref]
if not emptyp :lasteqn [output first butfirst last :lasteqn]
if equalp first :expr "this [make "expr butfirst :expr]
push "var :expr
output :expr
end


;; Solving the equations

to trysolve :shelf :wanted :units :aunits
local "solution
make "solution solve :wanted :shelf (ifelse emptyp :aunits [:units] [:aunits])
output pranswers :ans :solution
end


to solve :wanted :eqt :terms
output solve.reduce solver :wanted :terms [] [] "insufficient
end
```

```
to solve.reduce :soln
if emptyp :soln [output []]
if wordp :soln [output :soln]
if emptyp butfirst :soln [output :soln]
localmake "part solve.reduce butfirst :soln
output fput (list (first first :soln) (subord last first :soln :part)) :part
end


to solver :wanted :terms :alis :failed :err
local [one result restwant]
if emptyp :wanted [output :err]
make "one solve1 (first :wanted) ~
                (sentence butfirst :wanted :failed :terms) ~
                :alis :eqt [] "insufficient
if wordp :one ~
   [output solver (butfirst :wanted) :terms :alis
                (fput first :wanted :failed) :one]
make "restwant (sentence :failed butfirst :wanted)
if emptyp :restwant [output :one]
make "result solver :restwant :terms :one [] "insufficient
if listp :result [output :result]
output solver (butfirst :wanted) :terms :alis (fput first :wanted :failed) :one
end


to solve1 :x :terms :alis :eqns :failed :err
local [thiseq vars extras xterms others result]
if emptyp :eqns [output :err]
make "thiseq subord (first :eqns) :alis
make "vars varterms :thiseq
if not memberp :x :vars ~
   [output solve1 :x :terms :alis (butfirst :eqns)
                (fput first :eqns :failed) :err]
make "xterms fput :x :terms
make "extras setminus :vars :xterms
make "eqt remove (first :eqns) :eqt
if not emptyp :extras ~
   [make "others solver :extras :xterms :alis [] "insufficient
    ifelse wordp :others
           [make "eqt sentence :failed :eqns
            output solve1 :x :terms :alis (butfirst :eqns)
                       (fput first :eqns :failed) :others]
           [make "alis :others
            make "thiseq subord (first :eqns) :alis]]
make "result solveq :x :thiseq
if listp :result [output lput :result :alis]
make "eqt sentence :failed :eqns
output solve1 :x :terms :alis (butfirst :eqns) (fput first :eqns :failed) :result
end
```

```
to solveq :var :eqn
localmake "left first butfirst :eqn
ifelse occvar :var :left [localmake "right last :eqn] ~
                          [localmake "right :left  make "left last :eqn]
output solveq1 :left :right "true
end


to solveq1 :left :right :bothtest
if :bothtest [if occvar :var :right [output solveqboth :left :right]]
if equalp :left :var [output list :var :right]
if wordp :left [output "unsolvable]
localmake "oper first :left
if memberp :oper [sum product minus quotient] ~
   [output run (list word "solveq. :oper)]
output "unsolvable
end


to solveqboth :left :right
if not equalp first :right "sum [output solveq1 (subterm :left :right) 0 "false]
output solveq.rplus :left butfirst :right []
end


to solveq.rplus :left :right :newright
if emptyp :right [output solveq1 :left (simone "sum :newright) "false]
if occvar :var first :right ~
   [output solveq.rplus (subterm :left first :right) butfirst :right :newright]
output solveq.rplus :left butfirst :right (fput first :right :newright)
end


to solveq.sum
if emptyp butfirst butfirst :left ~
   [output solveq1 first butfirst :left :right "true]
output solveq.sum1 butfirst :left :right []
end


to solveq.sum1 :left :right :newleft
if emptyp :left [output solveq.sum2]
if occvar :var first :left ~
   [output solveq.sum1 butfirst :left :right fput first :left :newleft]
output solveq.sum1 butfirst :left (subterm :right first :left) :newleft
end


to solveq.sum2
if emptyp butfirst :newleft [output solveq1 first :newleft :right "true]
localmake "factor factor :newleft :var
if equalp first :factor "unknown [output "unsolvable]
if equalp last :factor 0 [output "unsolvable]
output solveq1 first :factor (divterm :right last :factor) "true
end
```

```
to solveq.minus
output solveq1 (first butfirst :left) (minusin :right) "false
end


to solveq.product
output solveq.product1 :left :right
end


to solveq.product1 :left :right
if emptyp butfirst butfirst :left ~
   [output solveq1 (first butfirst :left) :right "true]
if not occvar :var first butfirst :left ~
   [output solveq.product1 (fput "product butfirst butfirst :left)
                           (divterm :right first butfirst :left)]
localmake "rest simone "product butfirst butfirst :left
if occvar :var :rest [output "unsolvable]
output solveq1 (first butfirst :left) (divterm :right :rest) "false
end


to solveq.quotient
if occvar :var first butfirst :left ~
   [output solveq1 (first butfirst :left) (simtimes list :right last :left) "true]
output solveq1 (simtimes list :right last :left) (first butfirst :left) "true
end


to denom :fract :addends
make "addends simplus :addends
localmake "den last :fract
if not equalp first :addends "quotient ~
   [output simdiv list (simone "sum
                               (remop "sum
                                      list (distribtimes (list :addends) :den)
                                           first butfirst :fract))
                   :den]
if equalp :den last :addends ~
   [output simdiv (simplus list (first butfirst :fract) (first butfirst :addends))
                  :den]
localmake "lowterms simdiv list :den last :addends
output simdiv list (simplus (simtimes list first butfirst :fract last :lowterms)
                            (simtimes list first butfirst :addends
                                           first butfirst :lowterms)) ~
                (simtimes list first butfirst :lowterms last :addends)
end


to distribtimes :trms :multiplier
output simplus map [simtimes (list ? :multiplier)] :trms
end
```

```
to distribx :expr
local [oper args]
if emptyp :expr [output :expr]
make "oper first :expr
if not operatorp :oper [output :expr]
make "args map [distribx ?] butfirst :expr
if reduce "and map [numberp ?] :args [output run (sentence [(] :oper :args [)])]
if equalp :oper "sum [output simplus :args]
if equalp :oper "minus [output minusin first :args]
if equalp :oper "product [output simtimes :args]
if equalp :oper "quotient [output simdiv :args]
output fput :oper :args
end


to divterm :dividend :divisor
if equalp :dividend 0 [output 0]
output simdiv list :dividend :divisor
end


to factor :exprs :var
localmake "trms map [factor1 :var ?] :exprs
if memberp "unknown :trms [output fput "unknown :exprs]
output list :var simplus :trms
end


to factor1 :var :expr
localmake "negvar minusin :var
if equalp :var :expr [output 1]
if equalp :negvar :expr [output -1]
if emptyp :expr [output "unknown]
if equalp first :expr "product [output factor2 butfirst :expr]
if not equalp first :expr "quotient [output "unknown]
localmake "dividend first butfirst :expr
if equalp :var :dividend [output (list "quotient 1 last :expr)]
if not equalp first :dividend "product [output "unknown]
localmake "result factor2 butfirst :dividend
if equalp :result "unknown [output "unknown]
output (list "quotient :result last :expr)
end


to factor2 :trms
if memberp :var :trms [output simone "product (remove :var :trms)]
if memberp :negvar :trms [output minusin simone "product (remove :negvar :trms)]
output "unknown
end


to maybeadd :num :rest
if equalp :num 0 [output :rest]
output fput :num :rest
end
```

```
to maybemul :num :rest
if equalp :num 1 [output :rest]
output fput :num :rest
end


to minusin :expr
if emptyp :expr [output -1]
if equalp first :expr "sum [output fput "sum map [minusin ?] butfirst :expr]
if equalp first :expr "minus [output last :expr]
if memberp first :expr [product quotient] ~
   [output fput first :expr
                 (fput (minusin first butfirst :expr) butfirst butfirst :expr)]
if numberp :expr [output minus :expr]
output list "minus :expr
end


to occvar :var :expr
if emptyp :expr [output "false]
if wordp :expr [output equalp :var :expr]
if operatorp first :expr [output not emptyp find [occvar :var ?] butfirst :expr]
output equalp :var :expr
end


to remfactor :num :den
foreach butfirst :num [remfactor1 ?]
output (list "quotient (simone "product butfirst :num)
                       (simone "product butfirst :den))
end


to remfactor1 :expr
local "neg
if memberp :expr :den ~
   [make "num remove :expr :num  make "den remove :expr :den  stop]
make "neg minusin :expr
if not memberp :neg :den [stop]
make "num remove :expr :num
make "den minusin remove :neg :den
end


to remop :oper :exprs
output map.se [ifelse equalp first ? :oper [butfirst ?] [(list ?)]] :exprs
end
```

```
to simdiv :list
local [num den numop denop]
make "num first :list
make "den last :list
if equalp :num :den [output 1]
if numberp :den [output simtimes (list (quotient 1 :den) :num)]
make "numop first :num
make "denop first :den
if equalp :numop "quotient ~
   [output simdiv list (first butfirst :num) (simtimes list last :num :den)]
if equalp :denop "quotient ~
   [output simdiv list (simtimes list :num last :den) (first butfirst :den)]
if and equalp :numop "product equalp :denop "product [output remfactor :num :den]
if and equalp :numop "product memberp :den :num [output remove :den :num]
output fput "quotient :list
end


to simone :oper :trms
if emptyp :trms [output ifelse equalp :oper "product [1] [0]]
if emptyp butfirst :trms [output first :trms]
output fput :oper :trms
end


to simplus :exprs
make "exprs remop "sum :exprs
localmake "factor [unknown]
catch "simplus ~
      [foreach :terms ~
               [make "factor (factor :exprs ?) ~
                if not equalp first :factor "unknown [throw "simplus]]]
if not equalp first :factor "unknown [output fput "product remop "product :factor]
localmake "nums 0
localmake "nonnums []
localmake "quick []
catch "simplus [simplus1 :exprs]
if not emptyp :quick [output :quick]
if not equalp :nums 0 [push "nonnums :nums]
output simone "sum :nonnums
end


to simplus1 :exprs
if emptyp :exprs [stop]
simplus2 first :exprs
simplus1 butfirst :exprs
end
```

```
to simplus2 :pos
localmake "neg minusin :pos
if numberp :pos [make "nums sum :pos :nums stop]
if memberp :neg butfirst :exprs [make "exprs remove :neg :exprs stop]
if equalp first :pos "quotient ~
   [make "quick (denom :pos (maybeadd :nums sentence :nonnums butfirst :exprs)) ~
    throw "simplus]
push "nonnums :pos
end


to simtimes :exprs
local [nums nonnums quick]
make "nums 1
make "nonnums []
make "quick []
catch "simtimes [foreach remop "product :exprs [simtimes1 ?]]
if not emptyp :quick [output :quick]
if equalp :nums 0 [output 0]
if not equalp :nums 1 [push "nonnums :nums]
output simone "product :nonnums
end


to simtimes1 :expr
if equalp :expr 0 [make "nums 0 throw "simtimes]
if numberp :expr [make "nums product :expr :nums stop]
if equalp first :expr "sum ~
   [make "quick
         distribtimes (butfirst :expr)
                      (simone "product maybemul :nums sentence :nonnums ?rest)
    throw "simtimes]
if equalp first :expr "quotient ~
   [make "quick
         simdiv (list (simtimes (list (first butfirst :expr)
                                       (simone "product
                                               maybemul :nums
                                                        sentence :nonnums ?rest)))
                      (last :expr))
    throw "simtimes]
push "nonnums :expr
end


to subord :expr :alist
output distribx subord1 :expr :alist
end


to subord1 :expr :alist
if emptyp :alist [output :expr]
output subord (substop (last first :alist) (first first :alist) :expr) ~
              (butfirst :alist)
end
```

```
to substop :val :var :expr
if emptyp :expr [output []]
if equalp :expr :var [output :val]
if not operatorp first :expr [output :expr]
output fput first :expr map [substop :val :var ?] butfirst :expr
end


to subterm :minuend :subtrahend
if equalp :minuend 0 [output minusin :subtrahend]
if equalp :minuend :subtrahend [output 0]
output simplus (list :minuend minusin :subtrahend)
end


to varterms :expr
if emptyp :expr [output []]
if numberp :expr [output []]
if wordp :expr [output (list :expr)]
if operatorp first :expr [output map.se [varterms ?] butfirst :expr]
output (list :expr)
end


;; Printing the solutions

to pranswers :ans :solution
print []
if equalp :solution "unsolvable ~
   [print [Unable to solve this set of equations.] output "false]
if equalp :solution "insufficient ~
   [print [The equations were insufficient to find a solution.] output "false]
localmake "gotall "true
foreach :ans [if prans ? :solution [make "gotall "false]]
if not :gotall [print [] print [Unable to solve this set of equations.]]
output :gotall
end


to prans :ans :solution
localmake "result find [equalp first ? first :ans] :solution
if emptyp :result [output "true]
print (sentence cap last :ans "is unitstring last :result)
print []
output "false
end
```

```
to unitstring :expr
if numberp :expr [output roundoff :expr]
if equalp first :expr "product ~
   [output sentence (unitstring first butfirst :expr)
                    (reduce "sentence butfirst butfirst :expr)]
if (and (listp :expr)
        (not numberp first :expr)
        (not operatorp first :expr)) ~
   [output (sentence 1 (singular first :expr) (butfirst :expr))]
output :expr
end


to roundoff :num
if (abs (:num - round :num)) < 0.0001 [output round :num]
output :num
end


to abs :num
output ifelse (:num < 0) [-:num] [:num]
end


;; Using known relationships

to geteqns :vars
output map.se [gprop varkey ? "eqns] :vars
end


to varkey :var
local "word
if match [number of !word #] :var [output :word]
output first :var
end


;; Assuming equality of similar variables

to vartest :vars
if emptyp :vars [output []]
local [var beg end]
make "var first :vars
output (sentence (ifelse match [^beg !:pronoun #end] :var
                         [vartest1 :var (sentence :beg "& :end) butfirst :vars]
                         [[]])
                (vartest1 :var (sentence "# :var "#) butfirst :vars)
                (vartest butfirst :vars))
end


to vartest1 :target :pat :vars
output map [varequal :target ?] filter [match :pat ?] :vars
end
```

```
to varequal :target :var
print []
print [Assuming that]
print (sentence (list :target) [is equal to] (list :var))
output (list "equal :target :var)
end


;; Optional substitutions

to tryidiom
make "prob (sentence :beg last :idiom :end)
while [match (sentence "^beg first :idiom "#end) :prob] ~
      [make "prob (sentence :beg last :idiom :end)]
say [The problem with an idiomatic substitution is] :prob
student1 :prob (remove :idiom :idioms)
end


;; Utility procedures

to qword :word
output memberp :word [find what howm how]
end


to dlm :word                            to article :word
output memberp :word [. ? |;|]          output memberp :word [a an the]
end                                     end


to verb :word
output memberp :word [have has get gets weigh weighs]
end


to personp :word
output memberp :word [Mary Ann Bill Tom Sally Frank father uncle]
end


to pronoun :word
output memberp :word [he she it him her they them his her its]
end


to posspro :word
output memberp :word [his her its]
end


to op0 :word
output memberp :word [pluss minuss squared tothepower per sum difference numof]
end


to op1 :word
output memberp :word [times divby square]
end
```

```
to op2 :word
output memberp :word [plus minus lessthan percent perless]
end

to operatorp :word
output memberp :word [sum minus product quotient expt square equal]
end

to plural :word
localmake "plural gprop :word "plural
if not emptyp :plural [output :plural]
if not emptyp gprop :word "sing [output :word]
if equalp last :word "s [output :word]
output word :word "s
end

to singular :word
localmake "sing gprop :word "sing
if not emptyp :sing [output :sing]
if not emptyp gprop :word "plural [output :word]
if equalp last :word "s [output butlast :word]
output :word
end

to setminus :big :little
output filter [not memberp ? :little] :big
end

to say :herald :text              to lsay :herald :text
print []                          print []
print :herald                     print :herald
print []                          print []
print :text                       foreach :text [print cap ? print []]
print []                          end
end

to cap :sent
if emptyp :sent [output []]
output sentence (word uppercase first first :sent butfirst first :sent) ~
               butfirst :sent
end

;; The pattern matcher

to match :pat :sen
if prematch :pat :sen [output rmatch :pat :sen]
output "false
end
```

```
to prematch :pat :sen
if emptyp :pat [output "true]
if listp first :pat [output prematch butfirst :pat :sen]
if memberp first first :pat [! @ # ^ & ?] [output prematch butfirst :pat :sen]
if emptyp :sen [output "false]
localmake "rest member first :pat :sen
if not emptyp :rest [output prematch butfirst :pat :rest]
output "false
end

to rmatch :pat :sen
local [special.var special.pred special.buffer in.list]
if or wordp :pat wordp :sen [output "false]
if emptyp :pat [output emptyp :sen]
if listp first :pat [output special fput "!: :pat :sen]
if memberp first first :pat [? # ! & @ ^] [output special :pat :sen]
if emptyp :sen [output "false]
if equalp first :pat first :sen [output rmatch butfirst :pat butfirst :sen]
output "false
end

to special :pat :sen
set.special parse.special butfirst first :pat "
output run word "match first first :pat
end

to parse.special :word :var
if emptyp :word [output list :var "always]
if equalp first :word ": [output list :var butfirst :word]
output parse.special butfirst :word word :var first :word
end

to set.special :list
make "special.var first :list
make "special.pred last :list
if emptyp :special.var [make "special.var "special.buffer]
if memberp :special.pred [in anyof] [set.in]
if not emptyp :special.pred [stop]
make "special.pred first butfirst :pat
make "pat fput first :pat butfirst butfirst :pat
end

to set.in
make "in.list first butfirst :pat
make "pat fput first :pat butfirst butfirst :pat
end
```

```
to match!
if emptyp :sen [output "false]
if not try.pred [output "false]
make :special.var first :sen
output rmatch butfirst :pat butfirst :sen
end

to match?
make :special.var []
if emptyp :sen [output rmatch butfirst :pat :sen]
if not try.pred [output rmatch butfirst :pat :sen]
make :special.var first :sen
if rmatch butfirst :pat butfirst :sen [output "true]
make :special.var []
output rmatch butfirst :pat :sen
end

to match#
make :special.var []
output #test #gather :sen
end

to #gather :sen
if emptyp :sen [output :sen]
if not try.pred [output :sen]
make :special.var lput first :sen thing :special.var
output #gather butfirst :sen
end

to #test :sen
if rmatch butfirst :pat :sen [output "true]
if emptyp thing :special.var [output "false]
output #test2 fput last thing :special.var :sen
end

to #test2 :sen
make :special.var butlast thing :special.var
output #test :sen
end

to match&
output &test match#
end

to &test :tf
if emptyp thing :special.var [output "false]
output :tf
end
```

```
to match^
make :special.var []    output ^test :sen
end


to ^test :sen
if rmatch butfirst :pat :sen [output "true]
if emptyp :sen [output "false]
if not try.pred [output "false]
make :special.var lput first :sen thing :special.var
output ^test butfirst :sen
end


to match@
make :special.var :sen    output @test []
end


to @test :sen
if @try.pred [if rmatch butfirst :pat :sen [output "true]]
if emptyp thing :special.var [output "false]
output @test2 fput last thing :special.var :sen
end


to @test2 :sen
make :special.var butlast thing :special.var
output @test :sen
end


to try.pred
if listp :special.pred [output rmatch :special.pred first :sen]
output run list :special.pred quoted first :sen
end


to quoted :thing
ifelse listp :thing [output :thing] [output word "" :thing]
end


to @try.pred
if listp :special.pred [output rmatch :special.pred thing :special.var]
output run list :special.pred thing :special.var
end


to anyof :sen                         to always :x
output anyof1 :sen :in.list           output "true
end                                   end


to anyof1 :sen :pats                  to in :word
if emptyp :pats [output "false]       output memberp :word :in.list
if rmatch first :pats :sen [output "true]   end
output anyof1 :sen butfirst :pats
end
```

```
;; Sample word problems

make "ann [Mary is twice as old as Ann was when Mary was as old as Ann is now.
  If Mary is 24 years old, how old is Ann?]
make "guns [The number of soldiers the Russians have is
  one half of the number of guns they have. They have 7000 guns.
  How many soldiers do they have?]
make "jet [The distance from New York to Los Angeles is 3000 miles.
  If the average speed of a jet plane is 600 miles per hour,
  find the time it takes to travel from New York to Los Angeles by jet.]
make "nums [A number is multiplied by 6 . This product is increased by 44 .
  This result is 68 . Find the number.]
make "radio [The price of a radio is $69.70.
  If this price is 15 percent less than the marked price, find the marked price.]
make "sally [The sum of Sally's share of some money and Frank's share is $4.50.
  Sally's share is twice Frank's. Find Frank's and Sally's share.]
make "ship [The gross weight of a ship is 20000 tons.
  If its net weight is 15000 tons, what is the weight of the ships cargo?]
make "span [If 1 span is 9 inches, and 1 fathom is 6 feet,
  how many spans is 1 fathom?]
make "sumtwo [The sum of two numbers is 96,
  and one number is 16 larger than the other number. Find the two numbers.]
make "tom [If the number of customers Tom gets is
  twice the square of 20 per cent of the number of advertisements he runs,
  and the number of advertisements he runs is 45,
  what is the number of customers Tom gets?]
make "uncle [Bill's father's uncle is twice as old as Bill's father.
  2 years from now Bill's father will be 3 times as old as Bill.
  The sum of their ages is 92 . Find Bill's age.]

;; Initial data base

pprop "distance "eqns ~
  [[equal [distance] [product [speed] [time]]]
   [equal [distance] [product [gas consumtion] [number of gallons of gas used]]]]
pprop "feet "eqns ~
  [[equal [product 1 [feet]] [product 12 [inches]]]
   [equal [product 1 [yards]] [product 3 [feet]]]]
pprop "feet "sing "foot
pprop "foot "plural "feet
pprop "gallons "eqns ~
  [[equal [distance] [product [gas consumtion] [number of gallons of gas used]]]]
pprop "gas "eqns ~
  [[equal [distance] [product [gas consumtion] [number of gallons of gas used]]]]
pprop "inch "plural "inches
pprop "inches "eqns [[equal [product 1 [feet]] [product 12 [inches]]]]
pprop "people "sing "person
pprop "person "plural "people
pprop "speed "eqns [[equal [distance] [product [speed] [time]]]]
pprop "time "eqns [[equal [distance] [product [speed] [time]]]]
pprop "yards "eqns [[equal [product 1 [yards]] [product 3 [feet]]]]
```

Appendices

Bibliography

This book is a little like the previews of coming attractions at the movies; it's meant to whet your appetite in several directions, without giving you the complete story about anything. To find out more, you'll have to consult more specialized books on each topic.

There are a lot of books on computer programming and computer science, and whichever I chose to list here would be out of date by the time you read this. Instead of trying to give current references in every area, in this edition I'm listing only the few most important and timeless books, plus an indication of the sources I used for each chapter.

Computer science is a fast-changing field; if you want to know what the current hot issues are, you have to read the journals. The way to start is to join the Association for Computing Machinery, 1515 Broadway, New York, NY 10036. If you are a full-time student you are eligible for a special rate for dues, which as I write this is $25 per year. (But you should write for a membership application with the current rates.) The Association publishes about 20 monthly or quarterly periodicals, plus the newsletters of about 40 Special Interest Groups in particular fields.

Read These!

If you read no other books about computer science, you must read these two. One is an introductory text for college computer science students; the other is intended for a nonspecialist audience.

Abelson, Harold, and Gerald Jay Sussman with Julie Sussman, *Structure and Interpretation of Computer Programs,* MIT Press, Second Edition, 1996.

> The introductory computer science text at MIT, this book uses Lisp as the vehicle for an intense study of everything from data structures to machine architecture. Although it's not a book about artificial intelligence as such, this is the definitive presentation of the artificial intelligence view of what computer science in general is about, and the best computer science book ever written.

Hofstadter, Douglas R., *Gödel, Escher, Bach: an Eternal Golden Braid,* Basic Books, 1979.

> This book won the Pulitzer Prize for its success in explaining to readers who aren't computer scientists some of the deepest ideas of computer science, and it makes a strong case for the view that those ideas also have a lot to teach us about human intelligence.

Chapter 1: Automata Theory

The reference I used in thinking about this chapter was

Minsky, Marvin, *Computation: Finite and Infinite Machines,* Prentice-Hall, 1967.

> Part of the interest of this particular text is that its author is a leading figure in artificial intelligence research, and so the question of whether the insights of automata theory apply also to human intelligence is always visible as a motivating force in the presentation of the theory. Minsky's bibliography will refer you to the original papers by Turing, Kleene, Church, and so on as well as some left-field references to biological information processing from people like Lettvin and McCulloch.

Chapter 2: Discrete Mathematics

This chapter touches on several topics. An overall introduction for computer scientists is

Liu, Chung Laung, *Elements of Discrete Mathematics,* McGraw-Hill, Second Edition, 1985.

> This book requires no advanced mathematical background, but it does require that the reader feel comfortable with mathematical notation and the notion of formal proof. The topics include both purely mathematical ones, like set theory, combinatorics, and modern algebra, and related computer science ones like computability, formal languages, automata theory, analysis of algorithms, and recursion. This list is not unlike the one in the book you're reading now, and in fact Professor Liu expresses a goal similar to mine: to show computer science undergraduates the relevance of mathematics to their work. The difference is that I use actual programs to illustrate the ideas whenever possible, whereas his is a "straight" math book. (Of course another difference is that he treats all these topics in much more depth. But don't be scared away; he starts simply.)

On the topic of mathematical logic, there is a range of books that vary in accessibility. Among the most pleasant are

Smullyan, Raymond, *What Is the Name of This Book?* Prentice-Hall, 1978
—, *The Lady or the Tiger?* Knopf, 1982
—, *5000 B.C. and Other Philosophical Fantasies,* St. Martin's, 1984
—, *Alice in Puzzle-Land,* Penguin, 1984.

> These are books of puzzles based on logic, but they go beyond the simple propositional inference puzzles like the one in the text. Smullyan starts with some of the classic puzzle categories, like the Liars and Truth-Tellers puzzle, and builds up to an exposition in puzzle form of topics like self-reference, modal logic, and Gödel's Theorem.

"Logic programming" is the use of mathematical logic formalisms as a programming language. It is also called "declarative programming" because instead of issuing commands to the computer, the programmer makes statements about things known to be true. The algorithm by which the programming system makes inferences from these statements is not explicitly provided by the programmer, but is built into the language.

The most widely known logic programming language, although not the only one, is Prolog. An accessible introductory text is

Ennals, Richard, *Beginning Micro-Prolog*, Harper & Row, Second Edition, 1984.

> I list this book here because it's a Prolog text and therefore relevant to mathematical logic, but for me the main interest of the book is that it argues for the use of Prolog in teaching kids, as an alternative to Logo. The book gives examples of logic programming at work in various curriculum areas.

Chapter 3: Algorithms and Data Structures

To a software engineer, the issues in this chapter are among the central ones in computer science. That's not my own way of thinking, so it's possible that my presentation doesn't give the field all the pizazz that an enthusiast would manage. To compensate for that, you should read

Bentley, Jon, *Programming Pearls*, Addison-Wesley, 1986.

> This is a collection of monthly articles written by Bentley for the *Communications* of the Association for Computing Machinery. It requires virtually no formal mathematics and is extremely readable. If the book has a moral, it's "Think first, program later." It makes its case with a number of true-to-life examples of projects in which orders of magnitude were saved in the execution time of a program by rethinking its fundamental structure.

Chapter 4: Programming Language Design

There are textbooks in "comparative programming languages," but I'm going to stick to the strategy of the chapter by using Pascal as the example. *Structure and Interpretation of Computer Programs,* one of my must-reads, will be useful as a contrast here, giving the Lisp point of view.

Jensen, Kathleen, and Niklaus Wirth, *Pascal User Manual and Report,* Springer-Verlag, Third Edition, 1985.

> This is the official report of the international committee responsible for the design of the language. The book has two parts, a reference manual and the committee report itself. The latter includes some explicit discussion of the design decisions in the language.

Chapter 5: Programming Language Implementation

I really didn't have a reference for this chapter; I just sort of forged ahead on my own! But here's the book I *should* have read first:

Friedman, Daniel P., Mitchell Wand, and Christopher T. Haynes, *Essentials of Programming Languages,* MIT Press, 1992.

> This book uses the Scheme dialect of Lisp as the basis for a study of programming language interpreters. It's harder reading than most of the books in this bibliography, but it encourages the reader to think very deeply about how programming languages work.

Chapter 6: Artificial Intelligence

I'll list two references here; one on language understanding in general and one that contains a paper about the Student program specifically.

Winograd, Terry, *Language as a Cognitive Process, Volume 1: Syntax,* Addison-Wesley, 1983.

> A planned second volume on semantics was not published. This is a technically meaty book, but considering its depth it is quite readable.

The book strikes a good balance among technical programming issues, psychological issues, and the ideas of mainstream linguistics. It includes an extensive bibliography. When I attended Terry's course at Stanford in which he first presented the material that became this book, it was the first time I experienced a course that ended with a standing ovation for the instructor. The book shows the same clarity of explanation and the same enthusiasm.

Minsky, Marvin L., *Semantic Information Processing*, MIT Press, 1969.

This is a collection of early research reports. I include it here because one of its chapters is a paper by Bobrow on STUDENT, and you won't be able to find the more complete description in Bobrow's unpublished thesis. Other chapters describe similar microworld-strategy projects of the same vintage.

Computers and People

Last but far from least, some of the most fascinating reading connected with computer science is found outside of the technical literature, in the reactions of psychologists, philosophers, and sociologists to the computer as a social force. You owe it to yourself to understand the human context of your work; you owe it to everyone else to be strongly aware of the social implications of what you do.

Turkle, Sherry, *The Second Self: Computers and the Human Spirit*, Simon and Schuster, 1984.

A sociologist's view of the computer culture, this book explores both the psychology of computer experts and the ways in which a computer-rich environment has changed the thinking of non-experts not only about technology but about what it means to be human.

Weizenbaum, Joseph, *Computer Power and Human Reason: From Judgment to Calculation*, W. H. Freeman, 1976.

Weizenbaum is a computer scientist, and this book is in part a technical argument about the limitations of what computers can do. But it is more importantly a call to computer scientists to take responsibility for the uses to which their inventions are put. Weizenbaum argues that there are things we *shouldn't* do with computers, even if we *can* learn how to overcome the technical obstacles. Computer-based weapons of war are an obvious example, but Weizenbaum is also worried about things like automated psychotherapy, which was just a daydream when the book appeared but has since become a reality to a limited extent. Many computer scientists find this book offensive, and it is certainly possible to find flaws in the details. But the critics rarely present an alternative with an equally strong social conscience.

Dreyfus, Hubert L., *What Computers Still Can't Do: A Critique of Artificial Reason,* MIT Press, 1992.

Dreyfus is a philosopher who uses the phenomenological ideas of Heidegger and others to suggest a fundamental flaw in the assumptions AI researchers make about human intelligence. To try to sum it up in one sentence, the sort of thinking that people do in solving a puzzle is very different from the much more profound intelligence we use in carrying out our more customary activities. AI programs mimic the former but not the latter. This is a revision of an earlier book, taking into account more recent developments in AI research.

Weinberg, Gerald M., *The Psychology of Computer Programming,* Van Nostrand Reinholt, 1971.

This book studies programming as a social activity, programming as an individual activity, and the programming environment. In my opinion, its main contribution is the idea of "egoless programming," which means more or less that when your friend finds that impossible bug in your program for you, you should feel happy rather than threatened. Weinberg offers several good ideas for how to act as part of a programming community. On the other hand, I'm less enthusiastic about his manager's-eye view of the programmer as a cog in the machine, rather than as a creative artist. But overall I think this book is well worth reading; it's also entertainingly written.

Credits

Material on page xiv quoted from *The Second Self: Computers and the Human Spirit* by Sherry Turkle. Copyright © 1984 by Sherry Turkle. Reprinted by permission of Simon & Schuster, Inc.

Material on page 48 quoted from *Mind Benders B–2* by Anita Harnadek. Copyright © 1978 by Midwest Publications (now called Critical Thinking Press, Box 448, Pacific Grove, CA 93950). Reprinted by permission of the publisher.

Material on page 53 by Diane C. Baldwin quoted from *The Dell Book of Logic Problems #4*. Copyright © 1989 by Dell Publishing, a division of Bantam Doubleday Dell Publishing Group, Inc., reprinted by permission of Dell Magazines.

Material on pages 279 and 294 quoted from *Natural Language Input for a Computer Problem Solving Program* by Daniel G. Bobrow (unpublished Ph.D. thesis). Copyright © 1964 by Daniel G. Bobrow. Reprinted by permission of the author.

Material on page 295 quoted from *Mindstorms: Children, Computers, and Powerful Ideas* by Seymour Papert. Copyright © 1984 by Basic Books, Inc., publishers. Reprinted by permission of the publisher.

The illustration on page 313 quoted from *Language as a Cognitive Process, Volume 1: Syntax* by Terry Winograd. Copyright © 1983 by Addison-Wesley Publishing Company, Inc. Reprinted by permission of the publisher.

Index of Defined Procedures

This index lists example procedures whose definitions are in the text. The general index lists technical terms and primitive procedures.

General Index

This index lists technical terms and primitive procedures. There is also an index of defined procedures, which lists procedures whose definitions are in the text.

Bentley, Jon 344
bibliography 341
binary computer 69
binary number 25, 88
binary operator 223
binary search algorithm 143
binary tree 132, 144
binding, call by 199
binomial coefficient 82
bit 26, 28, 71
block structure 166, 177
Bobrow, Daniel G. xvii, 278
`Boolean` (Pascal) 187
bottom-up 175
bound reference 184
branch node 132
byte 147, 188

C

C 225
CAI, intelligent 294
call by binding 199
call by reference 197, 198
call by value 197, 198
call, procedure 178
category 49
`char` (Pascal) 187
checking, compile-time 223
Chinese food 46
circuit, integrated 230
Clancy, Michael xvii
closed form definition 80, 98
code generation 211, 245
coefficient, binomial 82
coefficient, multinomial 94
cognitive science 278
Colby, Kenneth 31
combination 74, 79
combination lock 74, 86
combinatorics 72
common subexpression elimination 109
community xv
compile-time checking 223
compiler 172

compiler compiler 219, 224
compiler, incremental 174
compiler, optimizing 109
compiler, Pascal 209
complexity ix
composition of functions 162
compound proposition 46
compound statement 177
computer assisted instruction 294
computer center xv
computer hardware 69
computer logic 71
computer science ix
computer, binary 69
concatenation rule 11, 17
conditional statement 177
constant string 189
constructor 137
context, limited 278
context-free language 310
continuous function 45
contradiction, proof by 34
contrapositive rule 61
correctness 107
correspondence, one-to-one 89
counting problem 45

D

data structure 107, 129
data type 187
Davis, Jim xvii
declaration part 176
declarative knowledge 16
declarative programming 168
declarative programming languages 16
declarative representation x
definition, closed form 80, 98
definition, formal 211
definition, inductive 80, 91, 94, 112
definition, recursive 12
descent, recursive 220
deterministic grammar 219
directed graph 22
discrete mathematics 45

Dreyfus, Hubert L. 347
dyadic 224
dynamic allocation 148
dynamic environment 184, 241
dynamic programming 115
dynamic scope 184, 185, 197, 198, 242

E

economics xiv
editor, text 9, 169
education 294
effective procedure 31
efficiency 107
elementary function 80
elimination rule 50
embedding 310
end (Pascal) 175
engineering, knowledge 278
English 278
Ennals, Richard 344
enumerated type 191
environment, dynamic 184, 241
environment, lexical 184, 198, 241
equation 281, 285
equivalence relation 68
ethics xiv
exclusive or 68
expansion, multinomial 112
experimental method 83
expert system 278
exponential 129
expression 223
expression, regular 11, 15, 211
extensibility 181
external memory 30

F

factorial 79
fence 205
Fermat, Pierre de 82
finite-state adder 25
finite-state machine 3, 15, 213, 309
first 110

food, Chinese 46
forest 133
formal definition 211
formal parameter 176
formal thinking ix
for (Pascal) 178, 181, 183
frame pointer 236
frame, stack 235
free reference 184, 185
Friedman, Daniel P. 345
function, continuous 45
function, elementary 80
function, generating 81, 98
function, predicate 67
function, sine 81
function, truth-valued 46, 67
functional programming 162
functions, composition of 162
function (Pascal) 194

G

gate 69
general knowledge 300
generated symbol 141, 239, 293, 304
generating function 81, 98
generation, code 211, 245
global optimization 111
global pointer 235
Goldenberg, Paul xvii
grammar, deterministic 219
grammar, predictive 219
graph 22
graph, directed 22
graphics xiii

H

half-adder 70
halting state 31
halting theorem 32
Hanoi, Tower of 169
hardware, computer 69
Harnadek, Anita xvii, 48
hash table 130

Haynes, Christopher T. 345
heap 131
heapsort 131
heuristic 294, 298
hierarchy 131, 146
hierarchy, syntactic 213
Hilfinger, Paul xvii
Hoare, C. A. R. 125
Hofstadter, Douglas R. 342

I

`if` (Pascal) 221
immediate 232
implication rule 60
incremental compiler 174
independent 72
index register 235
index variable 205
individual 49
induction, mathematical x
inductive definition 80, 91, 94, 112
inference system 47
inference, rules of 47
infinite loop 32
infinite set 89
insertion sort 119
instruction, computer assisted 294
integers, sum of the 119
`integer` (Pascal) 187
integrated circuit 230
intellectual property xv
intelligence, artificial 277
intelligent CAI 294
interactive language 169
intermediate language 173
internal state 30
interpreter 172
intractable 129
inverter 69
Iverson, Kenneth E. 224

J

Jensen, Kathleen 345

joke 112

K

keyword 219
Kleene, Stephen C. 16
knowledge engineering 278
knowledge representation 309
knowledge, declarative 16
knowledge, general 300
knowledge, procedural 16
Knuth, Donald E. 129

L

label 234
language, context-free 310
language, interactive 169
language, intermediate 173
language, machine 172, 209
language, non-interactive 169
`last` 110
leaf node 132
lexical analysis 215
lexical environment 184, 198, 241
lexical scope 183
limited context 278
linear 129, 286
linear search algorithm 143
Lisp 185, 196, 282
list, association 287
list, property 301
list, sorted 130
Liu, Chung Laung 343
`load` 147
local optimization 110
local procedure 176
lock, combination 74, 86
lock, Simplex 85, 114
logarithm 129
logic problem 45, 48
logic programming 168
logic, computer 71
logic, predicate 67
logic, propositional 46

logic, ternary 73
Logo 169, 294
Logo pattern matcher 283
Logo variable 199
lookahead 215
lookahead, one-character 216
loop, infinite 32

M

machine language 172, 209
machine, finite-state 3, 15, 213, 309
machine, nondeterministic 6, 22
machine, theoretical 1
mandatory substitution 280
matching, pattern 282, 308
mathematical induction x
mathematical model 1
mathematics, discrete 45
memoization 112, 312
memory 147, 230
memory, computer 28
memory, external 30
mergesort 126
Meteor 282
microworld 278, 297
Minsky, Marvin 342, 346
model, mathematical 1
modification, tree 139
monadic 224
multinomial coefficient 94
multinomial expansion 112
multiplication rule 72
mutator 141

N

nand 70
network, augmented transition 312
network, recursive transition 213
Newell, Allen 277
node, branch 132
node, leaf 132
node, root 132
non-interactive language 169

nondeterministic machine 6, 22
nor 70
null pointer 148
number, binary 25, 88
number, random 83
numerical analysis xiii
numof 281, 286

O

object-oriented programming 167
offset 235
one-character lookahead 216
one-to-one correspondence 89
operating systems xiii
operator precedence 223
operator, binary 223
operator, relational 224
operator, unary 223
optimization, global 111
optimization, local 110
optimizing compiler 109
optional substitution 304
ordered subset 74
ordering 146
ordering relation 68
ordinal type 188
overflow signal 71

P

P-code 173
packed array 188, 189
pair 147
Papert, Seymour x, 295
paradigm, programming 162
parameter, formal 176
parameter, value 197
parameter, variable 197
parentheses 227
parentheses, balancing 13, 28
Parry 31
parser 211, 212, 217
parser generator 217
partition sort 120, 204

Pascal 161, 310, 345
Pascal compiler 209
Pascal program 172
Pascal variable 199
Pascal's Triangle 82, 94
Pascal, Blaise 82
pattern matcher, Logo 283
pattern matching 282, 308
periodic 81
Perlis, Alan J. xi
permutation 74, 79
philosophy xiv
Piaget, Jean x
piracy, software xv
pointer 147, 190
pointer, frame 236
pointer, global 235
pointer, null 148
pointer, stack 236
portable 173
precedence 225, 285
precedence, operator 223
predicate function 67
predicate logic 67
predictive grammar 219
probability 73
problem, logic 48
procedural knowledge 16
procedural representation x
procedure call 178
procedure, effective 31
procedure, local 176
procedure, recursive 75, 80
procedure (Pascal) 176, 194
process ix
processor 147, 230
production rule 13, 212, 310
program verification 107
program, Pascal 172
programming languages, declarative 16
programming paradigm 162
programming, declarative 168
programming, dynamic 115
programming, functional 162
programming, logic 168

programming, object-oriented 167
programming, sequential 162
program (Pascal) 171, 172
Prolog 16, 68, 344
proof by contradiction 34
property list 55, 301
property, intellectual xv
proposition, compound 46
proposition, simple 46
propositional logic 46
psychology xiv, 277

Q

quadratic 129
quadratic formula 108
quantifier 283
quicksort 125

R

random access 148
random number 83
range 188
real (Pascal) 187
record 190
recursive definition 12
recursive descent 220
recursive procedure 75, 80
recursive transition network 213
reference, bound 184
reference, call by 197, 198
reference, free 184, 185
Reggini, Horacio xvii
register 230
register, index 235
regular expression 11, 15, 211
reject state 4
relation 67
relation, equivalence 68
relation, ordering 68
relational operator 224
repeat (Pascal) 178
repetition rule 11, 21
reserved word 183

retrieval time 131
robust 109, 146, 193
root node 132
round (Pascal) 190
RTN 213, 310
rule, production 13, 212
rules of inference 47

S

scalar type 187
science, cognitive 278
scope 239, 241
scope, dynamic 184, 185, 197, 198, 242
scope, lexical 183
search algorithm, binary 143
search algorithm, linear 143
searching 142
selection sort 117
selector 136
self-reference 32
semantics 180
sentence, simple 281
sentinel 205
sequential programming 162
set theory 89
set, infinite 89
sharable 150
sigma 91
Simon, Herbert A. 277
simple proposition 46
simple sentence 281
simple statement 177, 178
Simplex lock 85, 114
simulation 83
sine function 81
Smullyan, Raymond 343
sociology xiv
software engineering x, 174
software piracy xv
Somos, Michael xvii
sort, insertion 119
sort, partition 120, 204
sort, selection 117
sorted list 130

sorting 115
source file 171
space, time and 130
Spock, Mr. 72
spreadsheet 16
stack frame 235
stack pointer 236
start state 5
state 3
state, accepting 4
state, halting 31
state, internal 30
statement part 175
statement, assignment 178, 180, 195
statement, compound 177
statement, conditional 177
statement, simple 177, 178
statement, structured 178
storage time 130
store 147
string, constant 189
structure, block 177
structured statement 178
Student 278
subrange type 191
subset, ordered 74
substitution technique 285
substitution, mandatory 280
substitution, optional 304
sum of several terms 91
sum of the integers 119
Sussman, Gerald Jay ix, 342
Sussman, Julie 342
symbol, generated 141, 239, 293, 304
symmetric 68
syntactic hierarchy 213
syntax 179
system, expert 278
system, inference 47

T

table of values 81
table, hash 130
ternary logic 73

text editor 9, 169
theoretical machine 1
thinking, formal ix
time and space 130
time, retrieval 131
time, storage 130
timesharing systems xvi
token 214
tokenization 211, 214
top-down 174
Tower of Hanoi 169
tractable 129
tradeoff 130
transition network, augmented 312
transition network, recursive 213
transitive 68
transitive rules 51
tree 131
tree modification 139
tree, balanced 146
tree, binary 132, 144
`trunc` (Pascal) 190
truth-valued function 46, 67
Turing machine 30, 311
Turing machine, universal 33
Turing's thesis 31
Turing, Alan M. 30
Turkle, Sherry xiv, xvii, 346
two-stack algorithm 225
type, aggregate 187
type, data 187
type, enumerated 191
type, ordinal 188
type, scalar 187
type, subrange 191
type, user-defined 191
typed variable 187
`type` (Pascal) 191

U

unambiguous 217
unary operator 223
uniqueness rule 50, 67
unit 286

universal Turing machine 33
Unix xiii, xvi, 9
user-defined type 191

V

value parameter 197
value, call by 197, 198
variable parameter 197
variable, index 205
variable, Logo 199
variable, Pascal 199
variable, typed 187
`var` (Pascal) 176, 178, 197
verification, program 107

W

Wand, Mitchell 345
Weinberg, Gerald M. 347
Weizenbaum, Joseph 346
`while` (Pascal) 178
White, Dick xvii
Winograd, Terry xvii, 312, 345
Wirth, Niklaus 345
word 147, 189
word problems, algebra 278
word, reserved 183
workspace 171
workstations xvi
`writeln` (Pascal) 178
`write` (Pascal) 178

Y

YACC 219